Lutheranism and the Nordic Spirit of Social Democracy

ROBERT H. NELSON

Lutheranism and the Nordic Spirit of Social Democracy: A Different Protestant Ethic

AARHUS UNIVERSITY PRESS

Lutheranism and the Nordic Spirit of Social Democracy

Cover: Trefold
Layout and typesetting: Carl-H.K. Zakrisson
Publishing Editor: Karina Bell Ottosen
This book is typeset in Lyon and printed on 100 g Munken Pure
Printed by Narayana Press, Denmark

Printed in Denmark 2017

ISBN 978 87 7184 260 9

MIX
Paper from responsible sources
FSC
www.fsc.org
FSC® C010651

Aarhus University Press
Finlandsgade 29
DK-8200 Aarhus N
Denmark
www.unipress.dk

INTERNATIONAL DISTRIBUTORS:

Gazelle Book Services Ltd.
White Cross Mills
Hightown, Lancaster, LA1 4XS
United Kingdom
www.gazellebookservices.co.uk

ISD
70 Enterprise Drive, Suite 2
Bristol, CT 06010
USA
www.isdistribution.com

PEER REVIEWED

/ In accordance with requirements of the Danish Ministry of Higher Education and Science, the certification means that a PhD level peer has made a written assessment justifying this book's scientific quality.

Table of Contents

For Jill, Who Made It All Possible

Foreword

I met Bob Nelson in person for the first time in September 2016, when he came to give a keynote address at the University of Helsinki symposium 'Holy money? Economy as Religion', which I had helped to organize. I had read his work before, including a manuscript of this book, and was eager to meet the person behind it. Sitting in Café Engel by the Senate Square in Helsinki, Bob told me he was at a stage of his career where he had the privilege of choosing the topics he writes about based on his interests, including topics which may seem unconventional given his scientific background.

Nelson has an impressive career in and outside academia, and considering the topic of this book perhaps surprisingly in economics and public policy. However, in the 1990s he was already combining his background in economics with religious studies in his works on economics as a secular (or implicit or functional) religion, and has since continued to write broadly on this and other religious themes. In addition to the fact that Nelson is a 'non-theologian' writing about religion, he is also an American (although with Nordic roots) writing about the Nordic countries. Both of these facts make Nelson's book a bold endeavor, but boldness is needed for thinking beyond the ordinary boundaries.

And it seems sometimes things can be viewed better from a distance. The topic of this book, the influence of Lutheranism on the Nordic countries, is fundamental from the viewpoints of at least the social sciences, history, and religious studies. Yet it is far from common in Nordic literature. The influence of religion is often overlooked in many western contexts, at least partially because of the secularization assumptions of the 20th century. Furthermore, an approach such as Nelson's requires bold syntheses of viewpoints. Such multi-disciplinary work is challenged by the increasingly narrow specializations of academia today.

Indeed, Nelson's opportunity to write about what interests him has led to an ambitious project and a compelling book. It is rare in its comprehensive, multi-disciplinary approach to the role of Lutheranism in the history of Nordic countries, its perceptive analysis of the Lutheran version of the protestant ethic, and its ability to show how religion continues to be a penetrating cultural influence even in substantively secularized contexts.

From my viewpoint as a Finnish theologian, Nelson convincingly and perceptively analyzes the ways in which Lutheranism intertwines with a range of phenomena in Finnish culture and society. I read the manuscript of this book during the summer of 2016, when I was at Boston University as a visiting scholar. In Boston I had the privilege of discussing protestant ethics broadly with the renowned Weber scholar, Stephen Kalberg, who had recently applied it to American politics. These discussions, together with spending time in the US (amidst the early part of the presidential campaign that would later end in the election of Donald Trump), yielded a fruitful interaction with the manuscript of this book. The interaction was extremely stimulating for my own thinking and analysis, and indeed developed my research.

I believe a similar interaction between these contexts, American and Nordic, has been a key influence for Nelson too. He has Nordic ancestry, and has spent time in the Nordic countries, especially in Finland. This book was inspired by and at least partially emerged out of the activities of the Protestant Roots of Finnish National Identities (ProFini) network, which was established in 2014 when Nelson was visiting the Helsinki Collegium of Advanced Studies. This multidisciplinary network aims at examining the long-term effects of the Reformation, and especially those of Lutheranism, on the formation of Finnish society, culture, and national identity.

Strengthening such research approaches in Finland and other specific contexts is extremely important. But we also need further opportunities to illuminate our contexts by comparison with those of others. To understand multi-dimensional phenomena deeply, we need multi-disciplinary, international interaction – and bold thinking and writing. Nelson's book well demonstrates the indisputable benefits of such an approach.

Bob Nelson's book will be beneficial and, I believe, an enjoyable read for scholars and students in an array of disciplines. I hope it will reach a wide audience in the Nordic countries but also more widely, as its analysis of the Nordic case broadens understanding of the influences of (implicit) religion in general. Anyone interested in the historical and societal influence of religion should read this book, whether in Nordic countries or elsewhere.

Henrietta Grönlund
University Lecturer at the Faculty of Theology,
University of Helsinki, Finland
April 15, 2017

Preface

In February 2014, I arrived in Finland to spend seven months at the Collegium for Advanced Studies of the University of Helsinki, part of my 2013–2014 sabbatical year away from the School of Public Policy of the University of Maryland. Although I am by training an economist, I have long had a strong interest in the political and economic roles of religion in society, including the diverse forms religion has taken in the modern age.[1] I should say that this interest, moreover, is not driven by a longstanding traditional religious commitment of my own, but is more a matter of my intellectual curiosity, together with my view that the foundational role of religion has been much neglected in the twentieth-century scholarship of historians and social science professionals – much to their loss.[2]

Not long after I arrived at the Collegium, building on such previous thinking, I began exploring the hypothesis that social democracy in the Nordic countries is significantly a product of the secularization of their common Lutheran heritage. This book examines social democracy in all the Nordic countries but I make greater use of Finnish examples, reflecting the location of the book's origins. The intended audience includes economists, sociologists, cultural anthropologists,

1. My publications in this area include Nelson, *Reaching for Heaven on Earth*; Nelson, *Economics as Religion*; and Nelson, *The New Holy Wars*.

2. A recent book of mine, however, does represent an exploration of a more traditional and directly theological subject – what we can say rationally about whether a god exists. Following in the historic tradition of Aristotle and Aquinas, the book does not necessarily address the existence of a Christian God specifically, but more abstractly of some god, an argument now based on contemporary resources in physics, evolutionary biology, the philosophy of human consciousness and other current areas of inquiry. See Nelson, *God? Very Probably*.

students of Nordic history, students of the history of religion, theologians and indeed anyone interested in the role of religion in its diverse forms in shaping modern societies. I hope that the book will attract readers in Nordic countries who may learn more about the large impact of Lutheranism on what is often taken to be a secular outcome – the rise of Nordic social democracy in the twentieth century.

As I will also be arguing in this book, and perhaps surprisingly for some readers, Lutheran values and beliefs have not only been a foundational influence on the development of Nordic social democracy but also Nordic social democracy can itself be seen as a modern form of religion – a "secular Lutheranism." A number of theologians and other students of religion of the twentieth century have argued that "secular religion" (or some prefer the term "implicit religion") is a particular subcategory that falls within the general category of all "religion."[3] Some people may prefer the term "ideology" but I find that "secular religion" is more accurate and illuminating. Recognizing that many modern ideologies are actual forms of religion provides a better basis for understanding modern political and economic history. Indeed, the immense historic influence of belief systems such as Marxism and Social Darwinism can be fully understood only in a context in which they are seen to be modernized bearers of the heritage of traditional Christianity, including in the case of social democracy a Nordic secularization of traditional Lutheran religion. In the United States, as the sociologist Robert Bellah famously argued, the unifying national religion over the course of its history has been a "civil religion" – another term for a secular religion.[4]

Thus, for readers with wider interests in the general workings of religious phenomena, I hope by examining the role of Lutheran re-

3. A leading theologian of the twentieth century, Paul Tillich, thus defined religion as a belief system that offered answers to matters of "ultimate concern," thus extending the scope of religion well beyond the traditional Christian, Islamic, Buddhist, and other familiar faiths. See Brown, ed., *Ultimate Concern: Tillich in Dialogue*. A leading American legal philosopher wrote recently of the modern phenomenon of true religions that lacked any explicit mention of a god. See Dworkin, *Religion Without God*.

4. Bellah, "Civil Religion in America."

ligion in the Nordic countries in the twentieth century to provide a case study that will further illuminate the general relationship between traditional Christian religion and modern political and economic beliefs and developments.[5] Max Weber famously explored this subject about 100 years ago with respect to the impact of Calvinism – both in its early traditional and later secularized forms – in advancing the rise of capitalism and other modern developments.[6] I argue similarly in this book that Lutheranism – again in its earlier and then in its later secularized forms – has been a major contributing factor to the rise of social democracy in the Nordic countries in the twentieth century. There are thus two Protestant ethics of large historic significance: a Calvinist ethic that was the subject of Weber's investigations, and of many others who followed later in his path; and a Lutheran ethic that has been studied less, partly because the Nordic countries represent a much smaller part of the world than all the nations significantly influenced by Calvinism.[7] By the time that Nordic social democracy had risen to a leading world political force in the mid twentieth century, the idea that religion could be a major driving influence on modern social and economic outcomes was no longer part of the routine research agenda of mainstream history and social science.

As an American most familiar with American history, I am impressed by the many connections between nineteenth- and twentieth-century political and economic developments in the United States and the Nordic world – usually with somewhat of a lag in the Nordic case. Indeed, they could be described as two particular illustrations of a possible range of responses of a modern society to a common set of

5. This book draws on analyses of contemporary economics and other social sciences as themselves modern religious adaptations from traditional Christian religion. On economics in this perspective, see Nelson, *Economics as Religion* and Cox, *The Market as God*; on psychology, see Vitz, *Psychology as Religion*; on politics, see Gentile, *Politics as Religion*; on sociology, see Smith, *The Sacred Project of American Sociology*; and on American law, see Levinson, *Constitutional Faith*.

6. Gregory, *The Unintended Reformation*.

7. A Google search of "Lutheran Ethic" turns up few studies and little scholarly use of the term. One book titled *The Lutheran Ethic* turns out to be about the cultural attitudes of American Lutherans who had emigrated from Europe. See Kersten, *The Lutheran Ethic*.

scientific, economic and other fundamental challenges to the traditional western religious beliefs and institutions of the past. Both progressivism in the United States and social democracy in the Nordic countries were much influenced by the Protestant roots of these nations, but the former was shaped more by a Calvinist ethic, while the latter reflects a greater influence of a Lutheran ethic. American progressivism and Nordic social democracy thus might be described as Protestant theological, political and economic cousins.

In writing this book, I also had another very different type of motive. I was born and grew up in the United States; my mother (as of this writing 98) is the daughter of two Finnish immigrants who came to the United States and met there in the early twentieth century. My father, as a second-generation American, was the grandson of four Swedish immigrants who arrived in the late nineteenth century. Both of my parents were proud of their Scandinavian heritage, liked to talk about it and participated in the activities of the Finnish and Swedish communities that were still flourishing in the United States in their youth. I was baptized in what I recall was a Lutheran church. So this book is not only about the Lutheran roots of Nordic social democracy, but also about my own personal roots. I have discovered many fascinating things about this heritage in the course of writing this book.

Acknowledgments

During the seven months of my sabbatical year that I spent in 2014 at the Collegium for Advanced Studies of the University of Helsinki, I benefited greatly from the opportunity to explore Finnish and Nordic history – and the role of the Lutheran church in particular – in discussions with fellows of the Collegium. Kaius Sinnemaki was particularly generous with his time. I thank the Director of the Collegium Sami Pihlstrom who first extended an invitation to be a visiting fellow and then did much to make my stay both productive and enjoyable.

I also benefited that year from discussions with Anne Pessi and Risto Saarinen of the Faculty of Theology. Economics professor Esa Mangeloja of the University of Jyvaskyla undertook research and provided background that I have adapted in parts of this book. University of Helsinki historian Henrik Stenius offered valuable extensive written comments. I am now co-editing a forthcoming book with Kaius Sinnemaki, Anneli Portman and Jouni Tilli of the University of Helsinki in which chapters by leading Finnish scholars explore further the role of Lutheranism in shaping modern Finland. I have learned much from the opportunity to read drafts of these chapters.

Thanks to an invitation from Professor Stefan Schwarzkopf, I presented some of the main themes from this book to a seminar at the Copenhagen Business School in September 2016. That same month I made a similar seminar presentation at the Collegium for Advanced Studies of the University of Helsinki. I thank the participants in both seminars – too numerous to mention here by name – for their valuable comments.

I wish also to thank Karina Bell Ottosen of Aarhus University Press who smoothly guided me through the publication process.

INTRODUCTION

Two Protestant Ethics

In 1904 and 1905 Max Weber published a two-part article in the *Archiv für Sozialwissenschaft und Sozialpolitik* that would become *The Protestant Ethic and the Spirit of Capitalism*. A revised version appeared in 1920, shortly after Weber's death; it was this version that was first translated into English by Talcott Parsons in 1930. Weber himself began his university career in Germany as an economist, and regarded *The Protestant Ethic* as in part an alternative interpretation of the rise of capitalism to supplement the strict economic determinism of Karl Marx. Reflecting trends toward quantitative and other formal styles of analysis within American professional economics of the twentieth century, however, *The Protestant Ethic* was largely ignored by professional economists until recently. This recent interest reflects a growing recognition of the large limitations of mainstream economics with its traditional assumptions of "rational" behavior directed by self-interest, analyzed abstractly with mathematical and other quantitative methods that it is hoped will put economics intellectually in the same scientific category as physics.[1]

In a 2015 survey article in a leading American economic journal, however, Alberto Alesina of the Harvard economics department and Paola Giuliano of the UCLA management school define "culture" as that which "refers to those decision-making heuristics which typically manifest themselves as values, beliefs, or social norms." They then explain that "empirical investigation of the relevance of culture is fairly new in economics. So far, the goal of most cultural economics

1. The MIT economist Andrew W. Lo and MIT physicist Mark T. Mueller write that "WARNING: Physics Envy May Be Hazardous To Your Wealth."

papers has been to establish the relevance of culture."[2] Outside economics, in other professional fields such as sociology and intellectual history, *The Protestant Ethic*, despite many specific criticisms, has long been considered an essential work of the twentieth century. The great influence of *The Protestant Ethic* has one problematic aspect, however: Weber's book was not actually about a general "Protestant ethic."

By far the largest part of Weber's analysis and case examples were drawn from the history of Calvinism and other closely associated Reformed denominations. The book focused on the historical connections between Calvinist religion and economic events in historically Calvinist countries such as Switzerland, Holland and Scotland, and also on those countries with a large Calvinist influence within a greater religious pluralism such as England and the United States. The German social economist Alexander Ebner thus writes that the influence of "Protestant ethics in the institutional evolution of modern capitalism is [...] decisive." But it is not "the position [of] Martin Luther and German Protestantism in its Lutheranian blend but that of rather radical Protestant dissenters like Calvin which represents the essence of the Protestant ethics of capitalism."[3] The American theologian Max Stackhouse similarly explains that in *The Protestant Ethic* Weber focused on the ethical implications derived primarily from "Puritan attitudes as well as the later (Baptist and Methodist) traditions influenced by them."[4] It thus would have been more precise for Weber to have titled his book "The Calvinist Ethic and the Spirit of Capitalism."

The Lutheranism and Calvinism of the Reformation era did have many common features. Both saw the Pope and the large Vatican body of religious "experts" as heretically substituting a human creation for the true word of God, which could only be found in the Bible and in

2. Alesina and Giulano, "Culture and Institutions," pp. 901, 900.
3. Ebner, "Max Weber, the Protestant Ethics, and the Sociology of Capitalist Development," pp. 233, 240.
4. Stackhouse, "Weber, Theology, and Economics," p. 315.

God's own revealed design of the creation as could be discovered in the "Book of Nature." Both Lutheranism and Calvinism abolished the special religious status of the Catholic priesthood in favor of the Protestant "priesthood of all believers." Both Luther and Calvin denied any role for "good works" in the salvation of the individual person.

Despite such important common elements, Luther's message offered less support than Calvin's for the development of capitalism. Indeed, Luther was often scathingly hostile to a market organization of society based on the self-interested pursuit of profit. German sociologist Helge Peukert explains that Luther "was in favor of money as a medium of circulation but he fought against money in the function of money which gets independent in the form of capital." Unlike Calvin, Luther was opposed to the charging of interest. He thought that "the ethical code of the Christian demanded not to try to get what the market will bear." Rather, in market interactions "the central motive should always be the interest of our neighbor and not our personal gain. [...] Trade and sin are close together, a latent conflict exists between trade, money and being a Christian." Hence, in his social concept of its functioning, "he bombards the economy with ethical norms." All in all, "Luther offered western societies a concept of a practical moral economy [...] which is located in the interpenetration zone of economy and morals/religion. It is quite different from Weber's protestant ethics."[5]

Luther from 1525 onward, moreover, taught complete obedience of the Lutheran faithful to the German Prince – and later Lutherans would extend this way of thinking to other kinds of state authorities. In those places where Lutheranism later became the dominant national religion, there was typically a state church headed by a Prince, King or other holder of state authority who oversaw what amounted to a Lutheran theocracy. Calvinists, by contrast, typically made strong efforts to separate the institutional church of the Christian faithful from state control and were willing to rebel violently, if

5. Peukert, "Martin Luther: The First Modern Economist," pp. 53, 56, 54, 57.

necessary, against excessive state efforts to limit Calvinist religious freedoms. The American sociologist of religion Stephen Kalberg explains that, in contrast to Lutheranism, Puritanism (the English and American branch of Calvinism) "empowered the devout to act decisively in the political realm on behalf of a set of rules and principles. Required by religious belief, the devout *must* take action against secular authority and popular opinion" that strays too far from God.[6]

To the extent that readers of *The Protestant Ethic* took Weber's title literally, as promising an analysis encompassing all of Protestantism, this was bound to create some significant confusions. In places where Lutheranism was the dominant religious influence there would be no strong reason to expect that the Lutheran ethic – even though it was clearly also a Protestant ethic – would have the same strong positive relationship with capitalism or individual political freedom as Calvinism did. But this has not prevented numerous scholars, following after Weber, from speaking of a generalized Protestant ethic and then proceeding to explore the relationship between such a generalized Protestant ethic and capitalism.

It was possible to neglect the Lutheran ethic partly because there are only seven fairly small nations about which one can clearly say that they have been historically Lutheran – the five Nordic nations of Denmark, Finland, Iceland, Norway and Sweden, plus the two Baltic nations of Estonia and Latvia. In 2015, the total population of these seven nations was only about 30 million. In Germany many individual governing jurisdictions have had a Lutheran religious heritage since the sixteenth century but there has always been a large Catholic presence – historically around a third of the population – in the area of present-day Germany, and also a smaller but significant Calvinist presence. So any assessment of the historical role of Lutheranism in modern Germany, unlike the religiously homogenous Nordic countries, is complicated by the fact of its longstanding religious pluralism.

6. Kalberg, *Searching for the Spirit of American Democracy*, p. 44.

Another reason for the scholarly neglect of the Lutheran ethic is the marginal place of the Nordic countries in Europe, geographically and economically, until the twentieth century. Until the late nineteenth and early twentieth century, the Nordic countries were economically backward, to the extent that large parts of their populations felt it necessary to emigrate elsewhere, principally to the United States. Except for Denmark (from which there were fewer emigrants), the Nordic countries were located in the harsh climates in the northernmost parts of Europe, where they long existed in relative isolation, living at low population densities as compared with other parts of Europe.

But this all changed in the twentieth century. Modern technology and ideas did as much as – or more than – anywhere else in Europe to change the basic living conditions of the people of the Nordic countries. Electric lighting, for example, made more difference in those places where there was minimal sunlight for much of the year. Indeed, by the mid twentieth century, many people around the world were coming to see the Nordic countries as the forerunners of political and economic modernization. They seemed to have been uniquely successful in rapidly building modern societies that were egalitarian in spirit and at the same time economically prosperous.

Two of the leading American political scientists of the post-World War II era, Robert Dahl and Charles Lindblom, wrote in 1976 that most governments of the world had disappointingly failed to make much progress since World War II toward "political or economic or social equality," with the large exception of the "Scandinavian experience [which] suggests that under some circumstances the move can be made."[7] A recent 2012 working paper from the MIT economics department asks: "Can't we all be more like Scandinavians?" The authors state that "inequality at the top of the distribution has [...] been exploding in the United States, with the top 1% of earners capturing almost 25% of [increases in] total national income, while

7. Dahl and Lindblom, *Politics, Economics and Welfare*, p. xxii.

the same number is [admittedly still high] around 5% in Finland and Sweden."[8] Even though U.S. national income per capita is somewhat higher, as the working paper acknowledges, Scandinavia seems to many observers to be a nicer place to live.

In the 2015 *World Happiness Report* covering the period 2012 to 2014, and prepared under the auspices of the United Nations, the Nordic countries dominated the top ten rankings for overall national happiness, including Iceland (ranked 2nd), Denmark (3rd), Norway (4th), Finland (6th) and Sweden (8th). Interestingly, all the other top ten countries were historically Protestant – Switzerland (1st), Canada (5th), the Netherlands (7th), New Zealand (9th) and Australia (10th).[9] Perhaps we should be searching for a new Max Weber of our time to address a different and more contemporary set of social outcomes: Is the present state of the "Protestant ethic" now somehow responsible for making people happier; does it somehow today establish a powerful new "Spirit of National Happiness"? The economics profession claims to be seeking to understand how to "maximize individual utility" (the economist's term for happiness), but it seems that religious heritage may have more to do with levels of individual happiness (utility) in nations around the world than the workings of the economic system as systematically studied by professional economists with their formal technical methods (that we should recognize still reflect implicitly their own powerful underlying value lens).[10]

Following social democratic principles, the welfare states of the Nordic countries had seemingly found a way of achieving rapid economic progress while avoiding the class tensions between rich and poor – between capitalists and workers – that were common in other parts of Europe and the Americas. In early 2016, a prominent American political columnist, David Brooks of *The New York Times*, described the political program of a leading candidate in the Democratic Party political primary, the former socialist Bernie Sanders

8. Acemoglu, Robinson and Verdier, *Can't We All Be More Like Scandinavians*, p. 2.
9. Helliwell, Layard and Sachs, eds. *World Happiness Report 2015*.
10. See Nelson, *Economics as Religion*; McCloskey, "The Rhetoric of Economics."

– then engaged in a fierce struggle with the "establishment" candidate Hillary Clinton – as promising a "Danish dream."[11]

As the Nordic countries began to receive greater global attention in the twentieth century, leading scholars – inside and outside of the Nordic countries themselves – nevertheless continued for many years to give little attention to religious factors. If they did have anything to say about religion, they were more likely to attribute twentieth-century Nordic modernization to the shedding of an outmoded religious heritage of the past. A Northern heaven on earth would be a secular paradise, free of the many biases, pervasive ignorance, harmful tendencies toward violent conflict and other unhappy features of centuries of Christian history. Throughout the twentieth century, leading historians, economists and other scholars characteristically saw past and current world events though the powerful lens of a strict economic determinism. In this lens, there was little if any place for religion – or indeed for any ideas beyond the scientific understanding of the laws of nature and society that made modern technological and economic progress possible.

In this book, I will argue that, to the contrary, in the twentieth century a Lutheran ethic provided a powerful normative foundation that underlay the political and economic rise of Nordic social democracy. This Lutheran ethic originated in the writings and actions of Martin Luther himself in the first half of the sixteenth century. For the next 300 years in the Nordic world, the Lutheran ethic evolved within its Lutheran state churches. In the eighteen and nineteenth centuries, the pace of Nordic religious change accelerated as orthodox Lutheranism was increasingly challenged by Pietist and other new revivalist influences, partly reflecting a growing Calvinist presence in the Nordic countries (whose impacts were felt both within Lutheranism itself and in the spread of new "free" Reformed churches).

11. Brooks, "Livin' Bernie Sanders' Danish Dream," p. 9.

Beginning in the nineteenth century and then accelerating in the twentieth century, reflecting worldwide secularizing trends, this Lutheran heritage rapidly shed much of its traditional religious outward character and institutional forms. But the change for the Nordic countries was greater in outward appearance than most people in these countries recognized at the time. Indeed, as some Nordic scholars themselves have begun to point out with increasing frequency since the 1990s, social democracy in the Nordic world is appropriately understood as grounded in a Lutheran ethic; indeed, the result can be seen as a new form of Lutheranism, now mostly secularized and thus with its fundamental Lutheran essence unrecognized by many people. University of Helsinki sociologist Risto Alapuro wrote in 1999 that "after the Reformation [...] there was no rivalry between the state and the church and no protest movement from below," as all the Nordic nations ended up with top-down, Lutheran state churches. Although challenged in the nineteenth century, this continued into the early twentieth century, but then "the role of the Lutheran tradition in the development of the welfare state" took new forms. As Alapuro explains, the Nordic countries experienced the development of "a new 'secularized Lutheranism' in the form of the social democratic parties [that] continued the Lutheran tradition in the construction of the [Nordic] welfare state."[12]

Conclusion

It is not only Protestantism in its various forms that is now receiving growing attention as a decisive shaping force in modern political and economic developments. A British student of the continuing impact of Christian religion on the institutions of contemporary western society, Nick Spencer, finds that there are "different approaches to poverty – and by association work – and poor relief between Catholic, Lutheran and Calvinist traditions [that] have a powerful explanatory

12. Alapuro, "Comments on Sorensen's 'On King's, Pietism and Rent-Seeking in Scandinavian Welfare States'," p. 377.

potential when examining the influence of Christianity on welfare states." Within Protestantism, "Lutheranism could breed a critical attitude to poverty, [while] Calvinism could generate a positively hostile one." This was in contrast to the historical Catholic attitude in which "the poor were understood as especially acute images of Christ, whose prayers were therefore particularly efficacious and whose relief was a distinctly *Christian* duty, the giving of alms being inextricably linked to salvation" of the giver, not the recipient.[13] Most recently, Pope Francis has spread worldwide a similar Catholic message of the central religious significance of helping the poor and destitute in many of his public pronouncements.

The different Catholic and Protestant ways of seeing the poor had major consequences for the development of twentieth-century systems of public welfare in Catholic and Protestant countries. The social impacts of the differing views, moreover, extended to many other aspects of the modern welfare state, beyond the care for the poor.[14] In comparison with the rest of the world, nevertheless, Catholicism and Protestantism shared many beliefs fundamental to Christianity as a whole. Indeed, historians have been paying growing attention in recent years to the worldwide civilizational consequences of religion.[15] There has been an increasing recognition of the many critical ways in which Christianity shaped all of western civilization, so that western civilization might still be described as in essence a "Christian" civilization – even though its Christianity is now frequently presented in newly modern and thus partially disguised forms. For some devout Christians today, however, they consider the modern secular appropriations of large parts of the traditional Christian message as having created a "rival religion to authentic faith – it's a [new] brand of Christian heresy."[16]

13. Spencer, *The Evolution of the West*, pp. 175, 174.
14. Nelson, "Is Max Weber Newly Relevant?"
15. Huntington, *The Clash of Civilizations and the Remaking of World Order*.
16. "Requiem for Civil Religion," *Christian Century*, unsigned editorial.

CHAPTER 1

Lutheranism and the World of Nordic Social Democracy

The "Nordic countries" – Denmark, Finland, Iceland, Norway and Sweden – share a number of cultural, political and economic characteristics that distinguish them sufficiently that it is common to speak of a "Nordic world," within the overall international community of nations.[1] Culturally, the Nordic countries are distinguished by, among other features, higher levels of trust in other people than almost any other nations of the world (only the Netherlands – another Northern European Protestant country – is comparably high in world values surveys).[2] With respect to more narrowly economic matters, other studies have shown that "the Nordic countries are [...] different from other industrialized nations in a large number of criteria." They "differ from one another but differ still more from other nations" according to measures such as "expenditure for social welfare, tax rates, large public service sectors, a large public transfer sector and a more active labour market policy."[3] On the whole, as the director of the Swedish Collegium for Advanced Study Bjorn Wittrock wrote in 2012, "in the early twenty-first century, the Nordic countries form a rather unique part of the world, characterized by a unique form of common belonging arguably stronger than that which may be found among the other nations of Europe."[4]

1. In this book, I will not have much to say about Iceland, despite its many distinctively Nordic features, because of its small size and its unique geographic isolation among the Nordic countries.
2. Inglehart and Welzel, *Modernization, Cultural Change, and Democracy*, p. 72.
3. Marklund and Nordlund, "Economic Problems, Welfare Convergence and Political Instability," p. 51.
4. Wittrock, "The Making of Sweden," p. 108.

Henrik Kleven, an economist at the London School of Economics, recently offered a revealing example of the distinctive character of the welfare state in the Nordic countries. Economists define the "participation tax rate" as the total percentage loss due to taxation of income, loss of means-tested income transfers and loss of other means-tested forms of state support that result from newly moving into the labor force. In Scandinavia, uniquely high in the world, this participation tax rate is around 80 percent. This means that an average worker moving from outside the labor force to become a new member will be required to pay taxes and experience losses in state support equal in total to 80 percent of the income they earn in their new job. Stated otherwise, they will realize a net gain of only 20 percent of what they are being paid in the new job – as compared, for example, with a net gain of 67 percent in the United States.[5]

So why do average people in these countries work at all? If Nordic workers behaved according to the standard economic assumption that rational individuals pursue their self-interest, the economies of Nordic countries might collapse for lack of a labor force. Since this does not happen, there must be something distinctive happening in the Nordic welfare states (Iceland and Finland would likely be comparable in the above respect to Denmark, Norway and Sweden). Kleven does not reach any definitive conclusions but does offer strong suggestive evidence to support the idea that "the Scandinavian countries share some distinctive social and cultural attitudes and norms that could contribute to the willingness" to work hard for a small personal net gain economically.[6] Religion, historically, has been the most important way for a society to overcome the "free rider" effect of the obstacle of self-interest to successful collective action.

One possibility is that, rather than being motivated by economic reasons, work in Scandinavia is more like the fulfillment of a religious calling. It was not only in Calvinism but also in Lutheranism where

5. Kleven, "How Can Scandinavia Tax So Much?," p. 77.

6. Ibid., p. 95.

pursuit of a calling could stimulate seemingly irrational levels of work effort by ordinary private standards of maximizing personal gain. As one might say, it is seemingly part of the strong sense of "social solidarity" in the Nordic world that all able-bodied adults are morally required to work and thus to contribute to the economic success of the whole society, even when this is not in their self-interest narrowly defined, given alternative systems of state support. Indeed, failure to contribute to society will subject an individual to strong Nordic social sanctions, unlike in many other more "cynical" nations. To the extent that hard work is an "irrational" calling in life (by the conventional economic standards of rational self-interest), religion must lie at the very foundation of Nordic societies.

In another area of Nordic distinctiveness, the 2014 *Global Gender Gap Report* from the World Economic Forum ranks Iceland first in the world in gender equality, followed by Finland, Norway, Sweden and Denmark to fill out the top five.[7] Half of Finland's cabinet ministers in 2014 were women. Yet there is one revealing exception: the numbers of women in the Nordic countries occupying senior level executive positions in business. In this respect, the World Economic Forum ranks Denmark as 72nd in the world. Only 6 percent of Norwegian corporations had a female chief executive in 2013, as compared with 5 percent of the CEOs among the largest 500 companies in the United States as listed by *Fortune* magazine.[8] Becoming a high-level corporate executive requires making large sacrifices in many areas of life. The most capable Nordic women are seemingly willing to make such personal sacrifices to serve in callings in the public sector and other forms of public service, but seemingly do not see the profit-making private business sector in an equally "Godly" light. In this respect, they reveal one of the significant differences between a Lutheran ethic and a Calvinist ethic.

7. World Economic Forum, *The Global Gender Gap, 2014*.

8. *The Economist*, "A Nordic Mystery: In the World's Most Female Friendly Workplaces, Executive Suites are Still Male-Dominated."

Nordic Uniqueness in World Governance

Since 1996, the World Bank has been publishing "Wordwide Governance Indicators" that include virtually every nation and are updated each year.[9] World Bank researchers examine six different categories that are seen to bear significantly on the overall quality of the governance of a nation: (1) "Voice and Accountability," (2) "Political Stability and Absence of Violence/Terrorism," (3) "Government Effectiveness," (4) "Regulatory Quality," (5) "Rule of Law" and (6) "Control of Corruption."[10] Table 1 shows the 2008 rankings for the twenty highest-ranked individual nations in the world by each of these governance categories.

As Table 1 shows, the Nordic nations occupy an altogether disproportionate number of the top positions in the world for the six governance categories examined by the World Bank team. Of the nations ranked first in the world in their category of governance, three of the six top individual spots are held by Nordic nations. Among the first and second individual world rankings for their category, Nordic nations occupy seven – more than half – of the 12 total positions. In each of four governance categories – "voice and accountability," "government effectiveness," "rule of law" and "control of corruption," individual Nordic nations hold at least four of the top seven world rankings. Such

9. The indicators show the Bank's estimate of the quality of governance of a nation relative to all other nations in the world in that category. Such indicators should not be taken as the final word and are regularly revisited and revised. But the World Bank reports on these indicators are the most authoritative estimates available on a worldwide basis concerning the relative quality of governance of individual nations around the world within the six categories studied. For each category, the Bank assembles the most relevant national data that it can find and then aggregates it using a statistical model into a single numerical indicator for each nation in the world for each specific category. The Work Bank does not attempt to consolidate the six categories into a single overall governance quality measure by nation, but does make the individual nation governance indicators widely available for each of the six governance categories. See Kaufmann, Kraay and Matruzzi, *The Worldwide Governance Indicators*.

10. The indictors by nation and category of governance are available at http://info.worldbank.org/governance/wgi/index.aspx#reports.

TABLE 1

Top Twenty Ranked Nations in the World (2008), By Governance Category*

World Rank	Voice and Accountability	Political Stability and Absence of Violence/ Terrorism	Government Effectiveness
1.	**Norway(t)**	Luxembourg	Singapore
2.	**Sweden(t)**	**Finland**	**Denmark**
3.	Netherlands(t)	**Norway(t)**	Switzerland
4.	Luxembourg	Singapore(t)	**Sweden**
5.	**Denmark(t)**	Austria	Australia
6.	**Finland(t)**	Malta	**Finland(t)**
7.	New Zealand(t)	Switzerland	**Norway(t)**
8.	**Iceland(t)****	**Iceland(t)**	Netherlands
9.	Switzerland(t)	Brunei(t)	Hong Kong
10.	Canada	Ireland(t)***	New Zealand
11.	Ireland	New Zealand(t)	United Kingdom
12.	Belgium	**Sweden**	Austria
13.	Australia(t)	Hong Kong	Germany(t)
14.	Austria(t)	Australia(t)	Luxembourg(t)
15.	Germany	Germany(t)	United States
16.	United Kingdom	Slovenia	**Iceland**
17.	France	Portugal	France
18.	Malta	Canada	Japan
19.	United States(t)	Qatar	Belgium
20.	Spain(t)	**Denmark**	Israel

SOURCE: Daniel Kaufmann, Aart Kraay and Massimo Mastruzzi, *Governance Matters VIII: Aggregate and Individual Governance Indicators, 1996–2008*, Policy Research Working Paper 4978 (Washington, DC: The World Bank, Development Research Group, June 2009).

* In some cases, nations had the same numerical governance indicator, resulting in ties for positions in the rankings. I have nevertheless assigned such nations a sequential ranking, so that two nations shown one after the other in Table 1 may in some cases have actually had the same numerical indicator of relative governance quality. This is shown by placing a (t) after adjacent rankings that are tied.

World Rank	Regulatory Quality ***	Rule of Law	Control of Corruption
1.	Hong Kong	**Norway**	**Finland(t)**
2.	Singapore	**Denmark(t)**	Singapore(t)
3.	Ireland	Austria(t)	**Denmark(t)********
4.	**Denmark**	**Iceland**	New Zealand(t)
5.	United Kingdom	**Sweden**	**Iceland(t)**
6.	Australia	**Finland**	**Sweden**
7.	Netherlands	Switzerland	Netherlands
8.	New Zealand	New Zealand	Switzerland
9.	Luxembourg	Luxembourg	Australia(t)
10.	**Sweden**	Canada	Canada(t)
11.	Switzerland(t)	Netherlands(t)	**Norway(t)*********
12.	Canada(t)	Australia(t)	Hong Kong(t)
13.	Austria	Ireland	Australia
14.	**Finland(t)**	Singapore	United Kingdom(t)
15.	United States(t)	Germany	Germany(t)
16.	Chile(t)	United Kingdom	Ireland
17.	Belgium	United States	United States
18.	Estonia	Malta	France
19.	Germany	Hong Kong	Bahamas
20.	**Norway**	France/Japan(t)	Belgium

** Denmark, Finland and New Zealand were tied, ahead of Iceland and Switzerland which themselves were tied.

*** Iceland ranked 31st in 2008 in the category of "Regulatory Quality."

**** Finland and Singapore were tied, ahead of Denmark, New Zealand and Iceland which themselves were tied.

***** Australia and Canada were tied, ahead of Norway and Hong Kong which themselves were tied.

extraordinary Nordic dominance of the top ranks of measures of qualities of governance is obtained from among a total of about 175 total nation states around the world that each received a World Bank governance indicator for each of the six categories (I have excluded some very small nations such as Lichtenstein).

Three other countries that are typically almost as close to the top of the world rankings are Australia, Canada and New Zealand (one might describe them as Protestant parts of the old British empire); Switzerland and the Netherlands (Reformed Protestant nations of northern continental Europe); and Austria, Ireland and Luxembourg (Catholic nations of northern Europe). But none of these other clusters of world nations stand out in the world in nearly as distinctive a fashion as the five Nordic countries.

The quality of governance estimates as provided by the World Bank thus offer yet further strong evidence that there is something about the Nordic world that sharply distinguishes it from the rest of Europe and indeed the rest of the globe. Given the free flows of information around the world, it is unlikely that the Nordic countries have any special knowledge of methods of administration or other technical governance skills. Rather, it would seem that they must have national values and other features of their cultures that support exceptionally high qualities of governance – and historically the culture of a nation has been significantly rooted in its religious heritage and recent practice.

Conclusion

So what accounts for the extraordinary governance quality, social equality, high mutual trust and social solidarity and other unusually strong commonalities that have been widely observed among the Nordic countries? Many nations that are grouped together by social scientists and historians are defined by a common language but this does not apply in the case of the Nordic world – Finnish is radically different. A common history is another factor often giving a group of nations a shared sense of identity, but that also does not apply well in the Nordic case – Sweden and Denmark were major European powers for centuries, while Finland and Norway were never independent nations until the twentieth century. Finland, uniquely, was part of Russia from 1809 to 1917. One might argue that, except for Iceland, they do share the common features of having locations in the very north of Europe – but that does not apply to Denmark either, with its more southern location, somewhat milder climate, and closer geographic proximity to events in continental Europe.

There is one important feature, however, that the five Nordic countries, for all their other significant differences, do conspicuously have in common: All have been almost uniformly – about 99 percent for several centuries after the Reformation – Lutheran. Indeed, all have had Lutheran state churches since the sixteenth century, although Sweden ended the official state church status in 2000. All five Nordic countries have almost the same national flags, featuring a cross embedded in a single field of color, the national flags differing only by the colors of the cross and the field. All five Nordic countries today remain predominantly Lutheran in terms of official church membership, despite strong secularizing trends that have seen widespread declines in direct religious participation in the second half of the twentieth century.

In Finland, for example, about 75 percent of the population continues to belong voluntarily to the Lutheran Church, despite the fact that this membership obligates a person to contribute about one percent of their income to the Church, revenues that are collected by the national tax authorities and then turned over to the Finnish Lutheran Church.[11] Yet few of these members of the Finnish Lutheran Church regularly attend church services on Sundays, limiting their main participation to baptisms, coming of age ceremonies, marriages and funerals. As this book will argue, however, and despite their outward religious skepticism, the Finnish and other Nordic country majorities

11. Kaariainen, "Religion and State in Finland."

of the population are still Lutheran at their core. But their deep Lutheran convictions – often unknown to them – have taken new forms that might be described as a "modernized Lutheranism," or, as suggested previously, perhaps it should be called a "secular Lutheranism."

The modern religions that evoked the most passionate support and were the most decisive in shaping modern history frequently denied that they were religions at all – Marxism being a classic example.[12] This denial was a principal reason that these religions attracted so many followers and exerted such a large influence. The historic messages of Christian religion, confronted with the revealed truths of the scientific method and other startling new developments such as the discovery of ancient dinosaur fossils, could no longer sustain the old claims to be the one "truth of the world," thus creating a vacuum that others moved aggressively to fill. Yet outside the natural world, where it achieved astonishing successes, the scientific method did not do much better than historic Christianity in understanding and explaining matters of human affairs. Large numbers of people, moreover, while professing allegiance to a new god of Science, continued to adhere – sometimes explicitly but more often implicitly – to Christian beliefs and values. The result was often a severe modern case of religious confusion, actual Christian belief embedded in and justified by arguments supposedly based in science and sometimes overtly professing an antagonism to Christianity.[13] Social democracy in the Nordic world in the twentieth century was among the leading modern examples.

12. MacIntyre, *Marxism and Christianity*.

13. Nelson, "The Secularization Myth Revisited."

CHAPTER 2

Rethinking the Lutheran Roots of Nordic Social Democracy

As recently as 2008, it was possible for the German sociologist of religion Michael Opielka to write that "little research exists reflecting the religious foundations of welfare states" in Europe and elsewhere. The usual view of students of the welfare state had long been "to avoid treating religion as an external variable of decision makers or national cultures, or even as an independent variable belonging at the centre of social policy analysis."[1] This had started to change, however, even though Opielka seemed not to know much about it, around 25 years ago. Given the impact of the Iranian Islamic revolution of 1979 and other indications of a new prominence of religion in shaping key world events since the 1980s, it was inevitable that scholarly attention would shift to begin to examine the place of religion in driving world political and economic events.

Indeed, more recent world developments have even further emphasized the importance of religion. The Europe editor of the *Economist* magazine Matt Steinglass observed in 2016 that until recently "Europeans thought themselves long past the stage of resorting to violence over religion. That was premature." The new reality is that "intolerance, corruption and religious upheaval are all making a comeback, and not just in the Middle East." It was therefore, he recommended, "time to bone up on our Luther."[2]

Although Opielka regarded the amount of actual research on the role of religion in the development of the welfare state to be rather limited, he did report in another article in 2008 (writing in this case

1. Opielka, "Christian Foundations of the Welfare State," p. 98.

2. Steinglass, "Martin Luther, Church Splitter," p. 80.

with Dutch sociologist Wim van Oorschot and fellow German sociologist Birgit Pfau-Effinger) that the need for study of the importance of ideas and other cultural factors such as religion was becoming more widely acknowledged. As he and his co-authors wrote, by then "those who deny a significant relationship between culture and welfare policy [increasingly] take a lonely position." While economic considerations were still seen as critical, it had now become necessary to incorporate in welfare state analyses such cultural matters as "the struggle between such various ideologies as conservatism, liberalism, and socialism. In addition, it is acknowledged that Catholic and Protestant religious cultures have had an influence on the formation and design of European welfare states." Ideas, especially religious ideas, as more and more European scholars were coming to acknowledge, could work powerfully to shape not only economic events but the world.[3]

Opielka finds, moreover, that the impact of religion on the welfare state goes well beyond that of the traditional Catholic and Protestant divide, reflecting a "growing awareness of the complexity and plurality of religions in the sociology of religion and in the sciences of religion" that has expanded the concept of "religion" beyond "the traditional quintet or septet of world religions – Christianity, Islam, Judaism, Buddhism, and Hinduism, plus Confucianism and Daoism." Opielka explains that the American sociologist Talcott Parsons wrote in the 1970s about how "religion is the social subsystem which organizes, through 'ultimate values,' the society's relations to an 'ultimate reality'" (in this respect similar to the prominent German/American theologian Paul Tillich's emphasis on matters of "ultimate concern" in defining religion).[4] Opielka writes that "behind elaborated [contemporary] political and ideological values one always finds a realm of religious values."[5]

3. Habermas, "Religion in the Public Sphere."
4. Opielka, "Christian Foundations of the Welfare State," pp. 100, 101; see also Brown, ed., *Ultimate Concern: Tillich in Dialogue.*
5. Van Oorschot, Opielka and Pfau-Effinger, "The Culture of the Welfare State," p. 14; see also Gentile, *Politics as Religion.*

Lutheran Roots of Nordic Social Democracy

The appearance in 1997 of *The Cultural Construction of Norden* (an edited anthology) was something of a breakthrough in the study of Nordic history.[6] The very emphasis on "culture" as a primary driving force in "constructing" the modern world of "Norden" was itself revealing. Culture, the book suggested, is not just another byproduct of more fundamental economic and other material forces, as Marxists and many other economic determinists had long asserted.

Observations about the long and continuing historical importance of Lutheran religion appear throughout *The Cultural Construction of Norden*, including in a chapter by the Finnish historian Henrik Stenius titled "The Good Life is a Life of Conformity: The Impact of Lutheran Tradition on Nordic Political Culture."[7] Opening up new avenues for social science inquiry, the editors Oystein Sorensen and Bo Strath write that "it is not particularly difficult to imagine the social democrats as a secularized Lutheran movement" – indeed, as they summarize matters, a main message of the book is that in the Nordic world of the twentieth century "social democracy [is] a continuation/transformation of Lutheranism."[8] In another chapter, the Norwegian theologian Dag Thorkildsen writes that "the two pillars of the welfare state have been full employment and social security. These two pillars correspond with two central ideas in Lutheranism: daily work as the fulfillment of God's vocation, and a priesthood of all believers" that brings religious zeal into even the mundane activities of ordinary people. "The idea of full employment may be seen as [a Nordic] secularization of the [traditional Lutheran] emphasis on the importance of daily work, which was reinforced during the periods of Pietism and revivalism" in the nineteenth century.[9]

6. Sorensen and Strath, eds., *The Cultural Construction of Norden*.
7. Stenius, "The Good Life is a Life of Conformity," p. 162.
8. Sorensen and Strath, "Introduction: The Cultural Construction of Norden," pp. 13, 5.
9. Thorkildsen, "Religious Identity and Nordic Identity," p. 159.

By the twenty-first century, the importance of religion in shaping modern Nordic culture and history was being recognized more widely. Finnish historian Pirjo Markkola, now at the University of Jyvaskyla, has been a leader in such efforts; in 2000 she explored "the ways in which urban middle-class women in the Lutheran context of Finland redefined women's rights and responsibilities" in a key formative period from 1860 to 1920 – and she has since made further contributions examining the large overall impact of Lutheranism on the Nordic history of social democracy in the twentieth century.[10] In an important edited anthology published in 2009, *Religion, Class Coalitions, and Welfare States*, the Dutch political scientist Kees Van Kersbergen and the German political economist Philip Manow offer strong evidence that the European welfare state has taken characteristically different forms according to whether the historic religion of a nation was Roman Catholic, Lutheran or Reformed Protestant.[11] American political scientist Karen Anderson observes in this volume that "religion as an explanatory variable is conspicuously absent in most accounts of the historical development of the Scandinavian welfare states," a gap she seeks to help to fill in a chapter on "The Church as Nation?: The Role of Religion in the Development of the Swedish Welfare State."[12] As Sigrun Kahl sums up matters in the concluding chapter, different histories of religion in different European nations have "generated political consensus and affected the emergence of different welfare states – through the institutionalization of [different] religious doctrines into countries poor relief systems, and the secularization of these institutions" in the development of national welfare states in correspondingly different ways.[13]

10. Markkola, "The Calling of Women: Gender, Religion and Social Reform in Finland, 1860–1920,", p. 113. See also Markkola, "The Lutheran Nordic Welfare States."

11. Van Kersbergen and Manow, eds., *Religion, Class Coalitions, and Welfare States*. See also Van Kersbergen, "From Charity to Social Justice: Religion and the European Welfare State Traditions."

12. Anderson, "The Church as Nation?," p. 210.

13. Kahl, "Religious Doctrines and Poor Relief," p. 267. See Sigrun Kahl, "The Religious Roots of Modern Poverty Policy."

In another indication of the growing importance being assigned to religion in shaping the welfare state, two volumes were published in 2009 explaining and summarizing the research results of a large-scale study of "Welfare and Religion in a European Perspective: A Comparative Study of the Role of Churches as Agents of Welfare within the Social Economy (WREP)," organized by the Center for the Study of Religion and Society at Uppsala University in Sweden.[14] In describing the WREP project, Anders Backstrom and Grace Davie explain that "an important starting point" is a recognition that "the majority churches of Europe – as theologically motivated carriers of values – are related to the different welfare models that have emerged across the continent." They conclude in particular that Lutheranism offers the strongest form of religious support for the establishment of an all-encompassing welfare state, as reflected in the fact that "the Lutheran countries of Northern Europe, including Germany, were the first to develop systems of welfare and social insurance" in the late nineteenth and early twentieth centuries.[15]

The WREP project finds that the Roman Catholic Church has often perceived the national welfare state as a secular challenge to its own longstanding history of church provision of social services, thus causing it to resist the government-led process of welfare state expansion. Although WREP did not have a specific Reformed religious case study, Blackstrom and Davie agreed with the earlier work of Van Kersbergen and Manow, finding similar limiting effects of Reformed Protestantism, again due to concerns that the governmental established welfare state would be making large inroads into what is the proper domain of the Reformed churches themselves – and also reflecting the Calvinist determination to maintain a strong separation between church and state. This was much less of a factor in the Lutheran Nordic world because the social democracies of the Nordic welfare states

14. See Backstrom and Davie, eds., *Welfare and Religion in 21st Century Europe: Volume 1, Configuring the Connections*; and Backstrom, Davie, Edgardh and Pettersson, eds., *Welfare and Religion in 21st Century Europe: Volume 2, Gendered, Religious and Social Change.*

15. Backstrom and Davie, "The WREP Project: Genesis, Structure and Scope," pp. 5, 6.

could step into the shoes of the former Lutheran state churches, thus continuing a long Nordic tradition of one national political authority and one national religion bound together in a single national church, if now increasingly of a secular kind.

All this lends support to the core WREP conclusion that "religion is important as an independent, as well as dependent variable, in the evolution of welfare in Europe."[16] More broadly, WREP researchers state that "our results confirm the view that modernity does not necessarily entail the displacement of religion, but is more likely to mean a change in its form, function and content. 'Religious change' is therefore a more helpful label than 'secularization' when describing the position and role of religion and religious organizations in late modern European societies."[17] In other words, contrary to the secularization thesis that prevailed in the social sciences for much of the twentieth century, the growing view by 2010 was that, even in the supposedly Nordic bastion of secularization, religion had not been disappearing as much as changing its form.[18]

Social Democracy as Secular Lutheranism

Continuing this trend, a worthy successor to *The Cultural Construction of Norden* appeared in 2012, *Nordic Paths to Modernity* (again an edited anthology, some of the chapters being authored by the same scholars found in the 1997 volume). With the benefit of further research and reflection, it was now possible to make a still stronger statement with respect to the large role of Lutheranism in shaping the social democratic culture and political and economic institutions of the five Nordic countries. The editors, Johann Pall Arnason and Bjorn Wittrock, write in the introduction that "as for cultural developments, there can [now] be little doubt about the overriding importance of

16. Ibid., p. 6.
17. Pettersson, "Majority Churches as Agents of European Welfare: A Sociological Approach," p. 15.
18. Nelson, "The Secularization Myth Revisited."

Lutheranism." Indeed, "the Nordic world is not the only part of Europe where Lutheran influences have counted for something in modern history, but it seems to be the region where this version of the Reformation played the most decisive and durable role." Modern Nordic history, in short, shows a continuing strong connection between "Lutheran religious culture and [the] social movements of the nineteenth and twentieth century."[19] They do not use the term, but one might say that a "Lutheran ethic" was as important to the creation of the twentieth-century Nordic political and economic world as a "Calvinist ethic" was elsewhere (and earlier) to the development of capitalist systems of open markets under limited state control.

Arnason and Wittrock comment, for example, that Lutheranism was central to "the growth of universities and their role in the training of a new and disciplined clergy in the seventeenth century, and the [related] enhancement of state capacities in this period." In the twentieth century professional experts replaced the Lutheran clergy as the leading Nordic priesthood, and Nordic universities accordingly refocused their efforts away from traditional religion and towards providing the scientific bodies of technical knowledge and professional expertise necessary to the creation and management of the Nordic social democratic state. Instead of the old Lutheran preoccupation with salvation in the hereafter, the new twentieth-century clergy of professional experts sought the secular salvation of society along a path to a new heaven on earth guided by science and economics.[20]

Arnason and Wittrock write that Lutheranism also "for a long time supplied the moral backbone of an absolutist and semi-absolutist state." Yet it also was coming to "serve as a source of reading, critical thinking and movement in the course of the nineteenth century." During the nineteenth century in Sweden and Finland, the most important Lutheran influence was exerted through a more centralized

19. Pall Arnason and Wittrock, "Introduction," pp. 10, 11.

20. Nelson, *Reaching for Heaven on Earth.*

"state church," while in Denmark and Norway it was exerted more from the bottom up through the several branches of the "Grundtvigian people's church."[21]

Danish historian Uffe Ostergard describes how in the mid nineteenth century the young Danish Lutheran priest Nikolaj Frederick Grundtvig "took it upon himself to reestablish what he took to be the original 'Nordic' or 'Danish' 'mind.'" His critical thinking, including attacks on Lutheran orthodoxy, led him to be "banned from all public appearances and publishing," leading in the 1830s to an "inner exile" during which he "formulated a program for the revival of the critical stagnant religion" of orthodox Lutheranism. When he was free to publish again in 1839, he soon delivered a "massive production of sermons, psalms, and songs, a literary legacy which until at least a few years ago formed the core of the socialization of most Danes" – and whose writings would have a significant influence on other parts of the Nordic world as well, probably greater than that of any other single Nordic writer of the nineteenth century (and perhaps the twentieth century as well). At its heart Grundtvigianism was a renewed Lutheranism that offered a new "unity of land, country, God, and people (*folk*)" that in a secularized form established in the twentieth century the foundations of Nordic social democracy.[22] The Danish social democratic state thus took the place of the Lutheran state church of old; the "people" took the place of the traditional Christian God as a source of ultimate Danish authority; and the religion of Danish "nationalism" offered a modernized version of the traditional Lutheran faith.

Lutheranism historically had also had large practical impacts on the governing institutions of the Nordic world. Bjorn Wittrock explains that "since the seventeenth century the Swedish state had been characterized by an unusual level of efficiency, in the last instance based less on external control than on the internalization of a

21. Arnason and Wittrock, "Introduction," p. 11. See also Hall, Korsgaard and Pedersen, eds., *Building the Nation*.

22. Ostergard, "The Danish Path to Modernity," p. 63.

strong, partly Lutheran-inspired moral code."[23] Perhaps partly because it had the secure status of being a fully established state church, Lutheranism in Sweden was less defensive, posing less of an obstacle in the eighteenth century to Enlightenment trends. Elsewhere in Europe such as France, traditional religion – especially Catholic religion – saw itself as fundamentally threatened. As Peter Hallberg reports, however, "the 1720s were critical to the cultural regeneration" of Sweden, "specifically the growth of science." In Lutheran Sweden in the eighteenth and nineteenth centuries, "the connection appears to have been obvious" that a "modern and civil society [...] could not be created without the ordered application of the arts and sciences, and these could not fully prosper under unfree government. Thus, the state and science went hand in hand without major conflict in Nordic countries to create a new political order," culminating in the twentieth century in Nordic social democracy.[24]

In the first half of the twentieth century, with its long Lutheran history Sweden avoided the deep social divisions so common in other parts of Europe. Social democrats in Sweden by the early 1930s favored a single national "people's home" with the goal to "unite the whole people across class divides," embracing yet again a unifying faith that now took the form of a worship of professional expertise that would guide the future wellbeing of the whole nation.[25] Similarly, in Norway, as Norwegian professor Rune Slagstad finds, in the twentieth century the social democratic "Labour Party state was a knowledge regime in the sense that modern Norway was to be created through the mobilization of a positivist science, with the social science professions as the avant-garde in social democratic policies of reform."[26] It was based on a newly confident expectation that "the new social sciences [would be capable] of creating a new society – and, as the boldest added, a new man" of the Nordic world. Reflecting the trends of the times, Marxism also prophesied the looming arrival of a

23. Wittrock, "The Making of Sweden," p. 107.
24. Hallberg, "History and Ethics in Pre-revolutionary Sweden," p. 114.
25. Wittrock, "The Making of Sweden," p. 101. See Nelson, *Economics as Religion*.
26. Slagstad, "The Metamorphoses of Norwegian Reformism," p. 161.

"new man," but in its case this would occur as a sudden culminating event in history, the apocalyptic outcome of a final struggle among economic classes, yielding the final glorious triumph of the proletariat. In the social democratic countries of the Nordic world from the 1930s onward, however, the progress of society would have to be achieved more incrementally through political and economic actions in a democratic framework; heaven on earth was to be reached peacefully and by parliamentary means over a more extended period of time, rather than through the violence of class struggle.

As we now know, of course, the expectation of a looming heaven on earth proved to be overly optimistic – for Marxists, early Nordic social democrats and many other men and women of the first half of the twentieth century.[27] The disillusionment of the western world began to set in with the gross failures of political leadership leading to the senseless deaths of 9 million combatants and 6 million civilians in World War I. Matters then became even worse in the 1930s and 1940s. How a scientifically and economically advanced nation such as Germany – that had once led the world in mathematics, music, philosophy, and other main areas of knowledge – could descend into the hell of the Holocaust remains rationally incomprehensible even today for large numbers of people. Desperate for any explanation, some have even found it necessary to turn back to much older ideas, to invent new modern substitutes for the Christian devil of old, a pervasively irrational force for evil in the world as now spread by new servants of Satan such as Adolf Hitler.

The Finnish Case

In Finland, the same social democratic ideals were found in the twentieth century as in the other Nordic countries. The mood, however, was perhaps somewhat less radically optimistic; this might have been due to the greater disappointments and misfortunes experienced

27. Johnson, *Modern Times*.

by the Finns over the long course of their modern history. Already by 1918 Finland had witnessed a destructive civil war fueled by deep hatreds among its own people, the only Nordic country in centuries to experience such high internal levels of violent conflict.[28] Finnish historian Henrik Stenius observes that Finland is "a country with a political culture of realpolitik. It acknowledges and approves of political power relations in a national perspective: bide your time, and meanwhile be obedient, work hard, become educated, and be nationalistic." In comparison with many other parts of Europe with their revolutionary dreams of radical social transformation, in Finland to a greater degree one now finds "a realpolitik that does not give much guidance or many instruments for how to change the political structures." Stenius draws a connection to Lutheranism in that "the universalistic figure of thought in modern Nordic societies is rooted in the conformist ideals of their pre-modern Lutheran societies."[29] One might add that obedience to the authority of the Prince – now having been transformed to become the secular social democratic state – was a central tenet of Luther's theology.

Luther denounced, for example, the revolutionary crusade of the German peasantry in the name of the Reformation in 1525, even endorsing its ruthless suppression by the ruling authorities. For Luther, a people's revolution in a fundamentally sinful world was an impossibility, merely an invitation to greater evils. Accepting the authority of even a bad prince was for Luther therefore a better choice than the likely outcome of a popular mob. A good Lutheran should be prepared to criticize his prince but not to pursue a revolution. Eventually, God would take care of those German princes who abused their authority. With the 1918 civil war as a major exception – itself a terribly painful lesson – Finns even today often show a related Lutheran caution about expressions of revolutionary idealism.

The American theologian William Mueller thus writes that for Luther "it is God who has founded nations and empires, and by his

28. Alapuro, *State and Revolution in Finland.*

29. Stenius, "Paradoxes of the Finnish Political Culture," p. 219.

judgments they also come to nought." Hence, "the ups and downs of history and of nations are in God's hand." As Luther thinks, God has also chosen – however mysterious his full reasons for doing so must often seem to us – the secular rulers of our time, and hence the church "can never have a part in open rebellion against the God-appointed orders of secular rule" of the moment. Indeed, human persecution "is a divinely willed feature of the church's life on earth in every epoch of history." For Luther, therefore, "the possibility of resistance to [the] secular authority" of a governing authority is "entirely excluded" from his thinking.[30] For the people of the Nordic countries, their relatively peaceful history since the eighteenth century – compared with the rest of Europe – might have reflected a greater Nordic appreciation for Luther's way of thinking about the dangers of mass religious movements. A controlling state authority may offer greater governing advantages than modern democratic theory would suggest. Owing to their Lutheran heritage, the Nordic countries have shown a rare voluntary willingness to accept a powerful state management of society.

For western civilization as a whole, after the many horrors of the first half of the twentieth century in Europe, Asia and elsewhere, a similar dampening of revolutionary passions (some would say cynicism) would become newly influential in the second half of the twentieth century. Turning away from war and revolution, the post-World War II era would celebrate economic competition, prosperity, individual rights and the maximization of individual happiness. Much of Europe would come together for the collective peaceful achievement of such objectives by means of the newly created political and economic institutions of the European Union – though they have recently faced greater challenges.

Richard Lewis is an Englishman who over the course of his long career has lived in Finland, speaks Finnish, and received an award in 1997 from President Altisaari for his services to Finland. Lewis's

30. Mueller, *Church and State in Luther and Calvin*, pp. 52, 53.

business is writing about and advising international business corporations on the character of national cultures, based on the assumption that in a globalized business world it will be essential for companies to have a good knowledge of the distinctive cultural features of each nation in which they are operating. In 2005, Lewis authored *Finland: Cultural Lone Wolf*, at one point providing this amusing but nevertheless revealing anecdote as a good illustration of Finnish national character.

> I was once in charge of an English language summer course in North Wales. We had assembled adult students from 3 countries – 20 Italians, 12 Japanese, and 18 Finns. Intensive language instruction was relieved by social entertainment in the evenings and by the odd full-day excursion to places of scenic or historical interest.
>
> We had scheduled a trip up Mount Snowdon on a particular Wednesday, but on Tuesday evening it rained heavily. Around ten o'clock that night, during the after-dinner dancing, a dozen or so Finns approached me and suggested that we cancel the excursion, as it would be no fun climbing the muddy slopes of Snowdon in heavy rain. I, of course, agreed and announced the cancellation. I was immediately surrounded by Italians, disputing the decision. Why cancel the trip? They had been looking forward to it (escape from lessons); they had paid for it in their all-inclusive fee. A little rain would not hurt anyone, and what was the matter with the Finns anyway? Weren't they supposed to be tough people?
>
> A little embarrassed, I consulted the Japanese contingent. If the Italians wanted to go, they would go too. If, on the other hand, we cancelled the trip, they would be quite happy to stay in and take more lessons. The Italians jeered at the Finns, the Finns mumbled and growled, and eventually, in order not to lose face, agreed they would go. The excursion was declared on.

> It rained torrentially all night and also while I took a quick breakfast in my room. The bus was scheduled to leave at half past eight; at twenty-five past, taking my umbrella, I ran to the vehicle in the downpour. Inside were sitting 18 scowling Finns, 12 smiling Japanese, and no Italians. [...] They had sensibly stayed in bed. When the Finns [later] asked them why, they said because it was raining.[31]

While this may not be a scientific argument, it nicely illustrates what is plain for anyone with eyes to see – that there are large cultural differences among nations, some of the largest of which may be found among Finns, Italians and Japanese, and that these differences can significantly affect the real world behavior of the citizens of these nations. So what does this story say about the Finns? It will not come as much of a surprise that Finns are open to compromise, and that they prefer finding mutually agreeable solutions to protracted arguments – a national characteristic widely observed in Finnish political life, if often attributed to the homogeneity of the Finnish population. Another characteristic is to see the world rationally – if it is raining heavily, and the experience will be unpleasant, why go just because you had planned and paid for it. Yet the Finns seem to feel unusually honor bound to keep their agreements, once they are made (it is sometimes said in Finland that the Finns are one of the few EU countries to enforce all the many strict EU bureaucratic rules, no matter how irrational they may be). Italians drive their cars through red traffic lights when there are no other vehicles around; Finnish pedestrians wait in the middle of the night for the red walking lights to turn green. So in the end who is "rational?"

Because in Finland the laws and rules are actually enforced, the actual level of social control may be among the highest in the world. Stenius comments that the citizens of the Nordic countries willingly accept the fact that "all the doors are open – to the living room, the larder, the nursery, not to mention the bedroom – and they are not just

31. Lewis, *Finland*, pp. 192–193.

open: society marches in and intervenes" with the powers of government "sometimes brusquely" applied.[32] So the Finnish rules and laws have to be written and administered well – with at least a modicum of efficiency and rationality – or the whole country might fall apart in confusion and chaos (other countries solve the same problem by simply maintaining a collective national understanding that it is permissible to ignore many if not most of the official rules that in any case will not be enforced).

A Wider Assessment

Another important collection of writings about Nordic culture and the welfare state comes not from a book but from a surprising source, a 2014 special issue of the American *Journal of Church and State* (published at Baylor University in Texas) on "Lutheranism and the Nordic Welfare States." It is guest edited by Ingela Naumann of Edinburgh University and Pirjo Markkola of the University of Jyvaskyla in Finland. As they note in their Introduction, for many years it had been "the dominant understanding that [European] welfare states had developed along the axis of material interests and class conflicts," reflecting the familiar materialist foundations of the social sciences in the twentieth century. It has only been more recently, as the editors write, that "a new comparative scholarship on religion and the welfare state is emerging that seeks to systematically account for the role of all Christian denominations in the formation of the European welfare state."Focusing on the specific case of the relationship between Lutheranism and social democracy in the Nordic world, Naumann and Markkola affirm that there is now "extensive evidence that the churches and other religious actors in the Nordic countries were actively involved in welfare provision, as well as actively part of shaping [general] policy debate around welfare issues" in the social democratic period of welfare state ascendancy.[33]

32. Quoted in Hilson, *The Nordic Model*, p. 88.

33. Markkola and Naumann, "Lutheranism and the Nordic Welfare States in Comparison." pp. 3-4.

Until the second half of the nineteenth century, the Lutheran church itself directly provided education, hospitals, care for the destitute and many other social services. This direct role then began to decline significantly – in some cases almost disappearing altogether by the middle of the twentieth century. Naumann and Markkola affirm, however, that the powerful "cultural influence of Lutheranism goes well beyond the direct operations of the church" in the administration of the welfare functions of the Nordic social democratic state. Indeed, as places in which Lutheran beliefs and values had been part of the lifeblood of the Nordic nations for centuries, it should not be surprising "that the Lutheran inheritance has contributed to a certain understanding of work ethics and equality, ideas forming a cultural backdrop of welfare state development" in Finland and other Nordic countries, even in the "secular" twentieth century.[34]

For many centuries Finland was part of Sweden and Norway was part of Denmark, one factor explaining why historically somewhat different patterns of Lutheran influence have been seen in Sweden and Finland, as compared with such patterns in Denmark and Norway. In another 2014 article in the *Journal of Church and State*, Naumann focuses on welfare state developments in neighboring Sweden in the critical period of the 1920s and 1930s when the Social Democratic Party was taking the key steps that would lead to the dominant Swedish political role it would assume in the decades following World War II. As Naumann comments, "what does religion have to do with the Swedish welfare state? 'Nothing' has been the established view among social scientists" until fairly recently. But she agrees with observers such as the Danish political scientist Tim Knudson who are now finding that "the Lutheran Church was centrally involved in creating this [great] homogeneity in linguistic and religious terms" in Swedish (and Finnish) society in first the nineteenth and then the twentieth century.[35]

34. Ibid, pp. 6, 8–9.

35. Naumann, "Consensus, Conflict, or Compromise?," pp. 36, 37, 39.

Beyond Lutheranism's central role in shaping Swedish national culture, it was the "historical institutional and administrative structures developed by the Lutheran state church [that] provided a fundamental precondition for the universal welfare state" of today. It was especially in "the figure of the local pastor, who [for centuries] took on both secular and spiritual functions in the agrarian communities" that dominated daily Swedish and Finnish rural life, thereby providing "a link between state and society" that laid a basis "for the development of the [twentieth-century] expectation that the state should be responsible for social welfare." The political forces that appeared in the 1920s and 1930s in shaping social democracy in Sweden – similar developments were occurring in Finland with a small lag – should thus be seen as a "Social Democratic state/church alliance."

Conclusion

In its aspirations at least, this book seeks to follow in the spirit of the distinguished Norwegian political scientist Stein Rokkan (1921–1979) who, earlier than most, and with considerable international influence, wrote about the large role culture has had in shaping the workings of the national political systems of Europe. Rokkan saw a shared "language as a focal point of identity," providing the "most pervasive and obvious" indicator of shared membership in a common national community – and thus the study of linguistic developments must have significance in the political analysis of European political and economic events in the long run. For Rokkan, a second key factor defining a community is religion; he states that religious and other "roots are important because they help you to know who you are and whom you can trust: they are the lifeblood of cultural identity." In the European history of the nineteenth and twentieth centuries, he largely agrees with an "interpretation of nationalism as a civic religion, a body of conceptions, rituals, and rules of behavior linking local communities together in a wider system" – as in, for example, the social solidarity of the individual Nordic nations.[36] Austrian sociologist Peter Flora writes of the emphasis placed by Rokkan on establishing an identity "as an element of the nation-building process [which] [...] is 'culture-dependent', since nation-building means an 'accentuation of the cultural significance of borders between territories' and 'cultural unification and standardization': hence the term territorial identity."[37]

In the Nordic world, much of the history of the nineteenth century consisted of the various evolutionary steps in the development of newly powerful national identities. This was partly a consequence of the breakup of the Danish and Swedish empires in the nineteenth century, which would result by the twentieth century in the existence of the five separate Nordic countries with which we are today familiar. Replacing the Danish and Swedish linguistically pluralist empires of old with new, much smaller nation states worked to facilitate the rise of the individual Nordic national identities. Yet these strong national identities have been able to coexist with the presence of a strong collective Nordic identity, something that has proven more elusive in the rest of Europe – suggesting the continuing power even today of the common Nordic Lutheran heritage.

Thus, while Rokkan placed the greatest emphasis on a shared language in the development of a common identity, the fact that Finland readily fits within the Nordic world shows that language cannot be the main unifying force. In the Rokkan scheme of things, it would therefore seem that the long history of shared Lutheran religion must be the decisive factor in establishing the powerful sense of common Nordic identity that continues today – along with individual national identities – to be a large influence in shaping the political and economic workings of the five Nordic nations. As discussed in the previous chapter, the five individual Nordic countries exhibit striking similarities in comparison to the rest of the world.

36. Rokkan, "Nation-Building and Language," pp. 171, 172, 170.

37. Flora, ed., *State Formation, Nation-Building, and Mass Politics in Europe,* p. 67.

CHAPTER 3

Setting the Stage: From the Vikings to Lutheranism

When the Viking era began in the late eighth century, the Nordic countries had almost no knowledge of the philosophical genius of ancient Greece, of the engineering skills and well-developed legal system of the Roman Empire or of the large body of Christian theological and other writings that existed by then. Unlike much of the rest of Europe, in the Nordic world there were no monasteries or other large repositories for written historical materials inherited from ancient times and then reproduced in continental Europe. Indeed, it is difficult in today's globalized world to imagine the total isolation of the far European North.

Partly owing to increasing contact with other parts of Europe, the Vikings, however, developed more organized societies that began to create historical records; perhaps more importantly, their many raids left an indelible impression that was amply recorded in the written records of the victims themselves. The British historian of the Viking era John Harwood explains, for example, that one Anglo-Saxon scholar wrote of a contemporary 793 Viking attack that "never before has such terror been seen in Britain as we have suffered by this pagan people." In the Christian world, the Viking raids were widely seen as "an expression of the wrath of God," a view "generally accepted by early medieval Europeans and [that] was frequently reiterated by later writers."[1] Thus, although some traces of knowledge have earlier origins, recorded Nordic history really begins with the Vikings, whose activities eventually resulted in the creation of Denmark, Norway

1. Harwood, *The Vikings*, p. 28.

(long part of Denmark), Sweden and Finland (long part of Sweden; it served as a transit and staging ground, but few Vikings came originally from Finland).

Although the Vikings eventually began to settle in the areas that they attacked, their method initially was that of hit-and-run plunder. As Harwood writes, "the first phase of Viking activity was dominated by pirates not settlers" who were looking to capture gold, church altarpiece items, and other valuable objects – including human captives who could be exchanged for ransoms. As he further explains, the element of surprise was a key to their success; "like the modern terrorist, the Vikings usually held the initiative, being able to choose the time and place of their attacks." Also like terrorism today, "gratuitous violence [...] was very much to the taste of the Scandinavian warrior elite." As stories of their cruelty spread, it could have the advantage of reducing future resistance. It is "from the skaldic verse that we know of the 'blood eagle,' the Viking custom of hacking open a captive's rib cage so that his lungs could be torn out to form a pair of bloody wings," later interpreted by some Viking historians as a "sacrifice to the pagan war God, Odin." Overall, Haywood writes, the record shows that "the Vikings were tough people from a barbarian society in which violence was recognized as the surest way to wealth and power; there should be no surprise that they glorified it and were quick to resort to it" – if not altogether different from other parts of Europe in those days.

The "Viking Mystery"

As recently as the first half of the twentieth century, admittedly, the scale of violence of two world wars, the Holocaust, the dropping of an atom bomb on Japan and other such events greatly exceeded anything that happened in Viking times. Perhaps surprisingly, England aside, the greatest violence of the twentieth century occurred in those parts of Europe that many centuries earlier had been more likely to be the objects of "terrorist" Viking onslaughts. Indeed, since at least 1800 the Nordic world has been more peaceful and treated its European neighbors in a more "civil" fashion than most of the rest of Europe has behaved. This seeming anomaly might be said to be a "Viking mystery." How did such a cruel and violent part of Europe become in the space of only about a thousand years (a small blip in terms of the history of human beings on earth) the most peaceful and "rational" part of the continent?

A thousand years is much too short a time for any significant genetic evolution to have occurred. The largest flows of new people into the Nordic world occurred before Viking times, so large-scale migration of more peaceful newcomers does not seem to work as an explanation of the Nordic transformation. Following the prevalent economic determinism of twentieth-century historical analysis, a natural inclination might be to look to economic causes. Until the nineteenth century, the Nordic countries had in fact long been among the poorest parts of Europe, with small numbers of people living at low densities over comparatively immense geographic areas. So the Vikings may have had an unusually strong economic incentive to pillage their southern neighbors. It is also true that modern developments have probably improved living conditions in Nordic countries as much as or more than any other parts of the world, reducing the economic benefits of violent acts.

But these large economic benefits did not really begin flowing abundantly until the end of the nineteenth century, and they had their greatest impacts in the twentieth century, especially after World War II. For many hundreds of years after the Viking age passed, the Nordic world remained desperately poor, both absolutely and relative to other parts of Europe. So the timing of economic events does not fit well in explaining the end of the Viking era and the resulting radical change in the extent of Nordic violence. A similar problem arises with respect to any suggestion that modern changes in military technology may have sharply reduced the material benefits of aggressive warfare in Europe, since that would have to explain the end of the Viking age that occurred almost 1,000 years ago.

It is, moreover, difficult to contemplate that any economic or other material factors would be capable of pushing any Nordic country today – or at any point over at least the past two centuries – to anything like the extent of Viking violence. Rather, the scientific materialists of our time to the contrary, it seems that the Nordic countries simply have in recent centuries developed cultures within Europe less disposed to violence. For Americans, for example, it is startling to hear that Anders Breivik, the Norwegian mass murderer of more than 70 people in 2011, was subject to a maximum sentence in the Norwegian judicial system of 21 years (with some possibilities for extension). Judicial revenge is, apparently, not part of the Norwegian mindset in the same way as it is in most other places around the world. Until recently, in most places summary execution – sometimes judicially authorized, sometimes informally by police actions – would have been a standard response.

One large hint in explaining the "Viking mystery" is found in later periods of the Viking era when it became common for the Nordic raiders to settle in the lands they had been raiding. In England, York was a Viking city for close to 100 years and at the end of the ninth century Danish Vikings controlled almost half of the country. The Viking impact on England took another and even more important form when Viking-founded Normandy invaded England under William the Conqueror in 1066. In areas of Viking settlement, the occupants were gradually absorbed into the habits and culture of their new country, although some evidences of the original Viking impact can still be found even today. As Haywood explains, in Ireland and England the "main agent of [Viking] assimilation was conversion to Christianity and intermarriage" (the two often closely related).

The Christian End to the Viking Era

To become a Christian was to adopt a new set of ideals far removed indeed from the pagan practices of the Vikings. Jesus had been a poor carpenter rather than a great warrior. Some of the leading objects of

Viking attacks had been Christian churches and monasteries. For its first few hundred years, the history of Christianity was one of frequent repression and persecution – sometimes undertaken by people with attitudes similar to those of the Viking raiders. Christianity saw itself as a community of all the world; the goal should be to convert all people everywhere. For a group of Christians to plunder another part of the Christian world for personal gain would be the religious equivalent of attacking a neighbor or brother. By contrast, most other religions historically had offered an "us" versus "them" view of human existence; for the Greeks, the "others," the "barbarians," were well suited to be slaves. While not a message of total pacifism, an important teaching of the Bible was to "turn the other cheek." In short, it would be difficult to be at the same time a historic Viking raider and a true believing Christian. Conversion to Christianity therefore meant adopting new habits of thought and behavior. The Viking era was at its peak in the ninth and tenth centuries, rapidly fading at almost the same time as the spread of Christianity among the Vikings and their Nordic successors.

Although Viking assimilation first occurred in areas of Viking occupation and settlement on the European mainland, Christianity also soon began to spread to the Nordic world itself. A few individual missionaries arrived as early as the ninth century and one Swedish king even converted in the tenth century – but then relapsed. By the eleventh century Christianity was beginning to take a firm hold, including the arrival in Sweden of priests seeking conversions and craftsmen from England to build churches and other religious structures. Historian Neil Kent reports that "it was the arrival of Adam of Bremen, during the 1070s, which proved crucial for the solid establishment of the Catholic church in Sweden."[2] By the end of the twelfth century, Sweden had become a Christian nation, as Kent reports, beginning a period in which Christianity exerted "a profound influence not only on Swedish society and its spiritual life, but by assisting in

2. Kent, *A Concise History of Sweden*, p. 15.

the growth of the Swedish state itself over the following centuries" – developments that would extend later with a lag to Finland.[3]

Almost everything about life in Sweden was affected in one way or another by the spread of Christianity. In the twelfth century, for example, "foreign churchmen were [...] particularly useful in introducing coherent legal codes and administrative practices modeled on those in their own lands."[4] Swedish students began to go abroad to prepare for a future life in the Catholic church, numbering at least 800 over the next two centuries, studying at universities such as the University of Bologna and later Paris, thus furthering the integration of the Swedish and continental European worlds. A shared Christianity was the original greatest impetus to the development today of a common European identity (which has been newly emphasized by the difficulty today of assimilating Islamic immigrants into historically Christian nations). It was not until 1330 that the first Swedish literary writings appeared that were not about religious subjects. Serfdom was abolished in 1335 by a royal decree, partly owing to the fact that the Catholic Church in Sweden had been "ever more vociferously condemning the enslavement of Christians" – as was then the effective status of a serf.[5]

The Swedish king Erik the Holy in the twelfth century not only built many new churches and otherwise aggressively promoted Catholicism but also sent missionaries to Finland (then "Ostland" as the eastern sector of Sweden), where the spread of Christianity would have similarly significant consequences. In the thirteenth century, a Catholic episcopal see was establish at Turku, doing much to spread the Swedish language and culture to Finland – and today it is still the location of the Lutheran archbishop of Finland, and the nation's third largest city. This act was the beginning in many respects of the Finland we know today. As contemporary Finnish Lutheran church historian Kimmo Kaariainen writes (with four fellow church historians), the Roman-appointed "Bishop of Turku was the most powerful

3. Ibid., pp. 12–13.
4. Ibid., p. 16.
5. Ibid., p. 32.

man in medieval Finland," as the "Catholic Church brought European civilization to Finland," including the provision of many necessary practical functions.[6] In medieval Finland, the Catholic Church:

> united dispersed tribes into a single nation and provided an advanced system of administration. The Church ministered to the destitute and infirm by maintaining houses for the poor and hospitals. It fostered learning and the arts. Eighty stone churches, their frescos, wood carvings, sacred relics, altar cloths and vestments remind us of the high quality of both Finnish and imported art.
>
> Most of the 164 Finns registered at medieval [European] universities embarked on their studies with the support of the cathedral chapter [at Turku].[7]

In 1548 Mikael Agricola, who would later become the Lutheran bishop of Turku, translated the New Testament into Finnish, thus, according to University of Helsinki historian Henrik Meinander, "laying the foundation of the written Finnish language."[8] Indeed, in the secular societies of today it is difficult for many people to grasp the full extent to which the histories of the Nordic countries are the histories of Christianity in these nations, beginning at the end of the Viking era. The religious impacts went far beyond narrowly theological matters such as beliefs about the correct path of individual salvation or about the true character of God.

War and Religion

The impact of Christianity admittedly was not always peaceful. Christians were at least somewhat restrained in attacking other Christians for reasons of winning goods and glory. But Christianity did lead to another form of conflict: warfare fought over religious beliefs for the purpose of containing and suppressing heresy and other falsities.

6. Kaariainen, Ketola, Niemela, Palmu and Salomaki, *Facing Diversity*, p. 8.

7. Ibid., p. 8.

8. Meinander, *A History of Finland*, p. 24.

Ignited by religious passions and a sense of an "evil" enemy, religious warfare could be just as destructive – indeed more so – as compared with wars fought for more conventional economic, geopolitical, and other reasons. The Thirty Years war in Germany between Protestantism and Catholicism in the seventeenth century would be followed by another cataclysmic "Thirty Years War" of religion from 1914 to 1945, this time driven by conflicts among newly "secular religions" that might be seen as Christian heresies, such as Marxism in Russia and National Socialism in Germany.

The degree of deliberate individual cruelty may have been less but the overall levels of death and destruction in Europe of the religious wars of the seventeenth century exceeded anything from Viking times. By some estimates, a third of the population of Germany died in the fighting between 1618 and 1648. Little of the most intense fighting occurred in the Nordic countries themselves (aside from some battles between Sweden and Denmark). As in Viking days, Sweden under King Gustavus Adolphus again marched its armies southward, now mainly into Germany, achieving remarkable military triumphs for almost 20 years, led by an outstanding series of Swedish generals (many of the field soldiers were mercenaries). In a sense, we might say, they were the last of the Nordic "Vikings." The military successes were nevertheless partly attributable to the strict Lutheran morality and tight religious bonds holding together the Swedish nation itself, helping to make Sweden one of the most efficiently run nations of Europe in the seventeenth century. But, like the Vikings, seventeenth-century Sweden did profit from its military excursions, including large monetary payments from France (although a fellow Catholic nation, it was more important to France that the Catholic Hapsburgs were an ancient enemy), bringing back to Sweden important cultural trophies from the areas of Europe it conquered, and at the end at the Peace of Westphalia adding significant new territories to its Kingdom.

In the Nordic world itself, the many centuries of war and other conflict between Sweden and Russia – much of it fought on Finnish soil –

was often fought as a form of religious war. The bishop of Turku, as David Kirby writes, "was an enthusiastic supporter of the idea of a crusade against the Orthodox Russians."[9] Partly owing to the bishop's influence, Pope Alexander VI issued a bull in 1496 condemning the Orthodox forces who had "most grievously destroyed a great part of the [far extending] diocese of Turku, [...] burning churches, desecrating the name of Christ, [...] and placing the yoke of slavery upon many thousand Christians" of then Catholic Finland.[10] Swedish Catholics (including those living in Finland) were called in the name of God to protect against this satanic religious invader from the East.

The Lutheran hatred of Russian Orthodoxy later played a significant part in one of the most unhappy episodes of Finnish history, the military defeat of Sweden by Russia in 1709, resulting in a harsh Russian occupation for 12 years, and loss of Finnish territory at the eventual peace settlement in 1721. Led by king Karl XII, Sweden at first achieved major military successes. But the Swedish king refused to negotiate an end to the conflict at a moment when the terms might have been most favorable. As Meinander writes, as "the product of a strict theocratic education, the king was totally convinced that he was God's instrument." He thus would have nothing to do with the idea of entering into negotiations with the "morally inferior Catholic and Greek Orthodox believers" who were his Baltic religious antagonists.[11]

A Lutheran World

In 2006, Meinander devotes much of his analysis in *A History of Finland* to exploring the "economic and political realities [that] dictated the material conditions of everyday life" over the course of Finnish history. But he also reflects the growing interest of recent years in culture and religion – not only technological and economic developments

9. Kirby, *A Concise History of Finland*, p. 16.
10. Quoted in ibid., p. 16.
11. Meinander, *A History of Finland*, p. 52.

– as powerful explanatory factors in Nordic history. As he writes of Sweden and Finland in the seventeenth century,

> The population was also subject to an indoctrination which brought a unified culture to the whole realm over the course of the seventeenth century. The process was conducted by the Church and the administrative apparatus of the state, both of which had been polished into efficient tools in the hands of the monarch. The role of the Church in this regard cannot be overestimated. The ideological heart of the Lutheran church service was the sermon, which in the Great Power [seventeenth-century Sweden] increasingly included political content and reminders that respect for the monarchy was inseparable from fear of God. The destructive effect of sin on both the individual and society was another recurrent theme. According to the ever more orthodox interpretation of Lutheran doctrine [at that time], unatoned sins would incur the wrath of God, which at the very worst could strike the entire country in the shape of war, pestilence or famine.[12]

In the seventeenth century more than 85 percent of the people living in Finland were native Finnish speakers. Yet despite the separation from greater Sweden by the sea, and the large linguistic differences, the Finnish-speaking areas were by the seventeenth century thoroughly integrated into the Swedish nation. The University of Turku, founded in 1640 (moved by the new Russian rulers in 1828 to become the University of Helsinki), ranked with the University of Uppsala as the two leading Swedish centers of learning. Meinander comments that in all of Sweden the university in Turku "led the field of theological research" at the end of the seventeenth century.[13] Among those conscripted into the Swedish army from 1626 to 1630 to fight in the European wars of religion, almost a third were Finnish.[14] As a result

12. Ibid., pp. 46–47.
13. Ibid, p. 49.
14. Kirby, *A Concise History of Finland*, p. 31.

of many such close bonds, "the Finn's loyalty to the [Swedish nation and] Crown was not in doubt," a product not of shared language or ethnic history – in many societies the leading bonding agents – but of a common "homogeneous Lutheran culture" tightly controlled and overseen by the common Swedish king.[15] Without the shared bond of Lutheranism, the lands of Finland would have been closer to "colonies" of Sweden than to the integrated "provinces" of the same nation that they in fact were.

Lutheran religion would continue at the center of Nordic life, explicitly so to the end of the nineteenth century, and implicitly so even to the present day. To a surprising extent, religion did, and still does, drive the world, whatever the many self-proclaimed secular social scientists of the twentieth century may have once thought. For reasons that will be explored further in this book, the workings of Lutheran religion –admittedly along with other major historical influences – have been driving forces for the past three hundred years towards a Nordic world that, by the nineteenth century, had become for the most part the least violent and most peaceful among the nations of Europe – the antithesis of its Viking heritage. It all started with the Christianization of the Nordic world a thousand years ago – and continued in the transformation today of Christianity into new "secular" forms.

15. Meinander, *A History of Finland*, pp. 49, 50.

CHAPTER 4

Martin Luther: German Political Revolutionary

In assessing the twentieth-century impact of Lutheranism on the Nordic world, it is well to begin with the figure of Martin Luther himself. As will be seen, Luther was a complex individual who did and said many contradictory things over the course of his lifetime. The study of Luther is thus only one element of the study of Lutheranism as it would take shape over the following centuries. His historical legacy is in significant part a story of the interpretations of Lutherans and other Protestants who followed after him. Yet his influence was such that Luther himself is commonly ranked today among the five most important figures for the history of western civilization of the past thousand years.

Luther was more bluntly honest about himself than many of the Lutheran faithful would subsequently be in assessing his theological legacy. As the religious historian Charlotte Methuen writes, "Luther was aware that he was not a systematic writer."[1] The year before he died, in an introduction to his collected writings in Latin, he commented that his writings over the course of his lifetime were a "crude and disordered chaos, which is now not easy to arrange even for me."[2] For a more systematic treatment of many of the same subjects, he suggested that the works of his close friend and theological colleague Philip Melanchthon might be preferable.

Melanchthon was a child prodigy who entered Heidelberg University in 1509 at the age of 12, graduating 20 months later. At the age

1. Methuen, *Luther and Calvin*, p. 56.

2. Quoted in ibid., p. 56.

of 21 he was appointed to a professorship with a new chair for Greek language studies at Wittenberg University, only the second such chair to have been created at a German university.[3] Although Luther was 14 years older, he looked to Melanchthon for his own instruction and professional guidance in Greek and other languages of the ancient world (Melanchthon provided significant assistance, for example, to Luther in 1522 in finishing his translation of the New Testament from Greek into vernacular German as published that year). As a professor of theology, Luther was the star faculty member at Wittenberg University but Melanchthon played a leading support role as the university's second most important professor.

It was due in significant part to the commanding presence of Luther and Melanchthon as professors known throughout Germany that Wittenberg, founded only in 1502, had the largest number of students of any German university by the 1520s. When Frederick the Wise protected Luther from the Roman Catholic Church in the early 1520s, he had additional motives but an important consideration was the critical importance of Luther to the continuing success of Wittenberg University; it was originally founded by Frederick and he remained strongly committed to its scholarly success and reputation. Characteristically blunt, Luther stated that "I was born to fight and wrestle with gangs and devils. That is why my books are more stormy and bellicose. I had to root out clods and roots, hew away thorns and hedges, fill the puddles and I am the rough woodsman who has to cut the path and make it straight. But Master Philipp [Melanchthon] rides cleanly and quietly, builds and plants, sows and waters with joy all the plentiful gifts God has given him." Indeed, Luther at one point confessed that "I like the books of Master Philipp more than my own and likewise take greater joy in seeing his books in both Latin and German in place than seeing my own."[4]

3. See Rhein, *Philipp Melanchthon*.

4. Luther quoted in ibid., pp. 22, 26.

Luther's Often Contradictory Thought and Ways

The American theologian James Nestingen thus commented in 2003 that, while a few core beliefs lay at the heart of Luther's thinking, in his writings "he at the same time considered the particular situation that drew his attention and addressed it specifically without apparent regard for what might be required in another circumstance," thus often saying one thing now and then another thing in a later, different situation.[5] Diarmaid MacCulloch, a contemporary professor of the History of the Church at Oxford University, agrees with Luther's own self-assessment. In his magisterial *Reformation: Europe's House Divided, 1490–1700*, MacCulloch writes that "Luther was a passionate, impulsive man, who felt his theology rather than beginning with logical questions and answers about God, resulting in a theology full of paradoxes or downright contradictions."[6]

This extended to even such central elements of Luther's thinking as justification by faith alone. As MacCulloch explains, his coming to this belief after years of early struggle had allowed him to escape the demons of religious perfectionism as an Augustinian monk, and thus to achieve a powerful "sense of release." Even as Luther "clung on" to this comforting belief throughout his life, however, he never entirely succeeded in resolving "the contradictions of theology within his own mind, battling with the liberating simplicity of justification by faith" against other less happy implications.[7] In particular, the absence for Luther of any human role (any place for human "works") in justification led to the conclusion that the salvation (or not) of each individual was in the hands of God alone. It then further seemingly followed that God not only chose the elect but also condemned the damned (this doctrine is known theologically as "double predestination," to which Luther subscribed). The members of the elect, moreover, were likely to be a minority of the population. By the most common estimate of his fellow Protestant John Calvin, there would be only 1 cho-

5. Arne Nestingen, "Approaching Luther," p. 248.

6. MacCulloch, *Reformation*, p. 115.

7. Ibid., p. 120.

sen out of every 100, although he occasionally raised the estimate to 1 in 20 or in especially optimistic moments to 1 in 5.

Hence, as Methuen notes, "one consequence for Luther was that God can, and does, will actions which appear to human beings to have evil consequences." Luther could offer no better explanation other than that for fallen human beings their capacities were limited and thus they could not see "the hidden ways in which God works." Recognizing that this might not be a satisfactory answer for many people, Luther pragmatically sought to avoid extensive public discussion of the predestination conundrums. As Methuen observes, "Luther did not believe that an awareness of these matters would aid the faith of all believers."[8] When he did write about such issues, he typically resorted to the Catholic method of distancing his efforts from the laity, writing in Latin. In specific situations, moreover, Luther was capable of resolving such significant tensions by simply ignoring his own previous teachings about the meaningless of good works. He thus said in one case that "it is nothing to build churches, finance masses, or to do any other works compared with this matrimonial work of raising children. This is the most direct way into heaven, and there is no better means to attain heaven than this."[9] As Finnish theologian Sammeli Juntunen observes, this statement "seems to go directly against the core of his theology, if taken literally."[10]

Even on another matter as central to Luther's thinking as reliance on "Scripture alone," Luther departed selectively as the occasion seemed to demand. Juntunen thus observes that "Luther was not in all respects a biblicist." Even though in the Bible "Christ (Matt 19:8) forbids divorce, Luther teaches that in certain difficult situations divorce is allowed for a Christian."[11] MacCulloch writes that in 1520 "when preparing teaching material on the [Ten] Commandments, [Luther] showed his characteristic ability to play fast and loose with Scripture by omitting all references to the prohibition on graven images" – thus

8. Methuen, *Luther and Calvin*, pp. 80, 81.
9. Quoted in Juntunen, "Sex," p. 205.
10. Ibid.
11. Ibid, "Sex," p. 190.

allowing him to hold to his own preferred position that "images do not matter." In Zurich, by contrast, Huldrych Zwingli was applying the Protestant message uncompromisingly, even banning the playing of music in churches as idolatrous, while Luther would himself compose many hymns that would be among his most important contributions to Lutheran religion.

Luther denigrated the status of four books of the Bible, saying that the Epistle of James "contradicted Paul and all the rest of Scripture in attributing justification to works" and of Revelation that "Christ is neither taught nor known in it." Among the four gospels, Luther downgraded Matthew, Mark and Luke, saying that the Gospel of John "is the one, tender, true, chief gospel," much to be preferred. Seemingly in contradiction to "Scripture alone," Luther declared the necessity of prioritizing among the Scriptures: "I stick with those books that give me Christ pure and simply."[12] As MacCulloch compares the two, Luther was in contrast to Calvin whose "theology was based on the [strict] principle that God's revelation of his Word was definitively contained within the Bible, and unlike Luther, he was not prepared to pick and choose where the Word was best expressed within the Bible's covers."[13]

Infant baptism was another area where Luther departed from a literal understanding of Scripture because – while he strongly favored it – there was no clear example or other justification of infant baptism in the Scriptures. Luther had offered just such a lack of a Scriptural basis as his grounds for abolishing five out of the seven traditional Sacraments of the Roman Catholic Church. Seemingly, he was acting in a contradictory way in the case of infant baptism, although he sometimes offered the (less than persuasive) argument that infant baptism could be regarded as a new Christian interpretation of the Old Testament Jewish requirement for circumcision.

As was often the case for Luther, his misleading assertion of the definitive final authority of "Scripture alone" arose to meet a specific

12. Luther, quoted in Edwards, *Printing, Propaganda, and Martin Luther*, pp. 112-113.

13. MacCulloch, *Reformation*, p. 241.

practical problem that he faced. Early in the Reformation, Luther charged the Pope and the Catholic Church with substituting its own very human – and thus also corrupted by the Fall – truths in the place of God's divinely revealed biblical truths. But this exposed Luther to a charge that he might be simply substituting his own individual views about the Scriptures in place of the teachings of the Catholic church – themselves based on a very much longer and larger body of religious inquiry dating far back to Augustine and before. Luther of course would have to deny that his readings of the Scriptures were merely his personal thinking, that he might believe he was divinely chosen so as to allow him to seek to impose his own personal views on the entire body of the Christian faithful.

Luther resolved this potential theological quandary by arguing that the clear meaning of the Scriptures could be discerned rationally and objectively by an appropriate close reading and analysis of the Scriptural texts themselves, as he undertook to provide in numerous writings over the course of his lifetime. He claimed that, rather being than a jumble of competing messages, the true meanings of the Scriptures "reveal themselves." When Luther and other newly Protestant faithful studied the Scriptures, therefore, they claimed the result was not merely a set of subjective interpretations but a religious understanding that offered a uniquely correct knowledge of God's revealed Word.

As the Reformation progressed, fierce disagreements had broken out among the Reformers as to the actual correct interpretation of Scripture. Luther remained adamant that he was correct, often saying of his critics that they had been sent by the Devil to undermine the Reformation. As the authoritative interpreter, this amounted in practice to Luther claiming to be God's new, divinely chosen representative on earth – literally, even as this seemed to exempt Luther from his own teaching of the general fallen condition of all human beings. Indeed, as Mark Edwards of the Harvard Divinity School writes, as sometimes encouraged by Luther himself, his own followers commonly did believe that he "was a specially chosen instrument of God who had revealed the papal Antichrist."[14] It is no wonder that later Lutherans would have to engage in a large project to "clean up" Luther in order to discern his true meaning for the Lutheran faithful to follow.

The Political Revolutionary

Despite all this, Luther is often treated in history as a great "theologian." Compared with Calvin, however, even though he was extraordinarily prolific and a great literary stylist who significantly infleunced the development of the German language itself, Luther was much less rigorous as a theologian. Indeed, to his Catholic critics, he was a great "heretic" who spread false religious doctrines. Luther's immense historic impact is therefore best seen not as that of a systematic theologian, but one of the great "political revolutionaries" of history – having an impact on his own times that might be said to have been most comparable in the twentieth century to that of, say, Lenin (who himself also frequently wrote to fit the tactical needs of the moment, often resulting in contradictory statements in his interpretations of Marxist dogma). As many have said, Luther's greatest historic significance is that he led a political revolt by means of which large parts of Northern Europe broke away from the longstanding political as well as religious authority of the Roman Catholic Church. In England, when Henry VIII seceded from the Catholic church in 1534, it was not over questions of the details of Christian theology but his ability to obtain a divorce – and to acquire very large amounts of Catholic church property.

Henry VIII had already been preceded in 1527 in Sweden by King Gustav Vasa, whose own act of secession from the Roman church was similarly driven by financial and other practical considerations. As Swedish historian Neil Kirk writes, Gustav Vasa "saw that the vast material resources of the Catholic Church in Sweden could be used

14. Ibid., p. 132.

to the benefit of the crown, by their confiscation and redistribution, in particular, to himself and the nobility, whose loyalty, through material interest, could thus be secured." More broadly, it was also crucially important that "with the power of the Church undermined, both the independence of the Swedish state and his own authority in ruling over it would be strengthened."[15]

Indeed, it was clear from the earliest stages of the Protestant Reformation that it would be as much a political as a religious event. This should not be surprising; over the course of history it has often been the case that religion is politics, and also that politics is religion.[16] This would be no less true in the twentieth century, even though the outward form of religion was being radically altered. In this particular instance, given that Christianity was involved in almost every area of medieval life, there could be no such thing as a revolt against Rome that would be limited to religious matters alone. As American theologian Robert Kolb writes, "Luther's concept of the Word of God gave 'confessionalization' its name, his image and person helped shape the phenomenon, his ideas altered the paradigm for discussion." As a result, "it redefined society not only theologically and ecclesiastically, but also in terms of political, social, economic attitudes and structures."[17]

Luther and the German Nobility

In his 1520 *Appeal to the Ruling Class of German Nationality* (often translated as "Appeal to the German Nobility"), Luther thus complains that the political leaders of Germany have allowed the Roman Catholic Church to run roughshod over Germans, not only in matters of true Christian faith but in many other practical areas of life as well. As Luther himself writes, "if ninety-nine percent of the papal court were abolished and only one percent were left, it would be large enough to deal with questions of Christian faith." Instead, in the

15. Kent, *A Concise History of Sweden*, p. 53.
16. See Gentile, *Politics as Religion*.
17. Kolb, "Luther's Function in an Age of Confessionalization," p. 210.

Roman Church the other 99 percent did little to advance true Christianity but was employed to support the "more than 3,000 secretaries alone" that served the Pope, part of an immense and expensive papal bureaucracy composed of a "crawling mass of reptiles, all claiming to pay allegiance to the pope" (Luther was seldom sparing in his use of adjectives), as they all benefited from papal revenues to live in luxurious comfort themselves.[18]

As Luther further complains, "now that Italy is drained dry, they are coming into the German countries. [...] They think the drunken Germans will not understand what the game is, till there is not a single bishopric, monastery, parish or benefice, not a cent or farthing, left for them" – the funds will instead be redirected to Rome. Luther suggests that "Germany today is giving far more to the pope in Rome than she used to give formerly to the [ancient Roman] emperors" many centuries ago. The current version of imperial Rome is thereby impoverishing Germany not only religiously but financially, absorbing the resources that Germans need for their own temporal welfare. As Luther warns, after covering the costs of the Roman Church, "it is not at all astonishing if princes, aristocracy, towns, institutions, country and people grow poor. We ought to marvel that we still have anything left to eat."[19]

For Luther, the Roman Church is engaged in a grand act of deception in the name of Christian religion. It perpetuates its "robbery, trickery, and tyranny" over the Christian faithful by concealing its true self-serving purposes in a vast array of "religious" teachings including "indulgences, bulls, letters of confession, butter letters, and other *confessionalia*." Luther writes to the German princes that they have been fools to go along with it. "It came to pass," for example, "in former times that the good princes, emperors Frederick I and II, and many other German emperors, were shamelessly trodden under foot and oppressed by the popes whom all the world feared."[20]

18. Quoted in Dillenberger, ed., *Martin Luther, Selections from his Writings*, p. 420.

19. Ibid., pp. 419, 421.

20. Ibid., pp. 431, 430, 405.

The Pope could succeed in such intimidation because the German princes accepted the Roman claim that God revealed Himself not only in the Scriptures but in the history, teachings and other actions of the Roman Catholic Church. To defy the Pope would therefore be to defy God: a frightening prospect indeed, that might in the worst case lead to the fires of hell as the final destination. Even Holy Roman Emperors with all their earthly powers might tremble before the prospect of God's punishment, as the Pope claimed to be forewarning them if they failed to heed his demands.

But Luther could now, as he boldly informed them, reassure the German princes. Rome was not a place of God's revealed truths and instructions but was in actual fact the abode of the Devil, the "Anti-Christ." The Popes and their cohorts, Luther declared, "deal with Christian people, [by] robbing them of their freedom without any warrant from Scripture, but by sheer wantonness," thus showing how "the Anti-Christ has been at work" within the Catholic Church. But for Luther all people are equal in the eyes of God; none has unique spiritual authority over others and each person falls within the "priesthood of all believers." The supposedly authoritative pronouncements of the Roman Church are therefore false; German Princes should know that, as Luther explains, "there is, at bottom, really no other difference between laymen, priests, princes, bishops, or, in Romanist terminology, between religious and secular." Indeed, for Luther the secular Princes of Germany are chosen by God to have their governing authority no less than the Pope in Rome.

Luther therefore appeals to the German Princes to expel the false Roman "evil-doers, and to protect the law-abiding, so we ought to leave them [the Princes] to do their work without let or hindrance everywhere in Christian countries, and without partiality, whether for pope, bishops, pastors, monks, nuns, or anyone else."[21] The Roman Church is thus to be subject in Germany to the secular authority of the

21. Ibid., pp. 412, 409, 410.

Princes, not the other way around, and as such the Princes are duty bound to protect their subjects from Roman oppressions and corruptions. Since the Roman Catholic Church is for Luther the source of some of the greatest evils, the Princes should do their duty, including the use of force as may be required in the defense of their realms from the depredations of Rome. As Luther thus calls on them,

> The German nations, including their bishops and princes, should remember that they too are Christians. They should protect the populace whom it is their duty to rule; they should defend them by means of their temporal and spiritual possessions against these ravening wolves [from Rome] who come dressed in sheep's clothing as shepherds and rulers. Further, since the annates are so shamefully misused, and agreements are not kept, the German bishops and princes ought not to allow their country and people to be so pitiably harassed and impoverished without any regard for justice. Rather, by an imperial decree, or a national law, they ought to suspend payment [to Rome] of the annates, or abolish them entirely. Since the pope and his adherents do not keep agreements, they have no right to the annates; rather, the bishops and princes are under an obligation to punish this theft and robbery, as the law demands.[22]

This is a call for revolution against not only the religious but also the existing political authority of the Roman Church in Germany. Many Princes, long restive under Rome's exercise of power in Germany, including the associated large financial drains, were happy to learn that a political revolution was now commanded of them in the name of true Christian religion. As suggested above, the line between the religious and the political is always difficult to draw, and that was especially true in the Christendom of late medieval Europe. Some of the German Princes believed devoutly in the new religious arguments being made by Luther; others may have regarded them mainly as win-

22. Ibid., p. 422.

dow dressing for more practical political aims of their own. In his instance, and whatever his exact motive (there is no general agreement), Luther was from the early days of the Reformation protected from an otherwise almost certain Roman execution as a heretic by Frederick the Wise, the prince of Saxony, also known as "the Elector" (because Saxony held one of the seven votes for the selection of new Holy Roman Emperors). Luther's own lived experience is thus not one of a separation of church and state but of a joining of the two under the authority of his German Prince, on whom his very personal and religious existence depended.

One Kingdom, Not Two

Luther's personal situation would prove to be representative of the future course of the Lutheran state. Although Luther is widely known today as an advocate of the "two kingdoms" relationship of church and state, the practical effect of his 1520 appeal to the German princes detailed above, and of many other later writings and actions of his, would be a "one kingdom" outcome. Roland Bainton was for 40 years a professor of ecclesiastical history at the Yale Divinity School and is the author of a leading biography of Luther, *Here I Stand: A Life of Martin Luther*. Bainton writes that Luther was torn between two concepts of the church, "a confessional church" that brought together those who shared a "personal faith and experience" and the alternative of a "territorial church" that included all the residents "in a given locality." Fearing in part that the mixing of religious passions in the same jurisdiction would lead to great internal "strife," Luther eventually opted for the latter "solution [...] that one religion only should be celebrated in a given locality." For those who did not share this religion, they should nevertheless be "free to migrate to favorable terrain" elsewhere.[23] Luther would advance this way of thinking in 1525 in condemning the mass revolts that were spreading rapidly across central and southern Germany. Although commonly known as

23. Bainton, *Here I Stand*, pp. 318, 319.

"the Peasants' War," Swiss historian Peter Blickle finds that they are better characterized as "the Revolution of 1525."[24] It was in fact not only an uprising of rural serfs and other peasants but a struggle that also included many miners and other urban people. The peak of the upheavals took place between February and May 1525, when tens of thousands of Germans joined in rebelling against their Princes and other governing authorities. Thomas Muntzer, a former Franciscan who had once been a follower of Luther, was the leading figure. The decisive moment occurred in May 1525 when the landgrave (ruler) of Hesse and Duke George of Saxony combined their forces to defeat a rebel army, slaying all of its 6,000 soldiers and capturing Muntzer – who would soon be beheaded. It is estimated that as many as 100,000 Germans died in the 1525 revolutionary upheavals, which ended up with the Princes back in full charge of their domains.

Despite his vehement denials, Luther himself bore a significant responsibility for the events of 1525. Luther had early on acknowledged that in principle it should be the members of the congregations who chose their ministers and otherwise governed the church, requiring a church internal organization for this purpose. If Germany was to be divided into a number of distinct "territorial churches" according to religion, why not give the governing authority to the members of the dominant faith within the territory? It fell to the followers of Calvin and Zwingli, however, not Luther, to act on this implication – as, for example, in the early Puritan settlements of Massachusetts in America that were conceived by the Puritans to be a religious haven that would provide a Christian "beacon" for all the world to follow.

The German revolutionaries could also find approval in Luther's own early 1520s willingness to advocate violence, if it were necessary in separating Germany from Roman corruption. His bombastic rhetoric in the early 1520s with respect to the terrible heresies of the Roman church and its representatives in Germany was a further in-

24. Blickle, *The Revolution of 1525*.

spiration to revolutionary thought and action directed against the symbols of Catholic rule. Thomas Brady and Erik Midelfort write that "his personal example as a rebel against the two great authorities of Christendom, the pope and the Holy Roman emperor" was of greater practical significance than any contrary theological warnings he might have given that only God can bring heaven to earth.[25]

The mass revolt in 1525 was in part inspired by more radical Protestants who accepted the view that the faithful should band together in Christian communities of fellow believers, distancing themselves from the control of the Princes to the extent of refusing to accept their authority in matters of governance as well as religious practice. Luther would later complain that he had been misunderstood and had always strongly opposed any attempts of the faithful to create their own Christian kingdoms on earth. But other leading figures of the Reformation did encourage such thinking. Most importantly, some Reformers in nearby Zurich reinterpreted Luther's message to reach such a conclusion.[26] Even though it may have been in significant part unwitting, Luther's writings and actions in early 1520 thus set loose revolutionary forces in Germany – and eventually all of northern Europe – that he was later powerless to control. Blickle therefore finds that "the Revolution of 1525 was an unfolding of the Reformation itself," and thus as the founding figure of the Reformation Luther would ultimately have to bear a large responsibility for the consequences.[27]

Luther, not surprisingly, and like many revolutionaries in history, never foresaw such consequences and now found them reprehensible, even as he adamantly refused to accept any personal responsibility. In any case in 1525 he made his loyalties to the Princes clear beyond any doubt. As he infamously wrote in *Against the Murderous and Thieving Hordes of Peasants*,

25. Brady and Midelfort, "Introduction," p. xxiii.

26. Blickle, *The Revolution of 1525*, pp. 155–161.

27. Ibid., p. 161.

> If the peasant is in open rebellion, then he is outside the law of God, for rebellion is not simply murder, but it is like a great fire which attacks and lays waste a whole land. Thus, rebellion brings with it a land full of murders and bloodshed, makes widows and orphans, and turns everything upside down like a great disaster. Therefore, let everyone who can, smite, slay and stab, secretly or openly, remembering than nothing can be more poisonous, hurtful, or devilish than a rebel. It is just as when one must kill a mad dog; if you don't strike him, he will strike you, and the whole land with him.[28]

The German Princes were only too happy to hear Luther's message. Many of them acted, however, not only to subdue the rebellion but to drive out Lutheranism from their territories. As Bainton comments, among the resulting "debacles" of the Peasants' War was that the "Catholic princes held Luther responsible for the whole outbreak, and color was lent to the charge by the participation on the peasant's side of hundreds of Lutheran ministers." In the aftermath of the 1525 events "the rulers in Catholic lands thereafter used the utmost diligence to exclude Evangelical [Lutheran] preachers, and the persistent Catholicism of Bavaria and Austria dates not so much from the Counter-Reformation as from the [1525] Peasants' War."[29]

Bainton thus considers the whole 1525 episode to have been a disaster for both Luther and the Reformation; Luther had turned on his own religious children and things would never be the same again, for him or for the world. In its aftermath "fear was to make him undiscriminating, ready to condone the innocuous lest in them might be concealed incipient Thomas Muntzers."[30] A late notorious culmination of this unhappily growing side of Luther's persona was his hate-filled 1543 tirade against the Jews, *Of the Jews and their Lies*, in which he advocated that "their synagogues or schools should be burned down and what will not burn should be razed and covered with earth."

28. Luther, *Against the Murderous and Thieving Hordes of Peasants*, quoted in Bainton, *Here I Stand*, pp. 284–285.

29. Bainton, *Here I Stand*, p. 290.

30. Bainton, *Here I Stand*, pp. 285, 290.

Luther would no doubt have detested Hitler (yet another murderous, thieving peasant) but even a leading biographer of Luther, Heiko Oberman, is not willing to absolve him fully of responsibility, writing that the messianic aspirations of Christianity encourage a "Protestant triumphalism [that] permits heretics, papalists, Jews, and 'us wicked Christians' to be looked back upon as past history." When this Protestant eschatological element is combined with "the anti-Judaism found in Luther – as in the Christian faith as a whole – [it] becomes a pawn of modern anti-Semitism" and in its most extreme forms may even be susceptible to the making of arguments justifying "a racist final solution."[31]

Unintended Consequences of Luther

Among the many inescapable contradictions of Luther is that his 1525 views could equally well have been directed at the entire Reformation and its historically far-reaching rebellion against Rome. If he had consistently applied his 1525 thinking, Luther should never have begun the Reformation for fear, as he said of the peasants then, of the "great fire which attacks and lays waste the land" that will inevitably result from disobeying the existing authorities. In the framework of such arguments of Luther, it should not have come as a surprise to him that the Peasants' War would prove to be merely the first of many great religious conflagrations in significant part originally set off by his own writings and actions. Indeed, the greatest destruction of life and property would come 100 years later during the 30-year religious wars between Catholicism and Protestantism that laid waste to much of Germany. In this respect the Catholic critics of Luther would seem to have the better of the argument, even if in the long run the modern age historically had to be born out of the destruction of the medieval world of Europe, an outcome that Luther – seemingly inadvertently – had been instrumental in precipitating.

31. Oberman, *Luther*, p. 297.

Luther's theology and indeed his entire body of thinking was presented in prolific writings largely improvised according to the circumstances of the moment; his immediate polemical needs thus routinely triumphed over a concern for maintaining a systematic theological organization of his thought. This immediate pragmatism served Luther well in terms of his ability to influence the ongoing events of his time. As a political revolutionary, there have been few others to equal him in history. It can plausibly be argued that the very existence and character of our modern world – including the social democratic Nordic states of the twentieth century – owes more to Luther than to any other single individual. In the broadest view, Luther and his later Calvinist followers broke large areas of Northern Europe free of the firm hold of the Roman Catholic Church, thereby opening the way to wide new religious, political and economic freedoms and resulting experimentation, and indeed to whole new directions of thought and action in society that in the space of a few hundred years would yield the modern world.[32]

Ironically, given Luther's core aim to restore an earlier and truer Christian world, he might have regarded the actual modern consequences of his own efforts as an abomination, eventually resulting for many people, as Nietzsche predicted, in the death of (the traditional Christian) God. He might also logically have had to concede that it was an unhappy confirmation of his often expressed view – however much he ignored this in his own actions with respect to Rome – that rebellion and revolution lead in the end to chaos and disaster. Perhaps the Pope was another gravely flawed but divinely appointed ruler whose authority should nevertheless have been obeyed – as Luther in other cases was consistent in demanding obedience in Germany to the rule of even gravely flawed Princes, some of them seemingly no better than the many sinners who had occupied the Papacy.

32. Troeltsch, *Protestantism and Progress*;
Gregory, *The Unintended Reformation*.

The Revolutionary Consequences of Luther

From our own perspective in the early twenty-first century, admittedly, we might want to thank Luther profusely for the errors of his ways. The costs of the religious divisions Luther did so much to foment in Europe have been extraordinary. But the whole new element of individual human freedom Luther did so much to introduce, with its surprising modern consequences, may have yielded even more extraordinary benefits. The distinguished American student of legal history John Witte writes that Luther advocated "a radical new theology of freedom" that became "the rallying cry of the early Lutheran Reformation."[33] Its significance extended far beyond matters of theology and into church organization, law and governance as well. As Witte writes,

> It drove theologians and jurists, clergy and laity, princes and peasants alike to denounce the [Roman] church's legal strictures and structures with unprecedented alacrity. "One by one, the structures of the church were thrust into the glaring light of the Word of God and forced to show their true colors," Jaroslav Pelikan writes. Few church structures survived this scrutiny in the heady days of the 1520s. The church's canon law books were burned. Church courts were closed. Monasteries were confiscated. Benefices were dissolved. Church properties were seized. Clerical privileges were stripped. Mendicant begging was banned. Mandatory celibacy was suspended. Indulgence trafficking was condemned. Taxes to Rome were outlawed. Ties to the pope were severed.[34]

The new freedom introduced by Luther thus was not only theological, but a freedom from the institutions built by the Roman Catholic church over centuries. There was now a large vacuum to be filled; it was as though a house had burned down and there could be a brand

33. Witte, Jr., "From Gospel to Law," p. 53. **34.** Ibid., pp. 53–54.

new freedom of architectural design in replacing it. The many resulting Reformation legal and other institutional innovations proved to be the opening wedge for new features that we can still recognize today as characteristically modern.

There is of course no form of economic calculation that would permit a comparison of the precise magnitude of the benefits and the costs of the creation of the modern world. There was much social chaos and great loss of life in the transition from the medieval Catholic universe to the modern world. But ordinary people today live much longer and at a higher material standard of living than the royal families of a mere few hundred years ago. The development of modern science, as was significantly advanced by the Reformation, has revealed astonishing mysteries of the workings of the natural world never previously conceived by human beings.[35] Indeed, any effort at assessment of the benefits and costs of modernity itself belongs to the realm of theology.

The human freedoms for which Luther's writings and actions bore a significant responsibility include:

1. THE FREEDOM TO PURSUE RELIGIOUS TRUTH outside the limitations previously imposed by the Roman Catholic Church. Ultimately, Luther's greatest historical significance is that – whatever one thinks about the final results – he instigated a successful revolution against Roman authority (political as well as religious) over much of Northern Europe, later extending to the United States and other Protestant nations outside Europe. In the area of "natural theology," this proved especially important when the new freedom led to the development of the scientific method in the seventeenth century in order to discover God's truths as revealed in the natural order of the universe (Kepler's, Galileo's and Newton's own understanding of their scientific purposes).[36] Even in nations with state Prot-

35. Harrison, "Protestantism and the Making of Modern Science."

36. Nelson, *God? Very Probably*, Ch. 3.

estant religions, there was a greater tolerance for a diversity of religious expression within and among such nations themselves, thus opening brand new paths of inquiry in many areas of human thought and action across a newly decentralized Europe.

2. THE FREEDOM OF INDIVIDUAL CONSCIENCE in religious and other matters. As Diarmaid MacCulloch writes of Luther's 1521 actions at the Diet of Worms, "not long after [Luther's] death, the first editor of his collected works, Georg Rorer, felt compelled to construct two tiny summary statements in German, which have become the most memorable thing Luther never said: 'Here I stand; I can do no other.' This can stand for the motto of al Protestants – ultimately, perhaps, of all western civilization."[37] Luther would later fail sometimes to stand up for the rights of other people in similar circumstances – especially their right to publicly advocate their beliefs – but that does not detract from the immense historic significance of his courageous actions at Worms in defense of freedom of religious thought, which eventually extended to other areas of life.
3. THE FREEDOM TO LIVE A RELIGIOUS LIFE AT THE HIGHEST LEVELS WITHIN THE WORLD OF ORDINARY HUMAN AFFAIRS. The pastor of a Lutheran church functioned as an ordinary person; he (or, now, she as well) held no exclusive expert religious authority over other people; members of the clergy were free to engage in sexual relations and to marry. Ordinary people were fully equal and also able to satisfy their full religious obligations as part of the lay "priesthood of all believers." Hard work in the ordinary tasks of life could equally serve a divine mission or calling – as true for Luther as it was for Calvin (even though their views about the best main areas for a calling were different).

37. MacCulloch, *Reformation*, p. 131.

4. FREEDOM FOR THE CONGREGATION MEMBERS TO SELECT THE LEADERS and administrators of each individual church. Luther in the early 1520s recommended this in principle although his defense of the powers of the German Princes from the mid 1520s increasingly undercut it in practice. Other Reformed branches of Protestantism would put Luther's original thinking into actual practice. Much later, from the nineteenth century onward, the Lutheran churches of the Nordic countries increasingly moved to adopt the "early Luther" democratic procedures of church management, such as local parish election of their pastors. Modern democracy extended the concept far wider. The modern idea that democratic state power and legitimacy resides in "the people" reflects the legacy of Luther and the Reformation.

Luther not only wrote powerful polemics in defense of such ideas but, more importantly, he acted vigorously in defense of them. By one estimate, in 1525 "three quarters of the work in print in German came from Luther's pen."[38] Luther's 1522 translation of the New Testament into German (and later the whole Bible in 1534) was among the most important accomplishments of his lifetime, significantly influencing the later character of the German language, and making it possible (combined with the invention of the printing press) for ordinary literate people to read and think for themselves about fundamental questions previously reserved for priestly and other religious experts. German Luther (and Melanchthon) scholar Stefan Rhein states that "without the printing press, there would have been no Reformation."[39] Luther's personal courage in defiance of Roman authority, highlighted by his actions at Worms, captured the attention of all Europe. He himself married and had many children in what by all accounts was a happy domestic life, setting the Lutheran pattern for its clergy for the centuries to come. Such real-world examples had

38. Arne Nestingen, "Approaching Luther," p. 241.

39. Rhein, *Philipp Melanchthon*, p. 30.

an impact that abstract theological arguments could not match. But Luther's compelling personal example changed the world.

As examined above, there is, however, one less positive side to Luther's actions that must be included in the record. Many people were encouraged by Luther's revolution in human freedom of the early 1520s to boldly explore revolutionary change in other areas of German society. In some cases the results were significantly destabilizing of the established order, including in Luther's own time challenges to the Princes and other ruling authorities in Germany. However large a responsibility he himself bore for all the new assertions of human freedoms, Luther proved surprisingly unsupportive of the resulting German upheavals – a sign that he had never carefully thought through the full implications of his own message. Perhaps he was loyal to the German princes because they had earlier shielded him from a likely death at the hands of Catholic authorities. More broadly, the Princes had been indispensable to the survival of the Reformation and its further spread over large areas of Germany.

In this respect, 1525 proved to be a turning point, when Luther's overall influence as a defender of individual freedoms in the early 1520s was increasingly challenged in the Lutheran world by the impacts of his writings and actions as defender of state authority. Instead, other parts of the Reformation associated with Calvinism and Reformed Protestantism more broadly (and also Anabaptism) would become the leading Reformation spear-carriers after 1525 in defending individual freedom. To the extent that Luther set the stage for these other Reformation branches of Christianity that followed, however, we can still say that he had an immense long-term influence in advancing human freedoms. Among the many contradictions seen throughout Luther's lifetime, the shift from the pre-1525 Luther to the post-1525 Luther is perhaps the greatest contradiction of all.

The theologian Cyril Richardson thus wrote many years ago that in practical effect the post-1525 "Luther sanctified the secular power" of his own time – setting a precedent that would long be followed in the Lutheran world and even to some extent into the twentieth century. In the territorial churches of the Lutheran future, the worldly authority of princes and other rulers was imposed – by force if necessary – on the Christian faithful, following Luther's effective approval of "uniformity of worship, confession and ecclesiastical usage, " as imposed by the German Princes of the sixteenth century within each of their domains and by later state authorities. As Luther had insisted, it would always be acceptable that a man in his own thoughts could hold heretical views, but in the public arena "all disunity and division enforced by insubordinate preachers was [to be] suppressed by the civil power."[40]

Conclusion

In explaining why Max Weber gave much less attention to Lutheranism in *The Protestant Ethic*, Max Stackhouse comments that Weber "believed that Luther preserved too much of the ethic of obedience to ecclesiastical authority" – that in Lutheran practice would reside simultaneously in state authority. Like Calvin, "Luther also advocated hard work in one's station in life," but for Weber "he also thought Luther understood 'station' in too static a way," that there was a deep conservatism in the Lutheran message.[41] This admittedly may have been more true of the later stages of Luther's life and of the Lutheranism that would evolve after his death. There can be little doubt that as a revolutionary force for change that would open the way for capitalism and the modern world, the impact of the history of Calvinism was considerably greater than that of the history of Lutheranism. It was the former development of the Protestant message, even as it had originated with Luther, that was therefore the object of Weber's greatest interest and concern.

40. Richardson, "Prophesy and Politics," pp. 145, 146.

41. Stackhouse, "Weber, Theology, and Economics," p. 315.

CHAPTER 5

Lutheran Theocracies of the North

The message of Jesus was that the word of God as revealed in the Bible must be obeyed by the Christian faithful. But what about the commands of the Roman Empire as it existed in Jesus's time? How should a good Christian regard secular authority? In giving an answer once again to this question, Martin Luther looked to what he regarded as the most relevant of the Scriptural answers. In his letter to the Roman Christians, Paul writes (Romans 13:1–4):

> Let every person be subject to the governing authorities; for there is no authority except from God, and those authorities that exist have been instituted by God. Therefore whoever resists authority resists what God has appointed, and those who resist will incur judgment. For rules are not a terror to good conduct, but to bad. Do you wish to have no fear of the authority? Then do what is good, and you will receive its approval; for it is God's servant for your good. But if you do what is wrong, you should be afraid, for the authority does not bear the sword in vain! It is the servant of God to execute wrath on the wrongdoer.

Similarly, the Apostle Peter writes in his first letter (I Peter 2:13–17):

> For the Lord's sake accept the authority of every human institution, whether it be the emperor, as supreme, or of governors, as sent by him to punish those who do wrong, and to praise those who do right. For it is God's will that by doing right you should silence the ignorance of foolish men. As servants of God, live as free people, yet do not use your freedom as a pretext for evil. Honor everyone. Love the family of believers. Fear God. Honor the emperor.

These passages – cited by numerous Christian writers before and after Luther – convey the common-sense message that a faithful Christian should not expect to take the law into his or her own hands, since confusion and chaos in society would otherwise be the frequent result. But what if the "emperor" is a Hitler or a Stalin?[1] Has God really chosen such people to rule over others, and should forceful resistance to them therefore be forbidden? The Bible, as in many areas, has conflicting language about such matters as well; it also says in the Acts of the Apostles (5:29) that "we must obey God rather than men." Later interpreters would be left to weigh the various arguments.

While Luther himself seemed in 1523 in his most famous treatise on church and state, *On Temporal Authority*, and in other 1520s writings, to give the secular authorities almost limitless authority, in the 1530s he would partially reverse that position, declaring that resistance to some grave evils was warranted – in this case Roman Catholic rulers such as the Holy Roman Emperor attempting to forcefully impose Catholic religion on other religious believers in Germany who Luther now concluded could rightfully resist physically. Even here, however, Luther limited this right to another ruling (typically subordinate) authority, still refusing to countenance any civil resistance by the masses of ordinary people – this principle thus seemingly precluding, for example, the popular "velvet revolution" in Czechoslovakia and the other 1989 uprisings that in Eastern Europe ended the Soviet Empire there. It would, however, have allowed the Finns acting through their government to fight back against the Soviet Union in the Winter War or even to resist the Russian Czar before Finnish independence in 1917 in matters of fundamental religious truth.

Luther further confused the issue by writing of the "two kingdoms," one consisting of the body of true Christians of the world (drawing on Augustine's concept of the City of God) in which there would be no need among the saved for controlling laws and government, and a second, altogether different kingdom overseen by the

1. Hillerbrand, "The Legacy of Martin Luther," p. 236.

secular rulers of the world (again following Augustine's concept of the City of Man, which for him meant the Roman Empire and for Luther now meant the many German states of his day). But this distinction of Luther had little operational significance because the true Christians were few in number relative to the total population and were in any case known only to God, and thus could not be found in any identifiable organized group in society (even Lutheran churches inevitably held many sinners). Indeed, as discussed in the previous chapter, Luther condemned in harsh terms and sought the repression of any actual efforts of Christian believers to join together in movements to realize God's kingdom on earth – as many of his enthusiastic Protestant followers had initially interpreted his radically new Reformation writings as suggesting might be desirable (perhaps reasonably enough in light of Luther's own advocacy of rebellion from Rome – by violent means if necessary – and the many theological ambiguities Luther had himself brought to his writings).

The idea of "two kingdoms" may have become more relevant in a modern context as another way of describing the idea of the separation of church and state. In Luther's own time, any such separation would have seemed untenable. Indeed, the purpose of the state for Luther was in many areas the practical implementation in real-world settings of the moral and other guiding principles of Christian religion, though overseen by the secular ruler. Since the Enlightenment, however, the political trend has been to limit religion to its own domain – part of the widely noted "individualization" and "privatization" of religion. Rather than the teachings of Christian religion, in a new secular age public policy should be guided by science and other "objective" forms of knowledge, in contrast to a private and thus "subjective" Christian set of truths. These are the modern two kingdoms: the individual and his or her private conscience (possibly expressed in the private setting of a specific church community), and the public arena of government administration and policy-making.

In this modern context, the "two kingdoms" doctrine has thus served to partially disguise the tensions for those many conflicted people who sought to be loyal to both the Lutheran church of traditional religion and the modern church of science, now attributing the possibility of the separation of the two to Luther himself. The concept of "two kingdoms" thus plays a larger role in Lutheran theology today than it did in Luther's own time. As the Oxford historian of religious ethics Bernd Wannenwetsch writes, "in the view of interpreters such as Max Weber, Ernst Troeltsch, Herbert Marcuse" the distinction between the "inner" and the "outer" man "within Luther's theological anthropology comes down to a separation between the religious and worldly spheres – a separation that resurfaces again in Luther's social and political thought in the parallel distinction of the Two Kingdoms." In light of Luther's many other writings, however, as Wannenwetsch concludes, the contemporary "widespread understanding of Luther's ethics as dualistic or polarizing is bound to fail" – in the real world of human affairs, there can be no actual City of God that exists separately from the City of Man. The City of God can exist only when God's rule reigns on earth as in heaven, an event the Christian faithful are still hopefully awaiting.[2]

Thus, once again, what is most important for the history of Europe – and the world – is not what Luther said but what he actually did, and what was later said in his name. In the future areas of Europe where Lutheranism was the dominant religion, there would not be two kingdoms but one kingdom. As religions go, Lutheranism is a small part of the total world body of Christianity. In the sixteenth century it had initially spread into significant portions of Poland, Slovakia and Hungary but its influence there was later much diminished by the Counter-Reformation. In the long run, Lutheran Europe has consisted mainly of parts of central and northern Germany (a nation also including large numbers of Catholics as well as Reformed Protestants); and as noted previously, the Nordic countries of Denmark, Norway, Sweden, Finland and Iceland (today having a total population only of about 25 million); and the small Baltic countries of Estonia and Lat-

2. Bernd Wannenwetsch, "Luther's Moral Theology," pp. 127, 126.

via. Given the massive emigration of the late nineteenth and early twentieth centuries from Germany and Scandinavia, there are also about an additional four million Lutherans in the United States – 19 percent of "mainline" (the historically most important American denominations in setting the terms for American culture and governance) Protestants today, but only 1 percent of the U.S.population. But they have mostly blended into the dominant culture of that nation itself, derived in significant part from its Puritan (Calvinist) heritage, including the core American political idea of a strict separation of church and state that does in some respects – to a greater extent in America than almost anywhere else – mirror a two kingdoms concept.[3]

After Luther's death in 1546, it was for a while questionable whether Lutheranism would survive at all in Germany as a separate religion. (Indeed, Luther himself had often stated that his great purpose was the "reformation" of the Roman Catholic Church, not the creation of a new religion in his own name). The Holy Roman Emperor at the time, Charles V, was threatening to win back the entire territory of Germany for Catholicism (and without Germany, Lutheranism might not have survived in the Nordic countries as well). Eventually, however, Charles V was pushed back, finally agreeing to the Peace of Augsburg in 1555. This was a defining moment in the history of Lutheran religion, resulting in a compromise known as the principle of "*Cuius regio, eius religio*," usually translated as "Whose realm, his religion." The religion of the Prince would be the religion of his principality and all its inhabitants. Those inhabitants who could not conform to the Prince's religion were free to leave. Uniformity of worship, confession and ecclesiastical roles was enforceable by each Prince in his domain, and all disunity and division fostered by insubordinate preachers was to be suppressed by the civil power.

In his own lifetime, Luther himself once stated that "I have written in such glorification of temporal government as no teacher has done since the days of the apostles, except, perhaps, St. Augustine.

3. See Association of Statisticians of American Religious Bodies, *U.S. Religion Census, 2010*.

Of this I can boast with a good conscience and the testimony of the world will support me." As Cyril Richardson puts it, in his later years "Luther does not continue to be Luther. Under the Pope he divorced the church from politics, in these times he seeks to identify politics with the church." In the Nordic countries as well, King Christian III of Denmark (then including Norway and Iceland) decreed that Lutheranism was the state religion in 1536, imprisoning Catholic clergy and confiscating church properties. Gustav Vasa had already acted similarly in Sweden (then including Finland) in 1527. In the Nordic countries, the King was the equivalent of the German Prince whose authority in matters of religion as well as earthly affairs had been justified by Luther and would continue to be by his Lutheran successors. Karen Anderson thus writes that "after his death the Scandinavian pattern of church-state relations was established in the 1500s. In the wake of the Reformation, Danish and Swedish monarchs usurped church influence and wealth, incorporated the clergy into the state apparatus, and assumed the welfare functions that the church had previously performed, such as hospital care and poor relief."[4]

The Nordic countries, in short, became Lutheran state "theocracies," not only in a metaphorical but in the literal sense of the word. In Sweden a person was legally required to be a member of the Lutheran church until the second half of the nineteenth century – and still legally had to belong to at least some church as late as 1951. In Finland, a citizen had to belong to either the Lutheran church (the choice of the vast majority) or the Orthodox church (this option reflecting Russian control over Finland) until 1889; full freedom of religion did not arrive until 1923.

In Denmark, to this day there is no recognized separate Lutheran church body at the national level (though local Lutheran churches do exist). Instead, the national administration of the Lutheran church in Denmark is the responsibility of the state Ministry of Ecclesiastical Affairs. In the Nordic countries, the state tax collecting authorities not

4. Anderson, "The Church as Nation?," p. 211.

only collect the revenues to run the secular government but also what amounts to a church tax (typically about 1 percent) that is then turned over to the Lutheran Church to support its activities. A person is subject to this "tax" unless he or she deliberately opts out of church membership, and most people do in fact remain members and pay, thus generating hundreds of millions of dollars in church revenues annually, even as weekly attendance of the Lutheran church members in these nations has become minimal.

Perhaps surprisingly for some, the manner in which Lutheranism became a state religion in the Nordic countries parallels in key ways the actions of Constantine and his conversion to Christianity in the fourth century in the Roman Empire, leading to Christianity becoming the religion of the Empire. Even as he constructed many Christian buildings and showered other benefits on Christianity, Constantine did not require all Romans to become Christians (and chose not to be baptized himself until near the end of his life). The Roman Emperor Theodosis I in 380, however, imposed the requirement that all Romans must be Christians, as all citizens of Nordic countries would later be required for several centuries to be Lutheran. When the Roman Empire collapsed in the late fifth century, its territorial successor was the Roman Catholic Church, the Pope eventually assuming the Emperor's authority not only to administer church affairs but also to resolve many other essentially political – as they would be seen today – matters in Western Europe.

In a great irony of history, therefore, one might say that each kingdom in Lutheran Europe became its own small version of the universal Roman Catholic Church, the Nordic King or German Prince now having a similar degree of religious authority in his territory as the Pope in Rome had over his domain. After Luther's death, as Robert Kolb thus writes, "official confessions of faith in several Lutheran lands accorded the corpus of Luther's printed works as a whole [...] [the] status as a substitute for [Roman] popes, bishops and councils."[5]

5. Kolb, "Luther's Function in an Age of Confessionalization," p. 218.

Even in Luther's own day, many of his followers regarded him in terms of a new savior born of human flesh on earth. Luther scholar Mark Edwards comments, for example, that "given all that Luther had accomplished in revealing the 'true' meaning of Scripture, many [Lutheran faithful] were coming to think of him not only as a learned doctor of the Bible but also as a divinely 'chosen light of Christendom,' sent to tell of God's divine word and to reveal the sorry state of the present world."[6] Indeed, this would characterize much of the Lutheran Nordic world until strong Pietist, revivalist and other challenges to orthodox Lutheranism would emerge in the nineteenth century. As University of Helsinki theologian Eero Huovinen explains, "during the period of Lutheran Orthodoxy [from about 1600 to 1800], Luther was held by many to be unique, even infallible, as a teacher of correct doctrine."[7]

Luther sometimes saw himself in a similar light, a contributing factor to the astonishing levels of energy he was able to summon for his writings and other efforts to advance the Reformation. Luther himself wrote in 1521 in response to a critic that "I let no one attack my teaching without a counterattack, since I know that it is not mine, but God's."[8] As sometimes thus encouraged by Luther, this type of thinking was carried to the extent among his followers that "some were even coming to see him in biblical terms, as the prophesied 'Angel of the Apocalypse' sent by God [...] to begin the final, apocalyptic struggle between the forces of good and evil, Christ and the devil." Luther himself contributed to such expectations in that in his lifetime he "took on many of the trappings of a biblical saint or prophet."[9] It was another of the large contradictions of Luther that he also sometimes confessed to grave doubts and a powerful sense of his own sinfulness. His writings sometimes acknowledged his own fierce battles with the devil who had already captured his religious opponents for his own purposes – and who sometimes even sought to create inner

6. Edwards, *Printing Propaganda and Martin Luther*, p. 166.
7. Huovinen, "Doctor Communis?," p. 140.
8. Martin Luther, *Concerning the Answer of the Goat in Leipzig*, quoted in Eire, *Reformations*, p. 158.
9. Edwards, *Printing Propaganda and Martin Luther*, p.167.

temptations in Luther himself in hopes that Luther might personally succumb. Luther did not spend 40 days in the wilderness, but there were parallels that he saw. He oscillated between presenting himself as sent by God, and as merely another ordinary human being who happened to be endowed with special skills in Scriptural and other theological analysis, and who obstinately would not relent.

As a practical matter, after his death and in the centuries to follow Luther thus came to be seen by many Lutherans in practice as a great prophet of biblical stature who had saved essential Christian truths that had been lost for centuries owing to the wide presence and great influence of the Antichrist in Rome. Ironically, the result was that Luther and Lutheranism took on a Catholic quality in new places and in a brand new form. Kaariainen and his co-authors write that "in Sweden in the 17th and early 18th centuries the [Lutheran] Church again had a similar cultural monopoly to that [of the Catholic Church] of the Middle Ages." But now "the Pope's power was replaced by that of the King of Sweden." In the nineteenth century the Orthodox Russian Czar replaced the Lutheran King of Sweden as the ruler of Finland but nevertheless "the Lutheran Church remained the state church of Finland" even under the Czar (and Finns were now as loyal to the Czar as other Lutherans had earlier been loyal to their Protestant Kings and Princes, in contrast, for example, to the rebellious Catholic Poles who created no end of troubles for the Czar).[10]

Such was the remarkable result of the great revolution against Rome that Luther had begun in 1517; in the end – as it would seem, somewhat perversely – Luther's efforts had resulted in a new decentralized and thus more flexible – a "Lutheranized" – version of Roman Catholicism across Lutheran Europe. Unlike most Protestants, for example, Lutherans and Catholics agree that in the eucharist the actual presence of Christ existed in the bread and wine. One might ask whether it might not have been much less costly for Europe in the

10. Kaariainen et al., *Facing Diversity*, p. 9.

long run if the Roman Catholic Church itself had simply shown the flexibility to give each German state and Nordic nation greater religious autonomy within the Catholic Church. But such was not to be, radically altering the course of world history.

Lutheran Doctrinal Divisions

In the first centuries of Christianity, fierce disputes had often broken out among the Christian faithful, including matters not only of the correct understanding of the place of Jesus in the divine scheme but also of the true history of his life and times. Various gospel accounts were offered and it was not until about the year 200 that a full official body of accepted accounts was authorized by the Church, as is now found in the Christian Bible. Concerned by the continuing theological confusions and conflicts within Christianity, Constantine himself convened the Council of Nicaea in 1525, which succeeded in establishing the definitive Christian understanding of the dual role of Jesus as both God and man, and of the Trinity composed of God, Jesus Christ and the Holy Ghost, standard elements of Christian belief to this day.

A wide range of deeply clashing views similarly faced the Lutheran church in the decades immediately after Luther's death. By then, as noted, Luther had become more than a mere ordinary mortal; he was no longer a "reformer" of the Catholic Church but increasingly a great founder of a new religion himself (which was given the name "Lutheranism" for the first time in the second half of the sixteenth century). Thus, for Philip Melanchthon, John Calvin and many others, as James Nestingen comments, "Luther had been confirmed as a 'different order of man, God's prophet,'' thus "inflating his work with significance far beyond his own intentions." Luther's writings rank today with those of Paul and St. Augustine as the "most scrutinized" in Christian history.[11]

11. Nestingen, "Approaching Luther," pp. 242-243, 245.

As with early Christianity, it was important for the newly emerging Lutheran church of the late sixteenth century to come to some agreement as to what this great new prophet had actually said and meant. It did not take nearly as long as the four centuries required for early Christianity to resolve such matters, but the level of immediate dispute among Luther's followers was almost as great – owing partly to the vast body of Luther's writings (his collected works come to more than 100 folio volumes), and to his many conflicting statements from one time and place to another. Thus, as Hans Hillerbrand remarks, "in the generation after Luther's death" there was "stark disagreement among Martin Luther's own followers as to what was, in fact, the reformer's authentic teaching." For his heirs, all this infighting "had woeful consequences," the fierce disputes undercutting "the external vitality of German Lutheranism," as reflected in a failure to grow much beyond the original areas of dominant Lutheran faith, even as Calvinism at the time was achieving a "dramatic expansion [...] throughout Europe."[12]

As has been the case throughout the history of Lutheranism, here again the political rulers ended up playing a decisive role, as the "theological controversies were resolved not by the instigation of theologians but by the active intervention of the political authorities." Under these strong outside political pressures, Lutherans finally managed to work out an agreement among themselves, first in 1577 in the *Formula of Concord* and then in 1580 in the *Book of Concord*, the latter providing "the definitive statement of the meaning of Luther's theological legacy," a role that it has continued to play up to the present time.[13]

After 1580, Lutheran pastors were expected to give their allegiance, in their ordination vows, to *The Book of Concord*, which included a selection of a few historic documents of Christianity, some of Luther's own writings, and also some writings of followers such as

12. Hillerbrand, "The Legacy of Martin Luther, pp. 229, 231.

13. Ibid., pp. 232, 231.

Melanchthon that were now given a new religious authority. *The Book of Concord* became in effect the new Lutheran "bible," in practice read and studied more closely by many devout Lutherans than the actual Christian Bible. Its contents established the doctrinal basis for a long period of "Lutheran Orthodoxy" that lasted through the seventeenth century, until challenged on the one hand by Pietism in the eighteenth century and on the other by a growing secularization of European thought in the age of the Enlightenment. The events leading up to the 1580 concord were again reminiscent of the Christian role of Constantine, whose efforts at Nicaea and elsewhere had pushed the fractious theologians, bishops and other clergy of the early Church to come to an authoritative and lasting agreement.

As Hillerbrand explains, the large role of the political authorities in defining Lutheran Orthodoxy contributed to giving "Lutheran rulers in Germany [and elsewhere] a particularly powerful role in church matters," further encouraging the "fateful alliance of 'throne and altar, which tied the Lutheran churches to inordinate subservience to the ruling authorities." In Prussia, for example, King Frederick William I in the eighteenth century would prescribe the "liturgical details of the Lutheran worship service" within his domain.[14] A Prussian successor, King Frederick William III, early in the nineteenth century would compel a merger of the Lutheran and Reformed churches. In the Nordic countries the extent of theocratic practice if anything went even further, as church and state were effectively merged into a common political and religious body. Roger Jensen writes that,

> Since the sixteenth century the governing of the church as an integrated part of the governing of the state has been a characteristic of the Nordic countries. The power and authority of the king and the church came to be intertwined; the one came to lend authority to the other.
>
> In the Kingdom of Denmark-Norway, the [Lutheran] vicars were the main instruments in the local governing of the king-

14. Ibid., 232.

> dom, as the most prominent representative of the king in the local communities. The Lutheran clergy represented both God and king, seeing that not only gospel but also royal ordinances and new laws were preached from the pulpit. [...] The [Lutheran] confirmation came to be a precondition for obtaining civil rights such as right to marriage, right to property, etc., [thus serving as] a vital instrument in establishing citizenship.
>
> Religion gave legitimacy to the authorities. The king had his power and authority from God. The church was a central instrument in building the state and ensuring morals among the citizens, and religion also came to demarcate the territory of one state from another.[15]

It is possible that Luther would have personally strongly disapproved of much of this, but he nevertheless bears a significant responsibility for such a final outcome. It was Luther himself who had effectively married the church to the state in his own time, depending on the Princes of Germany for his own personal survival and for the spread of his teachings, and as a practical matter often putting himself at their service. The complete Nordic intertwining of church and state – the "church" as the main administrative branch of the state at the local level in addition to its traditional religious roles --did not really begin to break down until the middle of the nineteenth century, when Nordic states began to assume such administrative responsibilities for education, health and care for the poor themselves: the beginning of the process that in the second half of the twentieth century under social democratic governance would yield the Nordic welfare state.

Admittedly, the Nordic welfare state would itself still continue in the Nordic tradition of theocracy. As will be discussed further in later chapters, it would now, however, become a theocracy of a new secular social democratic religion of modern scientific and economic progress, the state having become a new kind of modern church

15. Jensen, "The Formation and Identity of the Church as a Present Challenge in Norway," p. 50.

itself that assumed both the core administrative and (as now secularized) religious responsibilities. In both Luther's time, and in the twentieth century, a principal function of the state as church was the education of the faithful in the truths (first Lutheran and now social democratic) of religion.

Lutheranism in the Twentieth Century

There is thus a great paradox in Luther. As noted in the previous chapter, he was among the great historic defenders of freedom, including the liberty of individual conscience. At the same time, he was also one of the great defenders of the authority of the secular rulers of his time – and his Lutheran successors carried matters even further, most of all in the Nordic countries. One of the most important historic consequences of the Protestant Reformation was that, having undermined the transnational authority of the Roman Catholic church over much of northern Europe, it boosted the emergence of powerful nation states. Perhaps not surprisingly, this has precipitated a modern debate concerning the most important side of Luther's historical legacy: whether it is the defense of human freedom or of governing state authority.

This issue became a large practical concern for Norwegian Lutherans on two occasions in the twentieth century. In 1905, Norway threatened, if necessary, to go to war with Sweden to gain its independence (an outcome that was in the end averted), seeming to violate the longstanding position of Norwegian and other Lutheran theologians that the Swedish King was an instrument of God intended to maintain order in society, part of the traditional support of Lutheran religion for the state church. Norwegian theologians now declared, however, that "secular authorities are not first of all persons of authority, but the institution of authority," depending for their ruling status and legitimacy on the will of the people, a view that in the early twentieth century, as Dag Horkildsen remarkes, "had obviously broken [...] with

[...] Luther."[16] During World War II, Germany occupied Norway in April 1940, leading Bishop Eivind Berggrav and the Church of Norway to lend their authority to the Norwegian resistance movement, again requiring them to approve a significant departure from traditional Lutheran teachings about obedience to the state.

In Germany, however, matters were less clear. Historian Victoria Barnett writes that "since its inception, the German Evangelical Church [...] had been shaped by nationalism and obedience to state authority. Influenced by these traditions, and relieved that a strong new leader had emerged from the chaos of the Weimar years, many Protestants welcomed the rise of Nazism" until the 1940s and the growing evidence of its looming self-destruction.[17] Ernst Troeltsch, among the leading German theologians of the twentieth century, had earlier offered the harsh judgment that "Lutheranism provided a most favorable setting for the development of the territorial state [and church]. It smoothed the way for territorial absolutism. [...] Its only service to the actual modern state has been to encourage the spirit of modern absolutism."[18] As Hans Hillerbrand states, "Troeltsch doggedly attacked the prevailing picture of Luther that had made him a champion of modernity and an ur-German. According to Troeltsch, [...] his worldview was medieval, as were his theological concepts. In regard to German political history, Luther was nothing short of catastrophic."[19]

The prominent American theologian Reinhold Niebuhr, partly influenced by Troeltsch, also blamed Luther for encouraging authoritarian tendencies in Germany. Partly reflecting his own origins in Calvinistic ways of thinking, Neibuhr wrote that for Luther, "evidently no obligation rests upon the Christian to change social structures so that they might conform more perfectly to the requirements of brotherhood," a troublesome feature compounded by Luther's "inability to define consistent criteria for the achievement of relative

16. Thorkildsen, "Unconditional Christian Loyalty Towards the Rulers?," pp. 265, 266.

17. Barnett, "Dietrich Bonhoeffer: Opposition." See also Barnett, *For the Soul of the People*.

18. Quoted in Siemon-Netto, *The Fabricated Luther*, p. 59.

19. Hillerbrand, "The Legacy of Martin Luther," p. 235.

justice" in society.[20] The controversy became particularly heated with respect to the degree of responsibility Luther and Lutheranism had in helping to support the Nazi regime in Germany from 1933 to 1945. It is an historical fact, as Luther historian Heiko Oberman comments, that "a whole series of Luther scholars" in Germany worked to bless the National Socialist cause in the 1930s.[21] Observing the tight hold of Hitler over the German people and their lack of greater resistance to his authority, more strident voices in writings such as *From Luther to Hitler* would recently assign a significant part of the blame to Luther.[22]

Luther, however, also has his contemporary defenders. In *The Fabricated Luther: Refuting Nazi Connections and Other Modern Myths*, Uwe Siemon-Netto concludes that Luther has frequently been misinterpreted and misunderstood. He states that "as a rule of thumb, Protestants in Hitler's Germany fell into three groups of almost equal size: the pro-Nazi 'German Christians,' the anti-Nazi confessional Christians, and an amorphous 'neutral' faction in the center." Siemon-Netto acknowledges that today "the most prevalent view of the Protestant church's role in the Third Reich holds that the church ingloriously failed in its duty to stand up to the demonic force of National Socialism." He nevertheless faults this view for ignoring other key German developments, including the "heroism, and in many cases, martyrdom of the resistance." He argues that, while they were a minority of German Protestant Christians, there were still many "bishops and pastors who spoke up precisely in the way Luther would have wanted them to" – offering a passive resistance in their words, the kind of resistance of which Luther would have approved, even as he had always condemned outright popular rebellion.[23] On the whole, the greatest resistance was offered by ordinary Catholic priests in Germany who saw in Hitler a fundamental challenge to western civilization, as their Catholic peers almost 500 years earlier had seen

20. Reinhold Neibuhr, *Nature and Destiny of Man*, 2:193, 197, quoted in Siemon-Netto, *The Fabricated Luther*, p. 58.
21. Heiko A. Oberman, "The Nationalist Conscription of Martin Luther," p. 71, quoted in Siemon-Netto, *The Fabricated Luther*, p. 53.
22. McGovern, *From Luther to Hitler*.
23. Siemon-Netto, *The Fabricated Luther*, pp. 149, 150.

in Luther. It is, in short, a paradox; Luther greatly advanced what we know now as modern freedoms, even as he at the same time defended state authority that nevertheless often sought to limit Christian freedom of conscience and expression.

The best known of Christian resistance figures against the Nazi regime was the Lutheran theologian Dietrich Bonhoeffer, martyred in April 1945 within days of the end of war, and described by the American theologian Jordan Ballor as having become a "Protestant 'saint'" (a further example, one might note, of the continuing "Romanizing" of Protestant religion).[24] While not an active participant in the attempt to assassinate Hitler in 1944, Bonhoeffer knew of the plans and had been involved for some time as a member of the German resistance, thus violating the traditional Lutheran stance. Indeed, Bonhoeffer was highly critical of the two kingdoms doctrine of Luther, writing that "this division of the whole of reality into sacred and profane, or Christian and worldly, sectors creates the possibility of existence in only one of these sectors: for instance, a spiritual existence that takes no part in worldly existence, and a worldly existence that can make good its claim to autonomy over against the sacred sector."[25] As Ballor writes, "Bonhoeffer is so concerned about the secularistic application of two kingdom's thinking in his own day," used by many of his fellow German Lutherans to claim a separation from the affairs of the state, thus avoiding any dangerous political involvements in resisting it, that he "contends that 'we must get beyond this two-realms image'." Bonhoeffer was so disturbed by the apathy of so many German Protestant devout in the face of Hitler's evils that he suggested at times that the world might better be served in the future by a "religionless Christianity" (perhaps new forms of "secular religion" that might actually be more "Christian" than the real-world Lutheran and other official Christian bodies as they existed in the Germany of the 1930s).[26]

24. Ballor, "Dietrich Bonhoeffer, The Two Kingdoms, and Protestant Social Thought Today," p. 73.

25. Quoted in ibid., p. 67.

26. Ibid., pp. 67, 74.

In his defense of Luther, Siemon-Netto, surprisingly, says nothing about the very different series of events in the Lutheran Nordic countries in the twentieth century. Reflecting in part the freedom-enhancing elements of Luther's theology, the Lutheran tradition there was often strongly supportive of individual freedom of conscience, even as it also gave legitimacy to unusually tight royal – and in the twentieth century social democratic – state social controls over many areas of individual behavior. Even with such tight controls, the Nordic countries have never become totalitarian states. What might be the explanation for these different results in Germany and the Lutheran countries to the North? This is a complex subject that is well beyond the scope of this book but a few speculations may be offered. It may simply be that the Nordic world somehow gave greater theological weight to the aspect of Luther that emphasized the individual freedom of religious conscience. Another factor might be geographic; the harshness of living in the far North meant it was always incapable of supporting any large class of nobility or other elements of a full-fledged feudal system.

One can probably say, moreover, that another significant factor was the presence of a large Catholic (and to a lesser extent Reformed Protestant) population in Germany, creating greater religious pluralism and resulting greater social tensions in comparison with the homogeneous Lutheran North, thus significantly complicating the tasks of national governance. While absolving Catholicism of any blame for Hitler, Siemon-Netto does offer in partial defense of Lutheranism "the Roman Catholic upbringing of National Socialism's worst Nazi villains, such as Adolf Hitler, Heinrich Himmler, Joseph Goebbels, Julius Streicher, Arthur Seyss-Inquart, Ernst Kallenbrunner, Auschwitz commandant Rudolf Hess, and the notorious Auschwitz doctor Joseph Mengele."[27] Once such figures had asserted tight dictatorial control over Germany in the early 1930s, too many German Lutherans seemingly regarded Hitler – whatever his non-Lutheran origins – as their new all controlling "Prince."

27. Siemon-Netto, *The Fabricated Luther*, p. 65.

Conclusion

All such arguments, admittedly, might be dismissed as beside the point. Luther was what he was in his own time and place, now 500 years ago. The Lutherans who followed him were free to pick and choose among his voluminous body of often conflicting writings. He was never a systematic theologian who laid down a clear body of guiding rules for the Lutheran faithful. So it would seem the main responsibility for the German horrors of the first half of the twentieth century must be assigned collectively to the German people themselves – Lutheran and non-Lutheran alike – who were living in those years (and not accepting their vindictive treatment in the aftermath of World War I by the allied victors as an excuse). Contemporary views of Luther's role in more recent history are perhaps best understood today as a "litmus test" that say as much or more about the historical commentator as about the actual influence of Luther himself on German (and Nordic) history. But this emphasizes the need for contemporary Lutheran theologians – and other Nordic political philosophers and theologians – to again rethink in the twenty-first century the implications of Lutheranism and its social democratic progeny for the relationship of church and state. In the Nordic world in practice, there have never been distinct religious and political worlds separately making up "two kingdoms" on earth.

CHAPTER 6

The Lutheran Ethic and the Spirit of Social Democracy

Although best known in its Calvinist context, the idea of having a "calling" to some type of activity in this world is an important part of Protestantism in general, including Lutheranism. Finnish social historian Pirjo Markkola writes, for example, that in the late nineteenth century in Finland the application of the Lutheran "concept of 'woman's calling' became central in women's organizations and new female occupations." In the late nineteenth century for Cecilia Bloomquist, "her work was vocation, a calling given by God, and she repeatedly reflected on her insufficiency as God's servant. [...] However weak she might have felt herself, the calling led her to a remarkable career in the service not only of Christian social work but also health care in Finland." For Lutherans as well as other Protestants, the importance of pursuing a calling extends to all members of society, another radical implication of the Protestant belief in a priesthood of all believers. As Markkola puts it, in Finland and elsewhere in the Nordic world, "according to the Lutheran concept of calling everybody was called to serve in his or her daily life."[1]

For Max Weber, the Calvinist understanding of a calling was central to his arguments about the rise of modern capitalism. Indeed, as noted above, in one of the most famous works of social science of the twentieth century, Weber argued in *The Protestant Ethic and the Spirit of Capitalism* that the Calvinist view of a calling had played a large economic role in early modern Europe. For Calvinists, the successful pursuit of a calling offered at least partial relief from an existential dread that they might be among the condemned. Calvin

1. Markkola, "The Calling of Women," pp. 115, 121, 122.

had suggested that only a minority of people could expect to be saved (even among the outwardly Christian faithful), a matter predestined by an omniscient and omnipotent God and therefore outside any human ability to influence it through individual actions in this world. God's thinking in matters of salvation, Calvin had emphasized, must remain a great and inscrutable mystery, known only to God Himself.

Weber argued, however, that such a view, whatever its theological merits in recognizing the all-powerful character of God, was psychologically untenable for many ordinary members of the human species. If literally believed, if nothing whatsoever within human control mattered in matters of salvation, if all was already predestined even before a person was born, it might easily lead to a deep fatalism, a lack of moral commitment or a withdrawal from the world – or perhaps instead to a selfish hedonism in unrestrained pursuit of worldly pleasures. The later Calvinist response in practice (if not that of Calvin himself), as Weber found, was to regard success in a calling as a good "sign" of God's favor. For the Calvinist devout, as they came to think in practice, those who were actually among the saved would have an inner peace of mind and grace that would manifest itself in worldly accomplishments in the pursuit of a calling – even though this could have no true significance regarding salvation. Yet having a promising sign was enough in itself to provide a powerful motivation for the behavior of many individual Calvinists. In a great paradox, the actual religious impact of Calvinism as perceived by its followers may have lain in the fact that its popular reinterpretation brought back a new form of salvation by good works. However much Calvin himself might have been horrified by the thought, one might even say that with this later Calvinist understanding there was created in practice a stronger expectation of salvation by good works than could be found in some of the earlier teachings of the Roman Catholic Church.

Calvinism was also distinguished by the fact that many of its most devout followers were actively involved in business and other affairs of the world. A good Calvinist thus had a strong motivation to pursue success in a worldly calling, such as a business enterprise, expressing this economic commitment with the full energy of a devout religious conviction. For Calvinists, a high level of profits achieved in business might therefore serve as a promising indicator of a heavenly future. High profits, however, could also pose a grave new threat. If a successful businessman began to use his monetary gains to live a life of pleasure and luxury, the prospects for his eternal soul might be poor – as had happened to some ex-Calvinists. It was not necessary, however, for the businessman to live in poverty. A devout Calvinist whose calling was in business could be as successful – could make as large a profit as possible – within the bounds of living with only modest pleasures and acting ethically in his personal relations with others.

As Weber emphasized, seen from a modern utilitarian point of view of maximizing personal happiness and enjoyment – indeed, perhaps the outlook of most people in the history of the world – the Calvinist businessman was behaving "irrationally." He was supposed to work very hard, impose severe personal discipline on himself throughout his life, and yet should not want to derive large outward personal benefits from any great material successes. Calvinism in this way produced, as one might say, a new human type of "ascetic entrepreneur and businessman." It amounted, as Weber observed, to a transfer of the religious zeal of the monk to the practical affairs of the world. As he wrote of the Protestant ethic, the Calvinist way of thinking

> acted powerfully against the spontaneous enjoyment of possessions; it restricted consumption, especially of luxuries. On the other hand, it had the psychological effect of freeing the acquisition of goods from the inhibitions of traditionalist ethics. It broke the bonds of the impulse of acquisition in that it not only legalized it, but [...] looked upon it as directly willed by God. The campaign against the temptations of the flesh, and the dependence on external things, was [...] not a struggle against rational acquisition, but against the irrational use of wealth.[2]

2. Weber, *The Protestant Ethic and the Spirit of Capitalism*, p. 171.

A 2003 study of the economic impact of Calvinism thus describes it as having brought about a "disciplinary revolution" in early modern Europe. In comparing Catholicism, Lutheranism and Calvinism, Philip Gorski notes that "while all three confessions advocated discipline – both religious and social – it was the Calvinists who did so with the greatest fervor and consequence."[3] With their heavy involvement in worldly affairs, individual Calvinists and indeed whole Calvinist societies were more likely to prosper economically and otherwise – including in one such area of newly religious importance to the Calvinist faithful, the early development of modern science as a way of better understanding God's design for the natural world.[4]

The Calvinist drive to fulfill a worldly calling persisted even after devotion to the original Calvinism had waned – and, in the nineteenth and twentieth century, after it had almost disappeared altogether. Thus, the American Benjamin Franklin in the second half of the eighteenth century was prominently mentioned by Weber as an example of the powerful motivating influence of a Calvinist calling, even though Franklin by then was skeptical about traditional Christianity. In the later nineteenth century, Andrew Carnegie, raised in Calvinist Scotland before emigrating to the United States, offered another similar example. As he wrote in 1889 in "the gospel of wealth,"

> It becomes the duty of the millionaire to increase his revenues. The struggle for more is completely freed from selfish or ambitious taint and becomes a noble pursuit. Then he labors not for self, but for others; not to hoard but to spend [his wealth for public benefit]. The more he makes, the more the public gets. His whole life is changed from the moment that he resolves to become a disciple of the gospel of wealth, and henceforth he labors to acquire that he may wisely administer for others' good. His daily labor is a daily virtue.[5]

3. Gorski, *The Disciplinary Revolution*, pp. 20, 21.
4. Harrison, *The Bible, Protestantism and the Rise of Natural Science*.
5. Carnegie, "The Advantages of Poverty," quoted in Nasaw, *Andrew Carnegie*, p. 361.

This Calvinist view of business as a divinely blessed calling was not a mere pretense for Carnegie (who like Franklin was himself skeptical about the original Calvinist formulations), a public relations gesture; he really believed that in his maximization of the profits of U.S. Steel he was serving his God. Carnegie actually did what he preached, moreover, eventually giving away almost the entirety of his vast accumulated fortune to a wide variety of public causes, including the establishment of many non-profit institutions (such as Carnegie Mellon University and the Carnegie Institute for International Peace in Washington), the building of more than 2,000 community libraries across the United States and the construction of 7,000 church organs, as well as Carnegie Hall in New York City, thus touching the lives of millions of ordinary Americans.

Like a good Calvinist, Carnegie's purpose was not to provide charity for the poor that would enable them to continue living in an economically deprived condition, but to give them education and other tools to empower their future lives. Partly illustrating the great Calvinist influence in American history, nineteen of the leading 20 American universities today are private, including Harvard, Yale and Princeton – all were founded in the seventeenth and eighteenth centuries as Calvinist institutions of learning. Partly reflecting the potentially different consequences of historic religion, in Lutheran Finland there was only one university at the end of the nineteenth century – the University of Helsinki – and the 20 universities found in Finland today are public, almost all created in the second half of the twentieth century (besides the University of Helsinki – which moved from Turku to Helsinki in 1829 – the other main exception is the reconstituted University of Turku in 1920).

After its 1905 publication, while widely recognized as an economic and sociological classic, *The Protestant Ethic and the Spirit of Capitalism* also attracted many critics, perhaps not surprising in a century in which social science was dominated by an economic determinism that saw little historical causal role for religion. Even if Weber had been correct, given the widespread expectation of social scientists and historians of the twentieth century that religion was fading, his argument seemed for such scholars to lack much contemporary relevance. As indicated above, such views have been changing, however, since the 1980s. Among the early signs of such change, a leading contemporary American macroeconomist, Bradford De Long, reported in 1988 that his statistical research into the historical causes of the relative economic progress of the more advanced nations of the world from 1870 to 1979 had shown little statistical support for the most common explanations. But to his surprise, there was "one striking ex ante association between growth over 1870–1979 and a pre-determined variable: a nation's dominant religious establishment." Indeed, the presence in a nation of "a religious establishment that is Protestant" or even contained a significant mixture of Protestants and Catholics, as opposed to predominantly Catholic, "is significantly correlated with growth."[6]

Among economic historians, after long neglecting the subject not only of religion but culture in general, a growing number of them were similarly coming to a new appreciation of the important role of religion.[7] Indeed, it was becoming a common view by 2010 that Weber had been broadly correct, that there was a significant association of Protestantism with national economic success, but that many other things were at work besides the Calvinist concept of a calling – such as the Protestant encouragement of literacy among both men and women to allow them to read the Bible.[8] By 2013, in a well-regarded journal of the American Economic Association, two contributors would find that "going beyond the 'work ethic' hypothesis, we show that [Max] Weber's classic can be seen to argue that the different religions will also lead to different political preferences, and our empirical results [in Switzerland] confirm this" – and political differences inevitably lead to economic differences as well.[9] Another 2013 article

6. De Long, "Productivity Growth, Convergence, and Welfare," p. 1146.
7. Nelson, "Max Weber Revisited."
8. Becker and Woessmann, "Was Becker Wrong?."
9. Basten and Betz, "Beyond Work Ethic," p. 89.

in the *Journal of Economic Literature*, also a leading publication of the American Economic Association, explains that "the recent literature on economic growth and development has increasingly focused on very long-run effects of geographic, historical, and cultural factors on productivity and income per capita" – long-run factors that, except for geography, historically have been much influenced by religion.[10]

Students of economic development processes have also increasingly been emphasizing the quality of governance – the rule of law, freedom of expression, democratic political processes, etc. – as decisive factors for sustaining long-term economic growth and development. This is at least as much a matter for political study and investigation as it is for economic research. Writing in the *American Journal of Political Science* in 2012, political scientist Robert Woodberry states that, within the social sciences, "traditional modernization theory [...] [assumed] that liberal democracy and other social transformations traditionally associated with 'modernity' developed primarily as the result of secular rationality, economic development, urbanization, industrialization, the expansion of the state, and the development of new class structures."[11] Since the 1980s, however, political scientists have increasingly been recognizing that religion can be either a large direct causal influence or a key underlying influence on basic political – and thus also economic – outcomes.

As Woodberry thus notes, "quantitative research consistently suggests that countries with more Protestants are more democratic and have more stable democratic transitions." Indeed, the historical record shows that "stable democracy first emerged in Protestant Europe and British-settler colonies, and by World War I every independent, predominantly Protestant country was a stable democracy – with the possible exception of Germany." In areas with less Protestant influence, however, "less stable versions of democracy developed in Catholic areas with large Protestant and Jansenist minorities, such as France." The establishment of democratic governance "lagged in

10. Spolaore and Wacziard, "How Deep are the Roots of Economic Development?," p. 361. See also Nelson, "Is Max Weber Newly Relevant?"

11. Woodberry, "The Missionary Roots of Liberal Democracy," p. 245.

Catholic and Orthodox parts of Southern and Eastern Europe where Protestants had little influence. A similar pattern existed outside Europe." Indeed, Woodberry's own detailed empirical investigations, as he reported in 2012, offered further confirmation, showing that in less developed nations of Africa, Asia, Latin America and Oceania there were strong statistically significant correlations between "the historic prevalence of Protestant missionaries" and an earlier time frame for the creation of democratic institutions and then a more successful later development of democracy historically.[12] Woodberry does not distinguish between Lutheran and other Protestant missionaries, but in all likelihood the largest part of them came from Calvinist and other non-Lutheran denominations in nations – for one thing they had much larger populations – such as England and the United States.

The Lutheran Calling and Hopes for Salvation

Lutherans were not exempt from the existential dread experienced by Calvinists with respect to their possibly slim prospects for salvation – as Luther was equally committed to full predestination and to a doubt that the saved will be the majority. The idea of a calling was also prominent in Lutheran theology. There has been less scholarly attention, however, given to the presence of similar psychological mechanisms relating to salvation, as examined by Weber, that might also be found among the Lutheran faithful. Where there was not a Calvinist ethic, a Lutheran ethic might still have been powerfully at work; the successful pursuit of a calling for a Lutheran as well as for a Calvinist might be seen in practice as a promising sign for salvation, even if no guarantee. But given the different Calvinist and Lutheran ethics, one might expect that the Lutheran pursuit of a calling would have considerably different overall social and economic consequences. In the Nordic countries, for one thing, the Lutheran faithful were more likely to be farmers and other rural people, as compared with the urban faithful more typically drawn to Calvinism.

12. Ibid., p. 245.

However contrary it was to Luther's own stated beliefs, his theology contained the elements necessary for an expectation among later Lutherans that the successful pursuit of a calling might well be a good sign for salvation. Indeed, these elements might have been even more prominent in Luther than in Calvin. Like all good Protestants, Luther taught that good works could themselves do nothing to advance an individual's prospects for salvation – that this was a matter for "faith alone" and the existence of an individual's faith is ultimately in the hands of God alone (in other words, it is strictly up to God whether an individual does in fact have genuine faith). Luther taught, however, that those who had such faith would also do good works, even if it was not the good works themselves that produced the faith and ultimate salvation, but necessarily the other way around. As he wrote, the "just have faith and every work will flow from you naturally."[13] And as it says in the Augsburg Confession of 1530, "in the power of the Spirit, faith renews the heart, and the renewed heart is clothed with new affects which, in turn, enable good works."[14]

In his understanding of the Ten Commandments, Luther therefore emphasized that it was the first Commandment – "I am the Lord your God, you shall have no other Gods except me" – that stood before all the others, because the following of this Commandment would by itself mean that a person had a full faith in God. As Wannenwentsch explains, "Luther's emphasis on the First Commandment is the strongest possible guard against the temptation that fulfilling the [other] commandments would be an achievement." Even if all the other commandments were obeyed, as God had revealed these laws to Moses at Mt. Sinai, it would not mean justification in the eyes of God. Once faith exists (the First Commandment is followed), however, obedience to the remaining nine commandments for Luther will follow as a matter of course: "the very way in which the [other] individual commandments are followed, by individual acts of hand and mouth and body," is merely an outward manifestation of the original faith in God. Wannenwentsch writes that for a true Christian their life

13. Quoted in Wannenwetsch, "Luther's Moral Theology," p. 128.

14. Ibid., p. 129.

must be "in the first place, a matter of the heart (i.e., of faith). This is why the Christian life does not fall apart into a 'spiritual' sphere on the one hand and a 'worldly' sphere on the other."[15] In contrast to so much modern thinking, for Luther there must be no separate realms of a private religious conscience and an individual's actions in the outside political and economic society – their separation is a modern misreading of Luther's two kingdom ideas. A Lutheran businessman must obey the Golden Rule as much as any other of the Lutheran faithful.

Princeton Theological Seminary professor of Reformation History Scott Hendrix similarly explains that "good works were expected from believers because beneficial deeds always followed genuine faith." He observes that "Luther wrote that faith was 'a living, busy, active mighty thing' that was incessantly doing works without asking whether they should be done or not. 'It is impossible,' he said, 'to separate works from faith, quite as impossible as to separate heat and light from fire.'" For the devout, they understood Luther as saying that "'you are saved by faith alone and not by good works, but you should be doing good works nonetheless. They do not [assure] salvation but they are necessary for living as a Christian.' That was the first nuance: good works were necessary, but not necessary [or sufficient] for salvation."[16]

This argument was, however, more a rhetorical way for Luther to try to resolve tensions within his own theology that he could not otherwise overcome. If a person performed good works, it could well mean that he had true faith first and thus was among the saved in the eyes of God. It could also mean, however, that he simply wanted to have faith and thus to be saved, which was therefore his motive for performing the good works. If this was the case, however, Luther strongly disapproved, since it meant that the good works were actually being done to try to bring about salvation itself. Yet the very act of wanting to be saved, however this might be accomplished, could in itself be taken to imply faith (otherwise, why worry about salvation?). In this way, though contrary to Luther's thinking, the desire to do good

15. Ibid., p. 123.

16. Hendrix, *Martin Luther* (2010), p. 50.

works could mean the possession of actual faith, and thus doing good works could be a sign that a person was actually saved – even in Luther's own terms of "by faith alone." There was thus no necessary conflict between salvation by faith alone and salvation by doing good works – they meant much the same thing. Whether they were explicit about it all, much as Weber had argued with respect to the Calvinist faithful, one would expect that many Lutheran devout would feel and behave this way in practice, and many of them would turn to good works as a legitimate path to salvation.

For Lutherans as well as Calvinists, moreover, it was difficult for many people to live with the idea that they might simply have been predestined to damnation, independent of the lives they lived and for reasons of which they could have no knowledge. How could a loving God be so seemingly harsh and arbitrary? Luther himself had no good explanation, other than that God was all-powerful and his ways inscrutable. Weber had conjectured that the devout Calvinist would therefore have been likely to look for indications that he or she was among the saved, as could be found in success in a calling, even if such a sign could never offer a guarantee. Following Weber, one might suggest that a similar psychological and religious dynamic would be at work in the lives of the Lutheran faithful. Luther had, after all, declared that the saved would be naturally impelled to perform good works. So, probabilistically, some percentage of those performing good works would in fact have to be among the Lutheran saved – even if this exact percentage and the fate of each specific individual remained known only to God. As Weber had argued, and again applied equally to Lutheranism, good works might therefore not be able to guarantee salvation but their presence must surely represent a promising sign. One thing could be known for sure; if a person did not perform good works, according to Luther's teachings, he or she was assuredly not among the saved. Luther's message would therefore have worked powerfully to motivate the Lutheran faithful to perform good works in the pursuit of a calling, much as Weber argued was the case for the Calvinist faithful.

A Lutheran Ethic of Social Welfare

There remained, however, a large potential area of difference in the political and economic consequences of the Calvinist and Lutheran ethics. For Calvinists, they were encouraged to find their callings in worldly matters such as the conduct of business affairs – though they should not excessively spend any large profits resulting from business success in the sinful pursuit of luxurious living – but Luther's view of the world of business was more skeptical and even antagonistic. Indeed, he was often outwardly hostile to the commercial developments of his own times, which were setting the stage for the future rise of capitalism in Europe. As the Boston University professor of church history Carter Lindberg writes, "Luther found the calculating entrepreneur extremely distasteful. He was convinced that the capitalist spirit divorced money from use for human needs and necessitated an economy of acquisition." As a result, he routinely "preached and wrote against the expanding money economy as a great sin."[17] Success in business for a good Lutheran was thus unlikely to be seen as a promising sign for salvation; indeed, it might more likely portend the opposite.

In his description of Luther's thinking, Lindberg comes close at times to finding an outlook characteristic of modern socialism, with its historic distrust of capitalism. Lindberg finds that "Luther's concern was not only about an individual's use of money, but also the structural social damage inherent in the idolatry of the 'laws' of the market." Any ideas of an "impersonal market" or of "autonomous laws of economics" – such as has long been found at the heart of capitalist thinking, dating back to Adam Smith – would have been "abhorrent to Luther." For Luther, long before the 2008 financial crisis, the community was "endangered by the rising power of a few great financial centers; their unregulated economic coercion would destroy the ethos of the community." For Luther, "early capitalism was doubly dangerous because it not only exploited people but also strove to

17. Lindberg, "Luther's Struggle with Social-Ethical Issues," pp. 172–173.

conceal its voracious nature and to deceive people" behind various false claims of public benefit – as Smith, himself a product of Calvinist origins, would later strongly assert. Governments should therefore learn how to recognize such claims and be wary of them, causing Luther to appeal "for government regulation of interest rates and business practices."[18]

Luther rejected any assumption that self-interest could play a legitimate role as a main driving force in society. He thus would have strongly objected to this main premise of Smith's *Wealth of Nations* – the pursuit of self-interest as an "invisible hand" that worked for the good of all. Contemporary historians of economic thought now increasingly do in fact understand that for Smith the "invisible hand" was actually the implicit "hand of God" – something that for Luther would have been a new form of heresy.[19] Sean Doherty thus writes, concerning one of Luther's early writings on commercial ethics, that for Luther "self-interest is always wrong. Luther eschews all syntheses of self-love and neighbor-love," even as this concept remains effectively at the heart of the Anglo-American tradition – reflecting an original strong Calvinist influence – in mainstream economics today. Doherty explains that Luther condemns "many economic practices" of his own day as masking "vested interests and avarice" that violate God's wishes. While there is no grand conspiracy, it is nevertheless the case that for Luther those who write about "financial matters tend to be *deliberately* obscure, and this opacity is a camouflage for duplicity." The apologists for the private marketplace follow a convoluted "logic which justifies greedy behavior," all the while ignoring the contrary "commands of Jesus [that] are refreshingly clear." As Luther thus considers, "trust in the gospel may appear naïve, but true naivety would be an uncritical acceptance of economic claims" as put forth by those who rationalize the pursuit of self interest in the economic system.[20] This is a message still widely heard today in the Lutheran north.

18. Ibid., p. 173.
19. Oslington, ed., *Adam Smith as Theologian.*
20. Doherty, *Theology and Economic Ethics*, p. 67.

Rather than business success and profits in a Calvinist calling, the guiding principle in the pursuit of a Lutheran calling is that it should – ideally at least – selflessly serve the Golden Rule: "do unto your neighbor as you would have him do unto you." Doherty thus writes that as part of its governing responsibilities the "civil power" for Luther must be the instrument to "enforce natural law – the Golden rule." In individual actions, Luther maintains that "one must exist wholly for one's neighbour's benefit. Thus one's handling of worldly goods is wholly configured as an opportunity to serve others rather than make a profit. Even earning a living is to be done so one can benefit others." Luther, as Doherty elaborates, does not press for the actual "enactment of the Sermon on the Mount" by means of the coercive measures of the civil authorities. Nevertheless, "his vision of the integrity of earthly justice yields far broader and higher standards than his disapproval" in other contexts of "ruling the world with the gospel" might suggest. For civil rulers, their "purpose and calling are to govern in accordance with God's will, to secure justice, and to provide for the needy."[21] Luther himself wrote that "to serve God means to keep his commands and not steal, take, charge interest, and the like, rather to live and lend to the needy."[22] Here are the roots of the sense of social solidarity that remains such a powerful influence in the Nordic world even today.

Serving your neighbors and the whole community thus should therefore be the guiding principle of the Lutheran state churches of the Nordic world; Pirjo Markkola and Ingela Naumann explain that "for many centuries, the Lutheran churches had a hegemonic status and the clergy represented both the state and the church in local communities" – local theocracies in effect in which the values of the Lutheran clergy were the values of the state.[23] In 1998, Harvard University sociologist Aage Sorensen similarly argued that in the twentieth century the Nordic social democratic ethic could be traced to Lutheran influences manifested much earlier. As he noted, "the gen-

21. Ibid., pp. 66, 67, 68.
22. Martin Luther, quoted in Edwards, *Printing, Propaganda and Martin Luther*, p. 50.
23. Markkola and Naumann, "Lutheranism and Nordic Welfare States in Comparison," p. 1.

erosity of the welfare state system" in the Nordic countries depended in the twentieth century on "the prevalence of beliefs in the efficacy of rules and intentions." In many other non-Nordic societies characterized by higher levels of "opportunism," "rule-violation" and "rent-seeking" (as economists speak of self-seeking behavior in the political arena), any attempt to create a Nordic welfare state would soon break down under the pressure of a growing popular tendency to exploit its ample public generosity for individual private benefit (something Sorensen fears may now actually be occurring with growing frequency even in the Nordic world itself).[24] Some powerful ethical understandings thus must have underlain the very successful functioning of the Nordic welfare state. Sorensen criticizes fellow social scientists and other welfare state analysts for their common failure even to recognize the centrality of such ethics to the workings of the whole social democratic system, or if perhaps they do recognize this centrality, their failure to seek to understand and explain the origins, validity and continuing basis for such necessary normative foundations.

Hoping to help to remedy this gap in understanding, Sorensen seeks to show how "basic elements were created in 18th-century absolutism and its spiritual support system Lutheran Pietism." It was the "conflation of autocratic and militaristic regimes with Pietism that created an emphasis on education, and support for the poor, orphaned and infirm that is quite consistent with the objectives and concerns of the modern welfare state." Pietism saw itself as a new "reformation" of the Lutheran church itself, a revival of the true message of Luther that had been lost in the intervening centuries within increasingly rigid Lutheran orthodoxies. Indeed, it was this eighteenth-century Lutheran state church "model for the relationship between king and subject that was to become the model for the relationship between state and citizen in the modern Scandinavian welfare state. It is a relationship of obedience and respect for the good intentions of the ruler and his agents, who want to help and support those in need."[25]

24. Sorensen, "On Kings, Pietism, and Rent-Seeking in Scandinavian Welfare States," pp. 364, 365.

25. Ibid., p. 364.

Unlike the Calvinist ethic of success in a business or other worldly calling, the Lutheran ethic – dating to Luther himself – thus seeks to succeed in serving the welfare needs of society and especially the poor. This Lutheran ethic was still present in the Lutheranism of the eighteenth-century Nordic world, and survived through the nineteenth century and into the early twentieth century in an explicitly religious form. Later in the twentieth century, however, it would be transformed outwardly to become the – now secular in form – implicit Lutheran ethic of social democracy.

In a 2014 study, Anneli Portman of the University of Helsinki analyzed the key public speeches of the top political figures in Finland over the past 200 years, including the Presidents of Finland from its independence in 1917 to 2000, thus making it possible to observe the transition over this period from traditional Lutheran messages to newly secular statements of the old Lutheran values. In terms of the actual language used, Portman finds that this period was marked by the decline of presidentially expressed values of "spirituality" and the ascendency of "universalism," this being the most important Finnish value of the 1980s and 1990s. Universalism, as Portman notes, is closely associated with "equality"; as she writes, "at the center of Universalism values lies the concept of 'others' and their concerns being welcomed, and their rights being regarded as important as those of the in-group. This means that the negotiation of the in-group vs. out-group is resolved in favor of the out-group being included."[26] In the language of Martin Luther and his understanding of a calling, this is obedience to the Golden Rule. In the vocabulary of the Presidents of Finland of the late twentieth century, there was little explicit mention of God, the Golden Rule as found in the Bible or other traditional messages of Lutheranism, resulting in a "secular Golden Rule" of Nordic universal equality that was part of a newly secularized Lutheranism, which in the twentieth century became the official creed of a new social democratic transformation from the old Lutheran state church.

26. Anneli Portman, *From Might to Mandate*, pp. 161, 197.

Recently, the special Nordic ethic of trust and compassion towards others was illustrated in one specific case by a journalistic experiment in which 192 wallets containing money and identifying information were intentionally dropped in 2013 – as though they had been lost – in 16 cities around the world. In Helsinki (the only Nordic city studied), 11 out of the 12 dropped wallets were returned to the owners, the highest such rate in the world. In total, about half the dropped wallets were returned worldwide; when the people who returned them were asked why they had done so, a common answer was a strong sense of personal sympathy for the individual wallet owner – an application of the Golden Rule. In societies apparently not sharing that sentiment as widely, at the bottom of the list were such cities as Lisbon (1 of 12 wallets returned), Madrid (2 of 12), Prague (3 of 12) and Rio de Janeiro, Bucharest and Zurich (4 of 12).[27]

Some of the Finns returning the wallets expressed pride in serving a national culture of honesty and trustworthiness. It is a common view, recently expressed by the winner of the Nobel Peace Prize in 2008 for his efforts to resolve international conflicts in Kosovo and elsewhere, former Finnish President Martti Ahtisaari. He believes that "the Finnish attribute [that] is the most conducive to generating personal and professional success [...] is Finnish honesty and trustworthiness."[28] To return the wallet, one might say, is to "do unto your neighbor as you would have him do unto you" – the essence of Luther's understanding of God's expectation for the pursuit of a calling. It would in fact be a promising sign for a future secular salvation.

In a 2006 case study of the role of the Lutheran church in the City of Lahti, Finland, University of Helsinki sociologist of religion Anne Yeung (now Pessi) reported that outside observers were impressed that "church social work seems motivated by free will and neighbourly love." One such observer put it in more personal terms: "If I needed food money for my family, I think I would choose church social work over municipal agency – I feel they work there more based on

27. Press release, *Reader's Digest Online*, http://www.rda.com/news/reader%E2%80%99s-digest-reveals-the-most-and-least-honest-cities-in-the-world-with-the-wallet-drop-project.

28. Martti Ahtisaari, quoted in Chaker, *The Finnish Miracle*, p. 216.

neighbourly love." Yeung writes that in surveying Lahti municipal officials responsible for social welfare, they admitted that in the provision "even of similar services the church does it better" than they did, something they attributed partly to the fact of "the church's role as a grassroots institution encountering people" often within their own neighborhoods, and thus it was easier for people to relate to them in a personal – and sometimes a shared spiritual – way.[29]

For Luther in his time, as Hendrix explains, "the opposite of faith was idolatry; trust in other gods of any stripe – idols made with hands, other human beings, noble ideals, or material goods," which modern thinking might seem to offer in abundance. For those who had true faith in God, however, they would surely pursue "all the genuine good works that were directed outward toward the neighbor in obedience to the remaining [nine] commandments. These good works were not religious activities" themselves, as was the common understanding in the Roman Catholic Church, but involved "the dedication of one's public and private lives to charity, honesty, sympathy, encouragement, aid, and justice" within the full community itself.[30] They resulted from true faith in God, but for Luther were not themselves the means to that true faith. Doherty sums this up well: "Based on this theological account of [civil] authority, Luther argues that it has a proactive role in actively assisting the needy. Government's role is not construed minimally or solely negatively (to restrain wickedness). It also carries responsibility for doing and promoting good. Hence, care for the needy is not a private affair left at one's personal discretion, but a public, collective responsibility" of civil government. This must not be achieved for Luther by any forceful or revolutionary means, but by the continuing spread of faith in God to more and more people in each nation and in the end throughout the world.

Luther himself not only preached this message but was involved locally in its practical application. In Wittenberg beginning in 1522, he helped to establish a "common chest" for welfare work. Lindberg

29. Yeung, "The Finnish Lutheran Church as an Agent of Welfare".

30. Hendrix, *Martin Luther* (2010), p. 51.

writes that it "was a new creation of the Reformation that transformed theology into social praxis," including the assumption in Wittenberg of responsibilities for "care of the sick and elderly in hospitals, a medical office for the poor whose doctor, Melchior Fendt, established prophylactic measures in times of hunger and inflation, and support of communal schools."[31] Such ideas and methods soon spread beyond Wittenberg to other Reformation cities. While Luther preached a social ethic of greater concern for others than oneself, he was also aware that trust could not be unlimited and that helping others required disciplined efforts. As Doherty explains,

> It is worth noting the effective practical implications of this aspect of Luther's thought in the common chest arrangements which he supervised. These reflect his so-called realism. Contributions were personal but mandatory. Recipients of disbursements were vetted to ensure that they were genuinely impoverished. Money from the chest was usually given to alleviate short-term need, for example, if crops had been poor. Newcomers were given money to launch themselves in trade, or to tide them over while seeking employment. Recipients could not become perpetually dependent, unless they could not work for a strong reason such as age or illness. The intention was to foster a culture of local accountability, preventing abuses.[32]

Here again, Luther has already offered a justification for some of the same values that would be central to the workings of the social democratic project in the twentieth century. In *The Nordic Model of Social Democracy*, three Norwegian political scientists thus explain in 2013 that the "social democratic worldview" is grounded in a "communitarian assumption" in which "everyone is assumed to contribute" to the common good. As Nik Brandal, Oivind Bratberg and Dag Einar Thorsen elaborate, "work is a foundational principle of the Nordic

31. Lindberg, "Luther's Struggle with Social-Ethical Issues," p. 172.

32. Doherty, *Theology and Economic Ethics*, p. 69.

model of social democracy, resting not so much on self-fulfillment as on collective obligation." Yet the social democratic "obligation to participate" in collective efforts to serve the community "extends only to where the possibility of [individual] participation does in fact exist." If this is not possible, social democracy recognizes the rights of each citizen and will take the necessary actions to offer them – however adverse their individual circumstances – the best opportunity possible to live a healthy and satisfying life. As with Luther, however, there is also "the insistence from the social democratic tradition that [social] rights must be accompanied by [social] responsibilities."[33] Those who can work must work; slackers will not be tolerated – in Luther's time and today in Nordic social democracy.

In the social democratic state this is partly because "a high rate of [individual] participation in the labour market is a precondition for sustaining the welfare state economically," with its high costs. If individual opportunism became widespread in the Nordic world, if large numbers of people sought to take advantage of the public generosity of the system, Nordic social democracy would be unsustainable. People should, therefore, be strongly encouraged to "stand on their own feet" as the "most effective path to self-help and autonomy."[34] Luther saw such efforts as a matter of fulfilling God's calling for each individual; Nordic social democrats 450 years later said much the same thing, though they left any explicit mention of God or a Lutheran calling out of the message.

Lutheran versus Catholic Good Works

While Luther formally taught that salvation is by "faith alone," and that "good works" are irrelevant to an individual's salvation, many Lutherans – like many Calvinists – have not thought or acted as though their own actions in this world were irrelevant to their eternal fate. Luther's message, moreover, encouraged them to think this way

33. Brandal, Bratberg and Thorsen, *The Nordic Model of Social Democracy*, pp. 102, 107, 103, 102.

34. Ibid., p. 103.

by teaching that the justified would necessarily be actively involved in good works. So doing good works technically might not assure salvation but a failure to do them would be a strong indication of God's negative verdict. The overall effect was that, whatever the official theology, many good Lutherans would feel as religiously compelled to do good works as many good Catholics had always done.

What was most radical about Luther thus was not the importance of good works but his transformed concept of their meaning. As described above, Luther called for the faithful to serve the welfare of their fellow human beings, beginning with the villages and other communities where they actually lived. The good works of the Catholic church more often focused instead on things that would serve the Church itself. In one extreme case that incurred Luther's wrath, the payment of indulgences, one form of good works, was designed to fill the coffers of the Roman church. But more broadly the Catholic Church has long promised the faithful that their prospects of salvation could be enhanced (or perhaps even assured) by making monetary donations, performing services and making contributions of land, property and many other things to the Church. Hendrix describes a range of such longstanding forms of Catholic good works including "collecting relics and depositing them in local shrines, promising miracles and indulgences to believers who made pilgrimages to those shrines, adding altars to specific saints that attracted more devoted worshippers than the main altar where Mass was celebrated, endowing fraternities and their chapels in the name of saints and hiring priests to say special Masses for themselves and their relatives."[35] The practice of confession offered numerous avenues for encouraging the faithful to do acts of penance in ways that would be practically beneficial to the Catholic Church.

The Reformation, however, meant the abolition of most of this. For a good Lutheran, good works should serve the people and the community, rather than being performed especially for the benefit of the

35. Hendrix, *Martin Luther (2010)*, p. 50.

Church. For the monastic orders of monks and nuns, they also showed their devotion to God – and contributed to their own prospects of salvation – by building Church structures and living in ways that often kept them separate from the main body of the community. Here again, Luther's revolution in theology and church practice swept all this aside. Luther's efforts were admittedly abetted by the opportunity created for rulers such as Henry VIII in England and Gustav Vasa in Sweden to confiscate large amounts of church property for their own use and benefit. In England, by some estimates a third of the land had been owned by the Catholic Church prior to Henry's secession from Rome in 1534 – this fact itself a testimony to centuries of lay donations and other historical offerings to the Church deriving from longstanding teachings about Catholic good works.

A further important Catholic form of good works was charity – almsgiving – to the poor. As Lindberg remarks, in Catholic thinking the many biblical messages declaring "God's preferential option for the poor gave them a decided edge in the pilgrimage to salvation (the rich can no more squeeze through the eye of a needle into heaven than can a camel). On the other hand, the [Catholic] church had long emphasized that almsgiving atones for sin." This form of good works created a symbiotic relationship as "almsgiving provided the poor with some charity, enabled the rich to atone for their sins, and blessed the rich with the intercessions of the poor." It was said that "God could have made all men rich, but he wanted poor men in this world, so that the rich might have an opportunity to redeem their sins."[36] Catholicism in this spirit had little objection to begging while Luther (and later Protestants) condemned it.

In contrast to the Catholic view, the Calvinist ethic instead strongly encouraged the poor to improve themselves, including by the pursuit of an individual calling that one could hope would result in some form of worldly success. In one respect the Lutheran ethic was closer to the Catholic understanding in that it encouraged direct support

36. Lindberg, "Luther's Struggle with Social-Ethical Issues," p. 171.

for the poor, but this assistance should be the responsibility of the entire community in the pursuit of individual callings, not a special responsibility of the rich. For Luther, being poor was not a desirable state in and of itself; indeed, it was a condition to be overcome with hard work. The differing Catholic emphasis on charity from the rich to benefit a permanent class of the poor has led in many Catholic nations to a lasting greater social stratification of rich and poor.[37] It was in Protestant nations that general public education was first introduced, for example, while even today the nations of Catholic Latin America lag well behind in the quality of public education provided to the broad masses of the people.

Public and Private Welfare in Finland

Henrietta Gronlund is a member of the Faculty of Theology of the University of Helsinki. In 2016 she prepared a paper for a "Symposium on 'Holy Money,'" held at the Collegium for Advanced Studies of the University.[38] In the paper she examined some fundamental questions about how Finns think about the provision of welfare and the role of private philanthropy relative to government actions. As she observed, in previous Finnish welfare scholarship "religion has not been a very central viewpoint in understanding philanthropic cultures or [state] welfare models. Both theories on welfare state regimes and theories on social origins of nonprofit sectors [...] build mostly on theories of class conflict." Hence, in order better to understand the entire Finnish welfare system, it would be necessary to examine "the Lutheran cultural background" including its core value of "love for one's neighbor."[39]

In Finland, as she explained, drawing partly on some of the literature examined here, "many ideas, values, and structures of social democracy and the universal welfare state" can be "seen as a continuation or a transformation of Lutheranism." Indeed, the "historical

37. Castles, "On Religion and Public Policy, Does Catholicism Make a Difference?"

38. Gronlund, "Between Lutheran Legacy and Economy as Religion."

39. Ibid.

institutional and administrative structures developed by the Lutheran state church provided a fundamental precondition for the universal welfare state of today, and the universalistic figure of thought in modern Nordic societies is rooted in the conformist ideals of their pre-modern Lutheran societies." It is important to recognize that "cultural values change slowly, and are rooted in historical developments in different contexts." The centuries in which the religious beliefs of Finns were dominated by Lutheranism were thus bound to have a strong staying power. But in the nineteenth and then especially the twentieth century, Lutheran beliefs assumed new forms and were embodied in the workings of new Finnish political and economic institutions. Nevertheless, as Gronlund wrote, even today "the cultural values of Finland intertwine with the Nordic version of Lutheranism." In its transformation of the Finnish Lutheran heritage, "the Nordic welfare state can be viewed as an expression of these values, and also the Lutheran form of Christianity."[40] The powerful Finnish sense of egalitarianism and social solidarity is ultimately rooted in the long Lutheran history of the nation.

For example, in Finland "the ways in which Lutheranism emphasized everyday work as a calling and secular authority as a result of God's will, developed into a particular social contract. In this social contract the secular authority carries out its 'calling' by looking after the people, and the people carry out their calling in everyday work, by paying taxes, and in this way participate in the common goal of equal well being." Following on from Luther's prescription that the Prince must be obeyed as he oversees the welfare of his subjects, Gronlund writes that for Finns "the role of the Lutheran people is to support the work of the secular authority and be obedient to it." Even if the original source of such thinking is a "now forgotten religious meaning" from the Lutheran past, for contemporary Finns "both secular authority and the role of everyday work gain an intrinsic value." As a result, "a vast majority of Finns think the role of the state should

40. Ibid.

be even stronger in providing and financing welfare, they want to pay more taxes in order for this to happen, and have exceptionally strong trust in secular authority."[41]

Yet "at the same time, individual responsibility is also called for. Again, a vast majority of Finns think that the role of individual responsibility should be stronger in his or her well being." This sense of individual responsibility to contribute to the greater good of Finland depends on "attitudes [that] can be viewed as reflections of Lutheran thinking, and especially the social contract rooted in the dual calling: both the secular authority and the individual citizen must take care of their task, ensure universal welfare and work and pay taxes to make that possible." As Gronlund further observes, such elements "of Nordic Lutheran thinking" can be contrasted "with another Protestant ethic, that of Calvinism." In the United States, for example, the form that Calvinism took "sharply differs from Nordic Lutheranism with regard to the relationship between government and the people, the responsibility or calling of the individual, the viewpoint towards business, and the role of philanthropy." In contrast to Finland, in the American model private "philanthropy is central in welfare and other arenas, and its societal role is highly visible and normative." Finns are expected to be modest about their private philanthropic contributions to society (which have a lesser overall social role) but in the Calvinist United States "names of big donors as well as the amounts they have donated are commonly visible on the walls of universities and cultural institutions – often so that the names of those having donated the biggest amounts are written with the largest font, which grows smaller with the amounts. Entire hospitals, libraries, etc. are named after the people who have founded them."[42] Much of the American university system is private, based on initial large founding grants and subsequent widespread private giving.

Gronlund characterizes some of these differing national religious influences in Table 2 below.

41. Ibid.

42. Ibid.

TABLE 2
Calvinist influences in the U.S. versus Lutheran influences in Finland

U.S. and Calvinism	Finland and Lutheranism
As little as possible power to government; Government and religion kept separate	Strong reliance on and obedience to the government; government and religion intertwine
Positive viewpoint towards pursuit of profit in the private field	Reserved viewpoint towards pursuit of profit and self-interest
Building a good society through individual success and philanthropy	Building a good society through work as a calling
Individual responsibility to succeed and then provide to philanthropy (universities, welfare, religious communities)	Individual responsibility to work and pay taxes
Visible, normative role of philanthropy	Invisible, modest culture of philanthropy

SOURCE: Henrietta Gronlund, "Between Lutheran Legacy and Economy as Religion: The Contested Roles of Philanthropy in Finland Today," paper prepared for a "Symposium on 'Holy Money,'" Collegium for Advanced Studies, University of Helsinki, Helsinki, Finland, September 15–16, 2016.

Conclusion

Although Max Weber was a significant exception, few social scientists or historians of the twentieth century followed after him in focusing on elements of Christian religion as a main explanatory factor in the social and economic history of the modern age. They seldom delved into the religious arguments to consider whether alternative theological interpretations might supplement or even improve on Weber's understanding. Even as a greater recognition of the importance of religion began to develop towards the end of the twentieth century, few (if any) social science or history departments introduced the routine study of Christian theology as part of their course offerings (some individual students of course did enter into such studies on their own). Indeed, most social science or history faculty members would not have had the religious knowledge to teach theological history. Within theology schools, it was the opposite: they mostly focused on the history of and intellectual debates within religion, seldom exploring the profound social and economic consequences of the religious beliefs themselves, both in earlier centuries and then continuing throughout the twentieth century. Overcoming this artificial separation will be a challenge for the strict disciplinary specializations – even theology has now become a "professional" field of its own – that today characterize the university world of both Europe and the United States.

Owing to Weber, the existence of a Calvinist ethic and a related understanding of good works and a calling is at least widely known. There has been much less study, however, of the "Lutheran ethic," even though Luther and his followers also had a great deal to say about the pursuit of a calling with inevitable implications in practice for good works. The Lutheran ethic, moreover, differs significantly from the Calvinist ethic, especially with regard to such matters as the legitimacy of worldly success in business, the role of the pursuit of self-interest in society, the role of the state in providing for the welfare of the community, the interpretation of the Golden Rule and many other matters. Ernst Troeltsch, the great German theologian and close friend of Max Weber, wrote that "right from the onset and in contrast to Luther, Calvin found capitalism acceptable, as a calling."[43]

Conversely, as long ago as Luther's time, the Lutheran calling encouraged the public and private fulfillment of those responsibilities which today, five centuries later, have under social democratic governance become among the main responsibilities of the Nordic welfare state (with the Lutheran church still contributing if in a much lesser role). If a Calvinist ethic is the source of "the spirit of capitalism" as Weber wrote, we can now speak of a Lutheran ethic that is the source of "the Nordic spirit of social democracy." As Luther scholar Lindberg sums this up, "Luther believed that the church was called publicly and unequivocally to reject exploitative economic developments, and to develop a constructive social ethic in response to them. This social ethic [much later] contributed directly to the enactment of social welfare legislation in areas that accepted the Reformation."[44] Contrary to Weber who confused matters by writing of a "Protestant ethic," there are actually two distinct ethics within Protestantism, the "Calvinist ethic," and the "Lutheran ethic," the former encouraging the development of capitalism throughout its religious domain, and the latter the development of the twentieth-century social democratic version of the welfare state in the Nordic world .

43. Troeltsch, *The Social Teaching of the Christian Churches*, Vol. 2, p. 643.

44. Lindberg, "Luther's Struggle with Social-Ethical Issues," p. 174.

CHAPTER 7

Luther and the Equality of Women

As noted previously, the five Nordic countries held all top five rankings in the 2014 Global Gender Gap Report from the World Economic Forum.[1] A woman, Tarja Halonen, was President of Finland from 2000 to 2012. Following the 2014 elections, 44 percent of the 349 seats in the Swedish Parliament were held by women. The highest decision-making body of the Church of Sweden, the General Synod, in 2015 had 125 women and 126 men on its board. Similar proportions of women have characterized government and other top leadership positions across the Nordic world (although not the private corporate sphere). Kautto et al. find that gender relations are one of the key features setting the Nordic world apart from the rest of Europe, explaining that comparatively "a systematic Nordic pattern of more pronounced gender equality was found in almost all aspects studied."[2]

The explanations offered for the exceptionally high degree of equality of men and women in the Nordic countries have not traditionally looked to religion. Indeed, it has more often been the opposite; the increasingly equality of women in Nordic society has been seen as the product of a general secularization of Nordic societies, as has been accompanied by and reflected in the twentieth century by the declining role of the Lutheran Church in Nordic public life. The role of women in Nordic society increased most rapidly during the period of Nordic social democratic political dominance from the 1930s to the 1980s. The role of women, however, is another area where, contrary to the usual assumption, religion played a large role.

1. World Economic Forum, *The Global Gender Gap*.

2. Kautto, Fritzell, Hvinden, Krist and Uusitalo, "Conclusion," p. 264.

A new form of Lutheranism – now assuming an outwardly "secular" appearance – worked significantly to advance equality.

As with other aspects of the impact of Lutheranism in shaping the modern Nordic world, it is only recently that the influence of Luther's views with respect to the place of women in society has begun to receive more attention. A leading American religious historian, Mark Noll, thus observed in 2011 that "for Protestantism as a whole, Luther's example" in his own writings and in his portrayals of his marriage "exalted the status of wives, mothers, and the domestic round." Indeed, this "contributed greatly to establishing a general Protestant conviction: the belief that any calling – whether in the home or in public, sacred or secular, taken up by men or by women – could be pursued honourably and for the glory of God."[3] Luther transferred the central point of religious life from the Catholic church to the Lutheran community and family, a momentous historical development whose full gender implications are still being worked out theologically and practically today.

Theologically, Luther gave a new emphasis to the longstanding fundamental Christian message that all people, men and women alike, are made "in the image of God" – and thus in their core essence they are fully equal. He wrote that "all Christian men are priests, all women priestesses, be they young or old, master or servant, mistress or maid, learned or lay. Here there is no difference, unless faith be unequal," regardless of gender.[4] Timothy F. Lull and Derek R. Nelson commented in 2015 that in Luther's "Sermon on Marriage," written in 1519 while he was still a monk and six years before his own marriage in 1525, Luther offered "one of the more positive interpretations of marriage – as opposed to celibacy – that had appeared in many centuries" in the Christian world.[5] The elevation of marriage to a higher religious status in society than monasticism did much to raise the overall social status of women.

3. Noll, *Protestantism*, pp. 18–19.
4. Martin Luther, *A Sermon on the New Testament*, quoted in Edwards, *Printing Propaganda and Marin Luther*, p. 67.
5. Lull and Nelson, *Resilient Reformer*, p. 92.

In the United States alone in 2016 there were three museum exhibitions in New York, Atlanta and Minneapolis celebrating the life and historic impact of Luther. Reviewing these exhibitions, Peter Schjeldahl commented that one common theme was that Luther was "unusually supportive of women." If a woman had "an impotent or unwilling husband [she] should seek a divorce," or as Luther said, at the least find another local sexual partner. But "failing that, she might leave and start fresh in another town" in search of such a person.[6] Luther from the beginning was anything but puritanical. His favorable attitudes about the pleasures of sex between men and women stood in contrast to the Roman Catholic Church – which had taught for many centuries that its one legitimate purpose was procreation – establishing yet another basis for greater gender equality.[7]

Religion and Women's Rights

In 1990 the Danish sociologist Gosta Esping-Anderson published *The Three Worlds of Welfare Capitalism*, a pioneering analysis arguing that the welfare states of the economically developed nations of the western world fit into three broad types based on the religious cultures of those nations: (1) the mostly Catholic nations in continental Europe with strong corporatist/statist traditions; (2) the nations mostly with an Anglo-Saxon heritage with strong liberal (in the classical European sense) traditions; and (3) the Nordic nations with strong social democratic traditions.[8] Esping-Anderson's book began a new era in welfare-state analysis, with its shift from longstanding economic explanations to a new acknowledgement of cultural roots. A number of subsequent studies addressed more specifically the importance of religion to welfare-state developments, an explanatory factor to which Esping-Anderson himself had given limited attention (mainly with respect to historically Catholic countries).[9] As examined in the pre-

6. Schjeldahl, "Knock on Wood," p. 93.
7. Eire, *Reformations*, p. 711.
8. Esping-Anderson, *The Three Worlds of Welfare Capitalism.*
9. See Backstrom and Davie, eds., *Welfare and Religion in 21st Century Europe: Volume 1, Configuring the Connections*; and Backstrom, Davie, Edgardh and Pettersson, eds., *Welfare and Religion in 21st Century Europe: Volume 2, Gendered, Religious and Social Change.*

vious chapter, a historic Protestant religion, however, was now also increasingly recognized as having been an important factor in national welfare state outcomes, differing, moreover, in its impacts between the Lutheran and the Calvinist Reformed traditions within Protestantism.[10]

As early as 1906, Finland (then a Grand Duchy within Russia, but with a large degree of regional political autonomy) adopted universal women's suffrage, the first country in Europe to do so. The next two nations in Europe were Norway in 1913 and Denmark in 1915, and then among the Nordic countries Sweden followed in 1921. Indeed, the timelines for the adoption of women's suffrage can be roughly grouped in national categories to match the "three world" welfare state model proposed by Esping-Anderson. The Nordic nations again represent one distinct European "world" where women's suffrage advanced more rapidly than elsewhere. The adoption of women's suffrage so early in the twentieth century in Nordic countries also suggests that the preconditions for this development must have arisen in significant part in the nineteenth century, well before the processes of secularization and modernization took a firm hold and at a time when religion – and Lutheranism in particular – still exerted a powerful influence throughout every area of Nordic society.

In nations historically dominated by Reformed religions and branches of Protestantism other than Lutheranism, however, the timelines in Europe tended to be more mixed. The Netherlands adopted universal women's suffrage in 1919, but it did not arrive in the United Kingdom until 1928. It was not until 1971 that historically Protestant (since the days of Calvin and Zwingli, although always having a Catholic minority) Switzerland adopted women's suffrage at the national level, the last nation in Europe to do so.

Within the last of Esping-Anderson's worlds, consisting mostly of historically Catholic European nations, the national differences are even more pronounced. The first adoptions of women's suffrage in

10. See Van Kersbergen and Manow, eds., *Religion, Class Coalitions, and Welfare States.*

historically Catholic nations were in 1918 in Hungary, Lithuania and Poland. But the largest and most important Catholic nations of Europe were much slower, including Spain (1931), France (1944) and Italy (1946). In Latin America, a number of historically Catholic countries were slower even than this, including Mexico (1947), Argentina (1947), Columbia (1954), and Peru (1955). In part, this reflects the lesser role of women in the general functioning of the Roman Catholic church, which inevitably created beliefs and values that carried over into other areas of society.[11] Indeed, such national historic differences relating to the status of women can still be found. In the late 1990s, world national value surveys asked the question "do men make better political leaders?" Among those nations surveyed, the leading countries in Europe in terms of responding negatively were the same Nordic countries that had led the way in women's suffrage early in the twentieth century – Finland, Norway and Sweden (Denmark and Iceland were not surveyed).

In summary, as political scientists Ronald Inglehart and Christian Welzel – two leading students of social value trends around the world – wrote in 2005, the "Scandinavian social-democratic welfare states show the highest level of gender equality" in Europe, exceeding that of the other Protestant states and by an even greater margin the historically Catholic and Christian Democratic "corporatist" states of central and southern Europe. As they comment, "a trend towards gender equality becomes a central aspect of modernization" and is "crucial to the quality of democracy," areas in which the Lutheran countries of the Nordic world advanced most rapidly in the twentieth century.[12]

Martin Luther as Advocate for Women

While Luther's immense historic impact cannot be doubted, as has been discussed previously, he was a complicated individual. Both his theology and his actions were often filled with tensions and even out-

11. Nelson, "Is Max Weber Newly Relevant?"

12. Inglehart and Welzel, *Modernization, Cultural Change, and Democracy*, pp. 279–280, 272.

right contradictions. When it came to his writings about the role of women in society, Luther did frequently offer a traditional patriarchal understanding including the necessary subservience of a wife to her husband. Oxford historian Lyndal Roper comments that "it is easy to plunder his works for sexist aphorisms."[13] In exploring Luther's writings about sex and marriage, Finnish theologian Sammeli Juntunen also finds that the implications for the role of women can be negative. Luther frequently portrays the sex act itself as a sinful outcome of the Fall in the Garden which reduces human beings to animal-like motives and behavior – acceptable only because God has given his approval within the institution of marriage. For Luther in his writings, as Juntunen finds, one can find suggestions that "sex in itself is something dirty and shameful." At one point Luther justifies marriage because it works as "a medicine and remedy for whoring" – a better outlet at least for the implacably sinful and lustful nature of human beings.[14]

Typical of Luther, however, Juntunen also sees significant positive sides. Luther could also take the position that "marriage is still a godly institution, one that God has blessed with his word." Moreover, rather than the church, it is "the family [that] forms the basis of a society," where women have the central role. Juntunen finds that "in a certain sense Luther's theological thinking allows a much more positive attitude toward sex than the thinking of Augustine or Thomas Aquinas."[15] While Luther's explicit writings about sex and marriage can thus be ambivalent, there are other more critical factors to consider such as his overall theology including matters that do not directly address sex and marriage but do have implications for the status of women in Lutheran societies.

Whatever he wrote about the role of women at one time or another, Luther's broader theology and actions thus worked in practice to encourage a more equal status. The two most important of these actions were his rejection of celibacy for the Christian clergy and the example of his own marriage. German Luther scholar Bernhard Lohse

13. Roper, *Martin Luther*, p. 282.

14. Juntunen, "Sex," pp. 200, 197.

writes that Luther rejected "the then commonly accepted principle that there were two sets of ethics: one for secular Christians and the other for monastics," including the religious orders for women who lived celibate lives as part of fulfilling their higher religious vows (they were to be married to God and the church, not to men). Luther advanced instead the revolutionary idea that instead of "the medieval assertion of the spiritual over the secular estate, [...] all baptized are priests," including ordinary women equally with ordinary men.[16] Only a man could be a Catholic priest, but a Lutheran woman could hold an elevated religious status as equally as a member of the priesthood (along with all other believers). Women admittedly did not become Lutheran pastors until the twentieth century, but a Lutheran pastor was just another ordinary human being, more church administrator and discussion leader than a holder of unique religious authority. To this day, a female Catholic priest remains an impossibility.

As Protestants abolished the Catholic monastic orders in the 1520s, the question of celibacy was also readdressed; Luther rejected celibacy in part because he saw it as another false form of "good works." When monks and nuns left their orders, it was often because they wanted to marry, and many did so. The issue of their freedom to leave was initially framed in terms of their right to reject monastic vows of celibacy. Luther historian Scott Hendrix explains that in 1521 it was Luther's fellow reformer Andrew Karlstadt "who took the first steps toward religious change. When three priests in the vicinity violated their vows of celibacy and took wives, Karlstadt supported them by declaring that vows taken by priests and monks were null and void." Philip Melanchthon readily agreed but Luther was initially hesitant. By the end of the year, however, "he was certain everyone could leave, and he started an attack on monastic vows in order to 'free the young people from that hell of celibacy.'"[17] The wives of Lutheran clergymen achieved a higher social status, and all women benefited from

15. bid., pp. 199, 189, 202.
16. Lohse, *Martin Luther*, pp. 151, 128.
17. Hendrix, *Martin Luther(2015)*, pp. 120–121.

the elevated religious significance of the family, meaning a healthy sexuality was now something to be praised. The American professor of Reformation history and theology Jane Strohl writes that for the Lutheran faithful – including its women – the pursuit of a calling would involve a religious act of "serving and praising God in and through their routine activities" in this world.[18]

For Luther himself, having a "particularity of vocation was a great comfort" to him. Luther felt not surprisingly that "he was called to be a doctor of Scripture in the service of the church." What is less well known is that he regarded his second great calling in his life "to be the husband of one particular woman and the father of her children," seeing his actions in this capacity as also serving God's purposes.[19] In this role, Luther himself "did not consider it unmanly for fathers" such as himself "to wash diapers and make beds" (ideas that admittedly have yet to be universally adopted by the fathers of the twenty-first century).[20] Typical of Luther's frequently bombastic style, he once wrote that "a maid who wraps a child with swaddling clothes and cooks porridge for it – even if it is the child of a prostitute – has a much higher calling from God himself than all the monks and nuns on this earth, who can't claim that their self-appointed holiness is from God."[21] A stronger statement of the full equality of all women and men would be hard to imagine.

It is sometimes suggested, however, that Luther acted against women's interests by abolishing the orders of nuns and other special women's roles in the Catholic Church, one of the few potential avenues at the time for women to gain a higher level of education and to advance to higher leadership positions in society, outside the home. Kirsi Sjerna, for example, criticizes Luther in general for not doing enough to challenge the patriarchal character and male dominance of public life of his day. Indeed, in that respect she argues that he did positive harm in that "with the rejection of the monastic way of life

18. Strohl, "Luther's Spiritual Journey," p. 161.
19. Ibid.
20. Treu, *Martin Luther in Wittenberg*, pp. 279, 277.
21. Quoted in Treu, *Katherine von Bora*, p. 27.

and convents in pro-Reformation cities, women lost significant opportunities for [independent] spiritual formation and vocations" (she also observes that the Protestant war on brothels had similar consequences, depriving Reformation women of another main way of functioning independently in society). Yet Sjerna does also acknowledge that "the declaration of the priesthood of all believers and the spiritual equality of all believers that the reformers espoused [...] in their preaching of the sacredness of daily 'ordinary' life had the most profound promise for women" – even if the full extent of this promise would not be entirely realized until the twentieth century.[22]

Even in Luther's time, however, only a small minority of women lived in convents, whereas Luther gave a new elevated religious significance to the routine household activities of the great majority of Lutheran women. He also opened up new avenues for all women to obtain better educations and to become more equal partners in church discussions of religious matters. Egil Johannson explains that "it was the Reformation which stimulated the popularization of reading" (writing was given less emphasis until much later).[23] By the end of the seventeenth century, an individual in Sweden unable to demonstrate proficiency in reading when tested was unable to be confirmed or to marry. Throughout Protestant Europe, an estimated 35 to 45 percent could then read, as compared with fewer than 20 percent in Catholic (and Orthodox) Europe.[24]

For Luther and his later followers, it was thus necessary that girls also learn to read the Bible, as they were expected to understand and to discuss with others (including men) the true meaning of the Scriptures. Luther scholar Andrew Pettegree writes that "Luther was [...] a notable pioneer in the field of female education. If the goal of an informed Christian people was to be realized, then for Luther this applied equally to girls as to boys." He therefore called for "the best possible schools both for boys and girls in every locality."[25] Pettegree

22. Stjerna, *Women and the Reformation*, pp. 32–33.
23. Johannson, "The History of Literacy in Sweden,", p. 33.
24. Ibid., p. 34.
25. Pettegree, *Brand Luther*, p. 265.

reports that in a 1587 survey conducted in Catholic Venice, only 0.2 percent of the students were girls, while surveys in Lutheran rural areas of Germany around that time found almost equal numbers of boys and girls.[26]

Until the Reformation, almost all serious writings about religion were in Latin. Very early in his publishing career Luther also normally wrote in Latin, but he soon turned increasingly to vernacular German; over his full lifetime, 17 percent of his publications were in Latin and 83 percent in German – and thus comprehensible to ordinary people who were literate (still a small but often a particularly influential minority).[27] Luther famously translated the New Testament into German while hidden in 1522 in Wartburg Castle, thus facilitating the efforts of many lay Germans to reach their own conclusions as to the true meaning of "scripture alone." The invention of the printing press made Luther's voluminous writings in German – often in many editions – widely and inexpensively available, something that is commonly seen as a key to the success of the Reformation. As in other areas, it was not Luther's specific goal in this case but his use of German in his writings again worked to advance the equality of women. In his time, the number of men who had learned Latin, and thus could follow religious and other intellectual debates in Latin, was larger than the number of women.[28] In summary, German Luther scholar Martin Treu writes of Luther's views of relations between the sexes that even "in their time they developed revolutionary explosive power" that worked to raise the religious status of women in society.[29]

Luther's View of Marriage

Luther's rejection of clerical celibacy and other traditional Roman Catholic practices and attitudes concerning the expression of sexual drives in society was powerfully symbolized by his own decision to

26. Ibid., p. 266.
27. Edwards, *Printing, Propaganda and Martin Luther*, p. 20.
28. Roper, *Martin Luther*, p. 36.
29. Ibid., p. 27.

marry in 1525. Treu explains that in the medieval Catholic world "everyone considered it a certainty that life in an order and celibacy were a more meritorious way of life in the eyes of God."[30] But fairly early in the Reformation, Luther "reversed the traditional order [...] since [marriage as he saw it] was expressly governed by God's sacred will to create," as seen in human desires readily visible in nature, "while the former [celibacy] was not commanded by God" but was an artificial requirement traditionally asserted by the Roman Catholic Church.[31] In the earliest years of Christianity, women had often played a significant role in its spread over the Mediterranean world – Constantine's mother was a Christian – but with the establishment of the Roman Catholic Church and its bureaucratic religious bodies the importance of women had diminished. As Luther saw matters, his fundamental objective in the Reformation was a restoration of an older and truer Christianity as it had existed before the many centuries of corruption in Rome, the Pope in the end having become the Anti-Christ.

Thus, in the common view of the Roman Catholic Church in Europe before the Reformation, as Heiko Oberman writes, the "sexual drives are confused with man's 'primeval sin' [in the Garden]. What nature wants is 'unholy,' something only for the dark hours of the night." But in rejecting this way of thinking, Luther showed a willingness "to speak plainly about the healthy elemental force of desire," even including the occasional "erotic passage" in his correspondence. Indeed, for his day Luther was sometimes remarkably frank about the strong sexual attraction and mutual pleasures he and his wife Katherine von Bora enjoyed. He wrote to a friend about to be married that "when you sleep with your Catharine and embrace her, you should think: 'This child of man, this wonderful creature of God has been given to me by my Christ. May He be praised and glorified' [...] I shall make love to my Katherine while you make love to yours, and thus we will be united in love.""[32]

30. Treu, *Katherine von Bora*, p. 24.

31. Ibid., p. 27.

32. Oberman, *Luther*, pp. 275, 276.

In their biography of Luther, Lull and Nelson observe that with his marriage Luther began "to explore the path he had recommended to so many others – serving God not in a set-apart religious life but in the ordinary structures of family and work."[33] Luther on one occasion expressed his happiness that "the local wine is good, and the Naumberg beer is very good," further examples of how "Luther's Reformation found God-given space for love and good living," attitudes that would not always be embraced by later Lutheran pastors and other followers who could be more fearful of worldly pleasures.[34]

The professor of church history Carter Lindberg similarly explains that "Luther rejected every form of flight from the world with its suspicion of creation including the human body. Humankind is not called to flee the world but rather to engage the world." In abandoning clerical celibacy, "this was not just a matter of breaking church law; rather, the public rejection of mandatory clerical celibacy encompassed the new evangelical [Lutheran] understanding of the relationship to God and the world." For its time, as Lindberg writes, "the thought that persons could serve God in marriage was revolutionary." Reflecting his broader thinking, Luther further intended as part of the new worldliness of Reformation religion that "with marriage and the household estate came multiple responsibilities to the larger community and vice versa."[35]

Lyndal Roper distinguishes between Luther's evolved religious understanding of marriage and that of Calvinist and other Reformed faiths – another aspect of the different impacts on European societies of a Lutheran versus a Calvinist religious heritage. As she explains, Luther's "married life had transformed his theology. He had shed asceticism for a remarkably positive conception of human physicality. [...] This vision would separate him not only from the old [Roman Catholic] Church but also from the rule-bound communitarian moralism of those influenced by the Swiss reformers and their heirs, the Calvinists."[36]

33. Lull and Nelson, *Resilient Reformer*, p. 222.
34. Oberman, *Luther*, p. 283.
35. Lindberg, "Luther's Struggle with Social-Ethical Issues,", pp. 167, 168, 169.
36. Roper, *Martin Luther*, p. 305.

Luther as Husband

Given the lack of consistency in his writings, Luther's actions could be as important as – or more important than – his words themselves. In his lifetime, Luther took individual actions on three occasions in particular that were critical to the ultimate success and impact of the Protestant Reformation, also showing his great personal resolve and strength of will. The first occasion was his decision to become a monk in 1505, thus defying his father (who had invested heavily in Luther's earlier more practical education) and resulting in an estrangement that lasted for many years. The most momentous of Luther's actions was in 1521, when he defied the Holy Roman Emperor in refusing to recant at Worms – thus literally changing the course of history in Europe and indeed the world.

Luther's third great act of defiance was his marriage in 1525. Luther scholar Treu reports that "for Luther's enemies his marriage was a scandal," some even suggesting that he had launched a crusade against the Roman Catholic Church in order to gain the freedom to satisfy his private lust.[37] His new wife was by many accounts a beautiful woman, descended from a noble – if now impoverished – family. Treu writes that "even his friends were critical," including his theological collaborator Philip Melanchthon, who was not invited to the wedding. Melanchthon was particularly unhappy that Luther had acted in the midst of the Peasants' War, when death and destruction were so prevalent throughout Germany. He wrote harshly in 1525 how surprised he was that "in such serious times, when good people everywhere suffer so much, that he [Luther] does not share others' suffering, but even more, so it seems, indulges himself and compromises his good reputation, at a time when Germany right now especially needs his spirit and his authority. [...] The man can be terribly easily misled, and the nuns who in every way lay in wait for him, have

37. Treu, *Martin Luther in Wittenberg*, p. 76.

ensnared him, [...] and caused the fires of passion to blaze up in him."[38] It was particularly provocative in that a former monk was marrying a former nun. Characteristically, Luther ignored all such innuendo, snide remarks and other harsh criticisms for this latest violation of the social expectations of his times, again with long-term historical consequences. Luther once declared in a 1517 sermon that "where Christ is, there he always goes against the flow," a message heeded by Luther once again in his 1525 decision to marry.

As far as we know, Luther had had little if any sexual experience with women as of 1525. He had been an Augustinian monk and fully absorbed by his struggles to reform the Church. Indeed, before his marriage he was concerned about his future ability to perform his husbandly duties. The possibility of marrying at the age of 42 was a low priority for him but Luther now found himself driven by circumstances. He had assumed the responsibilities of a matchmaker for nine former nuns who had fled their monastic life to come to Wittenberg with his assistance. He was successful in finding husbands or other suitable arrangements for all but one, Katherine von Bora, who was already 26 years old, well past the usual age of marriage. Luther made a suggestion or two for possible husbands but she rejected them – thus acting on the Christian principle that a woman entering into marriage is free to decide as a matter of individual choice (a right not recognized at the time for women over much of the world).

Katherine did suggest, however, that Luther himself would be acceptable to her, and he somewhat reluctantly agreed to resolve the problem by marrying her. As Luther historian Roland Bainton writes, he offered "three reasons for his marriage: to please his father, to spite the pope and the Devil, and to seal his witness before martyrdom" (which he was then expecting to come soon).[39] He did not in fact die until 1546, and by all accounts his new marriage proved a great success.[40] Luther fathered six children (two dying in childhood), as his

38. Quoted in Treu, *Katherine von Bora*, p. 32.

39. Bainton, *Here I Stand*, p. 294.

40. Stjerna, *Women and the Reformation*, pp. 51–70.

new partner "Katie" provided a happy and supportive home environment. Pettegree observes that his marriage put him "at the center of a growing, happy family." Although little of Katharine's correspondence has survived, Luther's own correspondence indicates "how much Luther had come to respect and love his wife" with whom he shared a "partnership of real depth and touching devotion." The feelings were reciprocated as "Katharina was, within a very few years, his trusted soul mate, with whom he shared his hopes and fears."[41] According to the thinking of his time, Luther may have been expected to fulfill the role of patriarch, but the reality was that he and his wife shared a close partnership encompassing most areas of family responsibility, an example that would become a lasting part of the lore of Lutheranism to this day.

Katherine also managed the household business affairs, maintaining the household revenue and cost accounts, supervising the acquisition of land and livestock and making other management decisions. She proved talented in this regard – as her husband had not – and by the 1540s Luther had become "one of Wittenberg's wealthiest citizens."[42] Oberman comments that "she ruled an extended family judiciously," including a "never-ending stream of visitors – friends, people curious to meet the great man, or people with theological queries."[43] Lull and Nelson comment that she also assisted Luther in matters extending well beyond family affairs; she was present "not only in the kitchen and the bedchamber," but was sometimes even a "theological advisor" to Luther. Luther was a moody person who was prone to times of deep depression and despair. By his own testimony there were only three people who could effectively "minister to his discouragement," his pastor and confessor John Bugenhagen, his wife Katharine and his close friend and long-time theological collaborator, Philip Melanchthon.[44]

41. Pettegree, *Brand Luther*, pp. 255, 256, 257.
42. Treu, *Martin Luther in Wittenberg*, p. 82.
43. Oberman, *Luther*, p. 279.
44. Lull and Nelson, *Resilient Reformer*, p. 217.

Luther's Powerful Example

Luther by his behavior in his marriage – unusual for the time – thereby offered a future model for Lutheran Europe; by his example he showed that even a great religious leader might enter into marriage, treat his wife with great respect, enjoy their sexual relationship together for its pleasures as well as progeny and indeed generally conduct the marriage as a partnership of equal and freely choosing individual adults. Later members of the Lutheran church did not necessarily follow this example in every respect (or sometimes even most respects) but Luther in his relationship with his wife had acted in what we might say today was a remarkably "modern" way. This side of Luther's legacy would become especially important in the Nordic world in the nineteenth and twentieth centuries, as more and more men and women followed Luther's lasting example (whether they knew it or not).

The importance of Luther for the rights of women was a neglected subject in the twentieth century but this has been changing recently. In *Resilient Reformer: The Life and Thought of Martin Luther*, Lull and Nelson write in 2015 that "in the main, he [Luther] held the same views as others in the sixteenth century. He thought that women were weaker, more prone to emotional outburst, and less reasoned."[45] In his relationship with his wife, however, there was little sign of this. Luther can be a bundle of contradictions, and his actions are often more important than his words. Indeed, in the broader view, Lull and Nelson conclude:

> In the ways in which Luther departed from his culture – which ought to signal something deeper about his thought than the defaults of his [societal] context – Luther often viewed women more favorably than one might expect. His many writings on marriage consistently took seriously the claims of women. And his defense of marriage as a noble Christian institution was

45. Ibid., pp. 327–328.

> generally good news for women. [...] His strong endorsement of a healthy sexuality extended to women and men, loudly condemning earlier views that "marriages fill the earth, virginity fills heaven." He went against the norms of German law and made his wife the executor of his will. [...] He strongly encouraged Argula von Grumback, a noblewomen in Bavaria who wrote and published Reformation pamphlets, including a letter to the faculty of the University of Ingolstadt who had arrested a student for Lutheran views. Women ordinarily would never do such a thing, yet Luther did not think twice about urging her on.[46]

Given his renown across Europe, as Pettegree explains, Luther thus made large contributions to asserting a new role for women in Lutheran societies. Pettegree writes that in his "home life, lived in a very public way, [Luther] provided the new church with the archetype of the new Protestant family." Many Catholic priests in Luther's time, by contrast, had had female partners but their relationships had necessarily been "furtive and clandestine. The priest's woman was often the subject of public mockery and faced a dismal prospect of dispossession and penury in the event that the priest died." With Luther as a towering example, "now the Protestant churches not only regularized these unions; they provided the potential for a stable family life at the heart of each local community" with its Lutheran church and pastor, educating the children "in the new faith and suited for a profession of their own." Pettegree writes that "the power of Luther and Katharina as a model and exemplar is demonstrated in the proliferation of copies of [Lucas] Cranach's double marriage portrait." It presented to the owners of these famous portrait copies an image of "sober Protestant homes, presiding over households where the Christian life was both lived and taught: the holy household as church."[47]

In summary, Lindberg considers that "no institutional change brought about by the Reformation was more visible, responsive to late

46. Ibid., pp. 328, 329.

47. Pettegree, *Brand Luther*, pp. 255, 256, 257, 259.

medieval pleas for [Church] reform, and conducive to new social attitudes than the marriage of Protestant clergy. Nor was there another point in the Protestant program where theology and practice corresponded more successfully." Luther radically rejected the traditional Catholic view that encouraged the "self-chosen religious callings of clericalism." Instead, in properly serving God "Luther focused on 'the ordinary.'" It meant "that we are not called to self-chosen extraordinary tasks, but rather to service [of God] in the world" of marriage, family and immediate community. This means also that "the center of Luther's ethic of vocation is not self-sanctification, but the neighbors' needs" – and the needs of a person's spouse as the closest "neighbor" of all.[48] With the reach of religion now fully extending into every area of life, this should include changes in ordinary male as well as female behavior: "Luther attempted to redefine his culture's understanding of male gender from uncontrollable impulse to social responsibility."[49] In Latin American and other parts of the world today where Protestantism is making large new inroads, the largest impact for family life is often a change in male behavior patterns.[50]

Luther's views about marriage and family can have a more contemporary feel than other areas of his writings such as the proper ethics of the commercial sphere. Indeed, in terms of the views he expressed 500 years ago, it might not even be much of an exaggeration to say that, despite his patriarchal thinking in some respects, there was also an element of "Luther the feminist advocate". Carlos Eire writes that "attitudes towards sex and marriage were the source of one of the sharpest differences between Catholics and Protestants." For Luther himself, "the Catholic Church's teaching on sex and marriage was a total inversion of values, and he based much of his criticism on natural rather than theological grounds. Marriage, he argued, was the only way to preserve chastity, the only proper way to handle uncontrollable natural urges." Indeed, "all of the magisterial Reformers took the same tack, arguing that celibacy was an impossible goal for most human beings, and therefore 'unjust and against God.'"[51]

48. Ibid., pp. 168, 170.

49. Lindberg, "Luther's Struggle with Social-Ethical Issues," pp. 168, 170.

50. David Martin, *Tongues of Fire.*

51. Eire, *Reformations*, pp. 711, 712, 713.

Lutheran Origins of the Swedish Women's Movement

By the 1990s, as in the case of scholarly explorations of the origins of the social democratic welfare state, a few Nordic researchers in the field of gender relations were beginning to pay more attention to religion. Once again, they found that the importance of religion had been neglected by twentieth-century scholars, and that Nordic religion had indeed been a key factor in the development of the early suffrage movements of the later nineteenth and early twentieth centuries. In 2000 Finnish historian Pirjo Markkola assembled an edited book containing a series of case studies on *Gender and Vocation: Women, Religion and Social Change in the Nordic Countries, 1830–1940*. Since all the Nordic countries had Lutheran state churches, and the great majority of the populations of these countries were Lutheran, much of the book focused on the role of Lutheranism in changing Nordic gender relationships over this period.

In one chapter, Swedish historian Inger Hammar examined the role of Lutheran religion in influencing leading nineteenth-century figures in the early development of the movement for women's rights in Sweden, focusing in particular on Fredrika Bremer. Bremer was a famous novelist – she is sometimes described as the Swedish Jane Austin – but was also, as described by Hammar, "foremost in the Swedish women's movement" as it was emerging in the mid and late nineteenth century; her literary fame enabled her "to carry the emancipation debate to a much wider audience." Hammar comments in 2000 that "since it has long been assumed that the emancipation of women and secularization went hand in hand, [existing] research into the history of Swedish women has spent little time in tracing the deeply Christian tone of the [early] feminist movement" there – resulting in "religion blind" gender research, as was characteristic of so much social science in the twentieth century. In reality, however, in the nineteenth century "Swedish society was permeated by a Lutheran view of society," which extended to thinking about the role of women as well. For the early leading feminist Bremer, "the demand for equality for both women and men was [...] derived from a Christian world view."[52]

Hammar observes that, as in many areas, the Bible was not clear about the proper place of women in society – it contains some passages that "give expression to a misogynist gender ordering, while in others one finds the equality of men and women."[53] For Bremer, however, the heart of the matter was the core biblical understanding that human beings, men and women alike, are all made equally "in the image of God." In this respect, and unlike most societies and cultures over the long course of world history, Christianity taught the fundamental equality of all human beings, whatever their gender, social status or other personal features. Bremer thus wrote for her Swedish audience that in this respect Christianity was "a fairly strong proclamation from on high of women's equality in right and worth with man, and without which our sex would still languish in its heathen infancy."[54] As she argued, the time had now come to abolish those remaining and ever more obsolete social, political and religious barriers that had in previous centuries limited the full application of the true Christian message to the place of women in Swedish society.

As Hammar explains, "in Bremer's eyes, this meant that the roles of society traditionally accorded to women were now doomed. In [the] future, women's 'human and social value' must be stressed far more." Women must newly recognize and act upon the radical "freedom of the individual [as] had existed from the moment of Creation" at the hand of God. Hence, women should view life "from the Christian citizenness viewpoint. By drawing on the 'individual powers' that [Christian] women possessed, Swedish society would be imbued with the 'feeling for the holiness, the sense of beauty, the maternal, the caring.'"[55] Bremer once wrote that "I sometimes go whole days with a peaceful joy in my soul over our Savior's communion with women in the Gospel, and hers with him."[56]

52. Hammar, "From Fredrika Bremer to Ellen Key,", pp. 36, 57, 58, 39.
53. Ibid., p. 31.
54. Quoted in ibid, p. 39.
55. Ibid., p. 39.
56. Quoted in ibid., p. 41.

Although Bremer saw Christianity as the fundamental source of the full equality of all women (and all men), she believed that the institutional Lutheran state church, as it had developed in Sweden after the Reformation, had often failed in practice to heed the actual teaching of the Bible. Much as Luther in his own times had offered a similar verdict with respect to the historic actions of the Roman Catholic Church, Bremer now called for a second reformation in the nineteenth century within the Swedish Lutheran church, including especially the establishment of a more equal role for women, as Luther had originally advanced by his emphasis on women's participation in the priesthood of all believers and by his own example in his marriage.

Bremer admittedly had a somewhat ambivalent view of Luther himself, once praising "Luther, the true interpreter of the Bible, the liberator" who had dared to challenge the traditional religious thought and practice of his time.[57] Hammar writes that "the thing she treasured most in Luther was his demand for freedom in interpreting individual Biblical passages."[58] Yet she could also offer a "bitter judgment" of Luther, blaming him for those parts of his theology dealing with the three estates in which women were confined to the "household" estate, leaving men to dominate in other areas of society such as church and government affairs, and to function even within the household as the ruling patriarch.[59]

Bremer recognized that Luther could admittedly be admired for his view that a person – man or woman – might be called by God to ordinary service within the household, thus elevating the religious status of ordinary men and women in their daily lives. As Hammar relates, however, Bremer here again believed that Swedish Lutheran church practice had "circumscribed women's calling by giving priority to the wifely and maternal roles, leaving them with a severely limited range of action which was to the detriment of both women and society."[60] The lines between the family and the rest of society, more-

57. Quoted in ibid., p. 42.
58. Ibid., p. 42.
59. Quoted in ibid, p. 42.
60. Ibid., p. 38.

over, were breaking down in the nineteenth century; the concept of the "household" – where women had traditionally had special responsibilities – thus needed to be greatly expanded. Bremer wrote that in the nineteenth century Swedish society must now open the way for a woman to function as "a good human being in all walks of life, and independent of marriage."[61] Instead of finding their calling exclusively within the domestic household, Swedish women of the future should extend the range of their potential callings far beyond the family setting alone to include many other acts of social improvement across all walks of Swedish life (one might say that the whole Swedish nation was to become the new greatly expanded Lutheran "household" in which women would become main participants).

Hammar explains that it was not only Bremer – such thinking was found among many other leading figures in the Swedish movement for women's rights of the nineteenth century. Indeed, it was not until the early twentieth century that many Swedish advocates for women's equality made their case in secular terms divorced from any explicit Lutheran religious context. Until then, as had been the case for Bremer "the feminist pioneers in Sweden did not confront Lutheranism; instead, they wished to gain emancipation with the help of Luther and liberal theology. For them it was a question of redefining and reinterpreting the [Lutheran] idea of women's vocation so that they achieved influence over public life, and not of throwing Lutheran ideas overboard." They were hostile towards the Lutheran state church of Sweden not because it had followed Luther but because it had failed to follow him consistently enough. It had acted "in direct contradiction of Luther's understanding of each Christian's freedom before the Bible."[62] Thus, contrary to the views of many secular historians and social scientists in the twentieth century, Christianity for early Swedish advocates of equality for women was not a large obstacle to a brand new place for women in society. Rather, it was in fact a

61. Quoted in ibid., p. 38.

62. Ibid., p. 45.

powerful source of support in seeking to advance the goals of the rising women's movement that in the late nineteenth century was working with increasing success to bring gender equality to Sweden.

Pietism, Revivalism and the Role of Women in Finland

Bremer herself considered her approach to religion to be more rational and was skeptical of what she saw as the emotionalism of Swedish pietism and other revivalist movements of the nineteenth century. In Finland, nevertheless, pietism and revivalism played a major role in providing a religious setting for the growing women's movement in the late nineteenth and early twentieth centuries. In 2009, a leading student of the historic role of women in Finnish society, Irma Sulkunen, sought to explain the reasons for the exceptionally early arrival of women's suffrage in Finland in 1906. As she wrote, "the case for the central significance of religious revivals in the chain of events" is a powerful one.[63] As Sulkunen elaborates,

> First, the revivalist influence reached from the grass-roots level to the highest systems of administration and control. Second, as was characteristic of revivalism, religious conversions based on personal experience undermined the local social traditions, which were rooted in patriarchal communality, and in their place created new voluntary forms of association. Third, the revivals presented a challenge to the spiritual hegemony of the [Lutheran state] church. [...] By breaking down the traditional order of society at all levels and emphasizing the responsibility and conviction of the individual as the basis of religious and social activity, the revivals thus played a significant part in creating the social and ideological conditions for the birth of the modern civil society [in Finland with its new, much greater role for women].[64]

63. Sulkunen, "Suffrage, Nation and Political Mobilization," p. 99.

64. Ibid., p. 99.

Sulkunen explains that it was particularly "significant from the point of view of the suffrage question that in Finland it was women who initiated the early religious movements" in the mid nineteenth century, "and in the early stages they played an important role as leaders of them."[65] Women then transferred their experience and confidence gained in the Lutheran revival and free church movements into wider areas of social reform such as the temperance movement, the woman's suffrage movement and organized efforts in society to help the poor and downtrodden. Pirjo Markkola, the editor of the aforementioned book *Gender and Vocation*, also contributed a case study of her own, focusing on the last of these areas in Finland. She examined the late nineteenth-century Finnish "deaconess movement" in which single Lutheran women joined together in societies committed to serving the needs of the less well off (sometimes called "Protestant nuns" because of the similarities to their Roman Catholic counterparts); other forms of private charitable work undertaken by women such as remedial homes for prostitutes, alcoholics and other "fallen women"; and the direct entry of women into the political arena to work to cure the evils of society.

Mirkkola explains that these "three forms of women's participation in social reform movements [...] represented the most significant part of moral reform in nineteenth- and early twentieth-century Finland."[66] They were regarded by the many female participants as ways of fulfilling the Lutheran idea of a calling that emphasized an important role in the eyes of God in taking care of the poor and other needy in society-- of obeying Luther's understanding of the Golden Rule of doing unto others as you would have them do unto you. In their newly modern pursuit of such a Lutheran calling, moreover, as Bremer had advocated in Sweden, women would no longer be confined to actions in their immediate household and neighborhood but now all of society could be their concern.

65. Ibid., p. 99.

66. Markkola, "The Calling of Women," p. 138.

The Finnish Women's Association, formed in 1884 as the first women's rights society in Finland, argued that it was necessary to study "which rules were ordered by God and which rules were only said to be God-given" by frail human beings falsely claiming to be able to speak for God – an old charge once directed by Luther at the Catholic Church but now directed at old-fashioned Lutheran traditionalists in Finland who opposed the new women's activities. Following Luther's example in this new nineteenth-century setting, the Finnish movement for women newly sought to lay "the foundation of women's rights on a [valid] Christian basis." As Markkola writes, they argued, for example, that "the same Paul, who told women to keep silence in the meetings or wives to be obedient to their husbands had also promoted gender equality: '... there is neither slave nor free man, there is neither male nor female; for you are all one in Christ Jesus'" – as one of the local Finnish leaders of the Women's Association in 1905 quoted Paul (in Galatians).[67]

Another organization in which nineteenth -century Finnish women worked actively in the political arena to address the moral failings of society was the Women's Christian Temperance Union (WCTU). Indeed, the temperance movement was the largest social reform movement in Finland of the late nineteenth century; its membership included large numbers of men as well but about half of its members were women, who often occupied leadership positions. Markkola writes that the WCTU was "an association based on Christian values. As clearly, many of the leading members supported feminist ideas of women's rights which according to their understanding had a solid foundation in the Christian social order. Women's suffrage was an important issue for the movement," along with controlling and reducing alcohol consumption. Issues such as temperance and suffrage necessarily brought many Finnish women into the political arena as they sought to advance their Lutheran callings. Women's advocates in both cases now argued that "Christian women were needed in politics and women who had a Christian worldview should vote for candidates

67. Ibid., p. 132.

who promoted the right issues and shared the correct values" – the ability to use the political process to make corrective social reforms being another strong reason why women's suffrage was so important to them.[68]

In this way, although Finnish women's political involvement sought broadly to "promote [the] common good; it also protected religion, abolished the curse of alcohol, promoted nationalism, uplifted [the] poor and suffering and made it possible for women to have more power in other areas of society." Markkola observes that the various Finnish social reform movements with women playing leading roles "built their arguments around older Christian tradition which, in the name of God, could give women an opportunity to promote [the] good cause" in many areas of society.[69] This was a greater element of the Lutheran calling, as compared with the Calvinist calling which reflected a more individualist ethic.

The leading Norwegian historian of Swedish and Norwegian social democracy Francis Sejersted further explains in this regard that, as one concrete realization of the newly liberated Nordic citizenry, a "series of women's associations were formed toward the end of the nineteenth century, partly to perform social work and partly to struggle for women's rights and women's suffrage." Drawing on Reformation teachings and examples, "the concept of [individual] rights revealed itself to be an important and explosive force in the long run" for the Nordic countries (as elsewhere). These rights must now be extended to women as well as men. As it would now be reinterpreted in the late nineteenth century and then the twentieth century, Sejersted explains, "the individual, whether man or woman, has the [full] right to participate in the life of the nation." It was significantly due to this legacy, beginning as far back as Luther and the Reformation, that Nordic "women, through their associations and through their topical actions" were carried over into the public sphere in Sweden and Norway, enabling them to win for themselves there a more prominent place in society in the twentieth century than in almost any other nation.[70]

68. Ibid., pp. 136, 137.
69. Ibid., p. 137.
70. Sejersted, *The Age of Social Democracy*, p. 88.

Conclusion

In our own time, it is easy to forget that the core values and beliefs of western civilization are originally Jewish and Greek, as then reinterpreted and transmitted by Christianity over the past two thousand years. More recently, despite the outward appearance of a decline in Christian influence, it is more accurate to say that in the modern age Christianity changed its outward appearance.[70] Indeed, in retrospect the modern age in western civilization might now be described as new era of Christianity, in which its most vital forms in society typically presented its beliefs without explicit reference to (or often even awareness of) the traditional Christian origins and messages. The British sociologist David Martin – the closest we have to a Max Weber of our times – regards ideologies such as Marxism as modern forms of "secular messianism." He writes that, while many of his contemporary sociologist and other social science colleagues once regarded modernization as "a transition *from* the religious *to* the [secular and rational] political, I regarded their politics as so much secularized religion."[71] Indeed, for Martin the typical secularist denial of a significant continuing role in society for religion is best understood as itself a key tenet of secular religious belief – an actual form of religion particularly characteristic of the modern age.[72]

From the original Jewish side came the belief that all people are created equal in the eyes of God, a radical concept for its time and one that even in our own day remains so in many nations around the world. This belief offers a fundamental challenge to all efforts to create permanent nobilities, ruling classes, castes, slaves and other social distinctions that see some people as inherently superior and other people as inherently inferior. In the United States, this principle was seen as so fundamental that the nation fought a terrible civil war in the 1860s – resulting in more than 800,000 deaths – to resolve the issue of slavery.[73] The American movement for women's suffrage and

70. Nelson, "The Secularization Myth Revisited."

71. Martin, *Religion and Power*, pp. 16, 17.

72. See also Smith, *The Sacred Project of American Sociology*.

73. Sinha, *The Slave's Cause*.

other rights emerged out of the movement to abolish slavery, as married and other women took up the fight against their historic status as legally the property of their husbands. The American civil rights movement in the 1960s was led by a Baptist minister, Martin Luther King, Jr., who drew heavily on his Christian background.

The fact that genuine equality often offers a basic challenge to the ruling authorities of a nation is of course one reason why the maintenance of full equality will always be a difficult task. Over the past 2000 years of western civilization, some societies have had greater equality, and others less, but in the Judeo-Christian tradition the ideal of full equality has never been lost. Although it has been difficult to realize in practice in this world, in the Christian heaven we will all truly be equal, including men and women (or whatever form their heavenly presence takes) alike. On earth some compromises will apparently be necessary, but in the Nordic countries with their Lutheran foundations these compromises have been less than almost anywhere else.

CHAPTER 8

A "Second Reformation"

The immense volume of Luther's writings, their great diversity of subject areas and perspectives and Luther's tendency to say contradictory things all meant that later Lutherans found it necessary to agree on an official Lutheran canon, including the Augsburg Confession and other writings included in the 1580 *Book of Concord*, establishing an authoritative Lutheran "bible" that prevailed in the Nordic world throughout the seventeenth and much of the eighteenth century. Indeed, this material was often read by the Lutheran faithful more than the actual Christian Bible. Nordic allegiance to this orthodoxy was defended by the Lutheran state churches of that period with the power of the state.

In Germany, however, critics of the rigidities of the Lutheran orthodoxy appeared towards the end of the seventeenth century, notably in the Pietist movement led by Philipp Jakob Spener. Pietists accused the Lutheran church of ironically having lapsed into a new Protestant scholasticism of its own, its practice of religion having become formulaic, and its theologians generating a large volume of writings but showing little real life. As British historian Christopher Clark writes, Spener argued that the Lutheran "orthodox ecclesiastical establishment [...] had become so absorbed in the defense of doctrinal correctness that it was neglecting the pastoral needs of ordinary Christians. The religious life of the Lutheran parish had become desiccated and stale." Hoping to revive Luther's original example, Spener called instead for a new "spiritual intensity" that would "transform nominal believers into reborn Christians with a powerful sense of God's agency in their lives."[1]

1. Clark, *Iron Kingdom*, p. 124.

Although it had some Nordic impact in the eighteenth century, Pietism was slower in reaching the Nordic countries and did not really become a significant force until the nineteenth century. After Russia had annexed Finland in 1809, and Norway had been taken from Denmark and given to Sweden in 1814, the end of the Napoleonic age began a century in which warfare was less central to the histories of the Nordic countries and developments in religion would become larger driving influences. In part this was due once again to events internal to religion itself, as had been the case for the Protestant Reformation of the sixteenth century. The nineteenth century in the Nordic world would witness what might be described as a "second Reformation," now directed at reforming Lutheranism and its state churches.[2] As with the First Reformation, the Second Reformation would have far-reaching consequences – not as much for the Roman Catholic world in this case, but for the Nordic Lutheran world itself. And as was the case with the First Reformation, some of the most important consequences were altogether unforeseen. The First Reformation set the stage for the rise of the modern world in Europe in the seventeenth century and onward.[3] The Second Reformation in the Lutheran North set the stage for the twentieth-century rise of a new world of social democracy. As the distinguished American student of law and religion John Witte writes, "the rise of the modern welfare state over the past [twentieth] century is in no small measure a new institutional expression of the Lutheran ideal of the magistrate as the father of the family called to care for all his political children."[4]

Besides the increasingly rigid character of the Lutheran church itself after the death of Luther, a further important driving factor in bringing about the Second Reformation was that developments in science and the spread of Enlightenment ideas posed new challenges to traditional religious beliefs across Europe, including the Lutheran North. The French and American Revolutions introduced further radical ideas and additional pressures for religious rethinking. The

2. Hope, *German and Scandinavian Protestantism, 1700 to 1918.*

3. Gregory, *The Unintended Reformation.*

4. Witte, "From Gospel to Law," p. 69.

religious meaning and significance of the industrial revolution and its transforming economic and other social consequences also needed to be addressed The American economic historian Deirdre McCloskey estimates that the average income per day of a person living in Norway was only $3 in 1800 but had grown to $137 by 2000 – and other European nations had similarly extraordinary increases if not quite of this magnitude.[5] In the nineteenth century and continuing into the twentieth century, the Nordic countries thus began to experience an unprecedented pace of change in many areas, which had large consequences for religion as well.

Norwegian historian Oystein Sorensen and University of Helsinki historian Bo Strath thus write of the impact of the Second Reformation on the Nordic world:

> Religion was nationalized [...] in the 16th century when Lutheran state churches were established. Lutheran orthodoxy and state orientation provoked [the reaction of 19th-century] pietism and revivalism [in the Nordic world]. For a long time revivalism has been interpreted as a popular reaction to the Enlightenment and modernization. [...] [However,] revivalism can also be seen as a movement that broke the unity of pre-modern agrarian society, created new social forms, and stood for modernity. Pietism and revivalism meant individualization and de-hierarchization of religion with a long-term secularizing impact when religion moved from the public arena to the private room and from confessional and religious unity guaranteed by the state to personal conviction. The world-view was religious but the emphasis on individual emotions and experiences represented modernity. The long-term impact of the criticism within and outside of Lutheran churches meant the abandoning of religious hierarchies and the [re]emergence of the doctrine of the priesthood of all believers.[6]

5. McCloskey, *Bourgeois Dignity*, p. 5. See also McCloskey, "The Great Enrichment."

6. Sorensen and Strath, "Introduction," p. 10.

In the nineteenth century in the Nordic countries, as they explain further, there were "countless religious doctrines and movements [that] emerged within established and pietistic forms of [Lutheran] Protestantism." Harking back to the First Reformation and its attack on Catholic medieval thinking and institutions, one of the major nineteenth-century consequences "of this religious awakening was a gradual abolition of the distinction between the sacred and the profane." New religious forces helped to spur the temperance, suffrage, trade union and other social movements that dealt with the affairs of the world. These movements now again sought fundamental changes in Nordic social and economic affairs. Sorensen and Strath thus consider that such "popular movements are difficult to imagine without their revivalist element. They represented much more than the labour movements and the rising working class." Indeed, in the countries of the Nordic world "the labour movements took form and content" in the second half of the nineteenth century "from this religious ambience and were lastingly influenced" by it – contrary to a common assumption among twentieth-century historians and social scientists.[7]

Radical change was thus not limited to the equality of women, as examined in the previous chapter, but extended over wide areas of Nordic society. As Sorensen and Strath put it, "the Nordic welfare state should be seen in a long historical perspective of homogeneous state Lutheranism." Indeed, like Witte, they consider that it is "not particularly difficult to imagine the Nordic social democrats as a secularized Lutheran movement" that arose in significant part out of the Second Reformation of the nineteenth century. This is in considerable contrast to Germany, where in the nineteenth century "the Lutheran churches [...] fulfilled little of the potential inherent in Luther's thought" that might have posed a strong grassroots challenge to existing authority, reflecting the fact that "pietism and popular protest eroded the compact between throne and altar much more in the North" than in Germany.[8] In the twentieth century, nationalist

7. Ibid., p. 11.

8. Ibid., pp. 13, 11, 12.

branches of German socialism would deviate disastrously in totalitarian directions that social democracy in the Nordic countries managed to avoid. The Norwegian historian of religion Dag Thorkildsen remarks that the evidence becomes ever more compelling that the Nordic historic understanding and practice of "Lutheranism has been one of several important factors that have contributed to building" of the "modern Nordic social democratic welfare states," as characterized in the twentieth century by social equality, political freedom and economic prosperity.[9]

Finnish Free Churches

At the beginning of the nineteenth century the Lutheran state church had enjoyed a religious monopoly in Finland for at least two centuries. Its dominant position slowly began to erode thereafter, however.[10] Although in Finland most challenges remained officially within the Lutheran state church, some "free churches" outside the state church also began to appear. But they did not gain a legally authorized status until the second half of the nineteenth century, thus holding back their full emergence. By the late nineteenth century, missionaries from non-Lutheran religions were coming to Finland, where they enjoyed a growing following. The Swedish Missionary organization, for example, sent Constantin Boije to Helsinki in 1879, who shortly thereafter invited English revivalists to assist him in his efforts, including Lord Radstock. Such free church forms of revivalism spread especially among the upper classes and academics. A wealthy landlord, Edward Björkenheim, became an enthusiastic preacher who gained growing numbers of followers in Finland during the 1880s.

Other new kinds of Protestant churches came to Finland as well. The Baptists were early arrivals, beginning with revival meetings in Åland in 1856. The first Baptist congregation was established in Luvia,

9. Thorkildsen, "Religious Identity and Nordic Identity," p. 159.

10. Professor Esa Mangeloja of the University of Jyvaskyla provided assistance with this section.

close to Pori, in 1871. The first Methodist congregation was established in Vaasa in 1881. Although most revivalist preachers originally spoke only English or Swedish, a Finnish-speaking Free Church had been established by 1885 and there was a Finnish-speaking Methodist congregation in Pori in 1887. The Pentecostal movement came to Finland during the 1910s after visits by Methodist preacher Thomas Ball Barratt from Norway.

The religiously-inspired Finnish temperance movement was more than just a crusade against alcohol. In the late nineteenth century it was embedded in a larger project to greatly improve the quality of life of the working classes and the poor – as Pekka Sulkunen and Katarina Warpenius explain, "abstinence from drink was embedded in a Utopian vision of authentic living and independent emotional life in the individual family."[11] In Finland, the temperance and labor movements were initially joint participants in advancing a wider social reform agenda. Although this alliance would fairly soon break down in the twentieth century as socialism attacked traditional religion, the joint efforts of the temperance and labor movements brought together new allies – including large numbers of women from the temperance side – and would play a key role in Finnish politics into the first decade of the twentieth century, including the adoption of women's suffrage in Finland in 1906.

Irma Sulkunen thus concludes that in the nineteenth century in Finland "the revivalist movements are important in view of later developments because they considerably eroded the traditional social order, providing the mental and social conditions for the emergence of modern civic society." With their powerful individualism and emphasis on private faith, the new "religious solutions started to break the ideological hegemony closely associated with the [Lutheran] state church system" of old. As examined in the previous chapter, the fact that "women were active participants, even spear-

11. Sulkunen and Warpenius, "Reforming the Self and the Other," p. 423.

heading social change in the form of religious revivalism" would be an important factor in the later large-scale changes in the role of women in Finnish society in the twentieth century.[12]

After Finland's independence in 1917 and the Freedom of Religion Act in 1923, the free churches in Finland would split into Finnish- and Swedish-speaking groups, gathered together into the Swedish-speaking Fria Missionsförbundet and into the Finnish-speaking Suomen Vapaakirkko (Evangelical Free Church of Finland). While the numbers of free churches belonging to these organizations remained small, their influence as forerunners and strengtheners of individualistic life norms in Finland has been significant. They brought new cultural influences and ideas from outside Finland, as free churches have often been connected to the emerging revival movements in the United Kingdom and the United States. Because of these connections, the Finnish – as well as the entire Nordic – world of religion is more diverse and encompassing than would have been the case under a continuing exclusive presence of a Lutheran state church. Although the Lutheran state churches were not especially hospitable to these emerging competitors, no real religious violence was ever directed against them.

Revivalism in Sweden

Such trends were not confined to Finland. As Deane Lagerquest writes, during the peak years of emigration to the United States from 1870 to 1914 all of "Scandinavia was awash in [...] waves of pietism. [...] Many immigrant's trunks contained a copy" of the inspirational Pietist book *True Christianity* "as well as a prayer book, a catechism, and a Bible. Though each wave [of immigration] had distinctive characteristics, most shared the concern for right feeling and right action." Some forms of Scandinavian Pietism took on a "particularly austere

12. Sulkunen, "Suffrage, Gender and Citizenship in Finland," p. 41.

tone," as in the messages of the Norwegian Hans Neilsen Hauge, who "traveled the length of the country preaching the need for a profound conviction of one's sin, a concomitant sense of God's grace, and a reformed life free from such sins as dancing, card playing, and drinking."[13]

Emigration from Sweden was particularly large, including 1.4 million people who went to the United States between 1851 and 1930 out of a Swedish population that in 1900 was only about 5 million. The decade of the 1880s also "marked a breakthrough in the intellectual life of Sweden: the cultural and religious orthodoxy under Lutheran state-church auspices was challenged by a heterogeneous European-influenced counter culture which included natural scientists, artists and social philosophers."[14] It worked to undermine the traditional state church system with its "strong ties between the state and the church: [in which] the state's interests became also the church's interests, and the Swedish Church became to some extent a state bureaucracy, taking on important secular functions alongside religious ones."[15] Rather than the Lutheran church as the intermediary between the state and the citizenry, the Swedish secular state from the second half of the nineteenth century increasingly moved to provide for the welfare of the population by its own direct means.

Long an economic laggard in Europe, the processes of industrialization took off in Sweden in the last decades of the nineteenth century. The sociologist Ingela Naumann explains that in the nineteenth century in Sweden such "great transformations and the concomitant social problems they created triggered the mobilization of a series of social movements, the so-called popular movements: the temperance movement, religious freethinkers, feminists, consumer cooperatives, and the workers' movement," all of which existed apart from and thus posed new challenges for the traditional Lutheran state church of Sweden. In its basic disagreements with the religious status quo, as

13. Lagerquest, *The Lutherans*, p. 15.
14. Olsson, *Social Policy and Welfare State in Sweden* (1993), quoted in Anderson, "The Church as Nation?," p. 229.
15. Naumann, "Consensus, Conflict, or Compromise?," pp. 41–42.

she notes, "Pietism [re]emphasized the Protestant concept of a 'priesthood of all believers' and in its radical form maintained that 'there was no authority except from God,' thus questioning the established Lutheran social order." Naumann concludes that in the nineteenth century "religious revivalism became an influential social movement in Swedish society [...] and played an important role in transforming a premodern agrarian society into a modern one." In the early twentieth century, Swedish revivalists were around 10 percent of the population, not much different from the number of participants in the labor movement. In 1910, fully 22 percent of the members of the Swedish parliament belonged to a free church outside the Lutheran state church.[16]

In the face of such rapid change, the Lutheran state church in Sweden eventually sought to slow the pace, having come to perceive its own longstanding central role in Swedish society as endangered. For those who supported the modernizing trends, however, they found religious allies in the free churches outside the Lutheran state church. The free churches were closely associated in particular with the rise of the classical liberal political movement and the liberal party in Sweden. Although the liberals had different ideas about the appropriate role for private markets and other institutional arrangements in society, they would ally themselves with social democrats in working to modernize Sweden, both seeking to sweep aside the more conservative forces within the Swedish state church and thus helping to open the way to the welfare state of the twentieth century. Karen Anderson explains that "most scholars of Swedish welfare state development cite 1884 as the decisive year for the emergence of genuine debate about social policy." A liberal member of the Lower House, S.A. Hedin, who had "ties to free churches and the temperance movement" was the central figure.[17]

16. Ibid., pp. 46, 47, 42.

17. Anderson, "The Church as Nation?"

Grundtvig and the Second Reformation in Denmark

Probably the most charismatic and influential figure in the Second Reformation among any of the Nordic countries was Nikolai F.S. Grundtvig. He has been described as "the Moses of the Danish nation."[18] Danish historian Uffe Ostergard writes that he is "the single person most responsible for the national culture and political thinking that came to characterize the Denmark of the late nineteenth and twentieth centuries."[19] Denmark began the nineteenth century as a major European power with an empire that included Norway, the German duchies of Schleswig and Holstein, Greenland, Iceland and other smaller possessions. On the losing side of the Napoleonic wars, it lost Norway to Sweden in 1814. In an 1864 war, it lost Schleswig and Holstein to Germany. Iceland remained part of Denmark until 1918, but the current boundaries of Denmark were essentially set by the last decades of the nineteenth century. Rather than a major power covering areas of substantial linguistic diversity, Denmark was now a small European state where a newly homogeneous population all spoke Danish as their native tongue. It fell in significant part to Grundtvig to lay out the terms of a new Danish national identity to fit its much changed circumstances.

As with the Second Reformation in other parts of the Nordic world, Grundtvig sought not to reject Lutheran religion but to reform it. As Ostergard observes, his fundamental objective, beginning in the 1820s, was "to formulate a program for the revival of the stagnant official religion" of the Danish Lutheran state church. When this put him at odds with the authorities, he was banned from public life for many years but was allowed to return in the late 1830s. By then he had "produced a massive number of sermons, psalms, and songs" that would now become newly available to the Danish public and with other writings would constitute "a literary legacy that, until a generation ago, was the core of the socialization of most Danes."[20] It reflected "an

18. Hall and Korsgaard, "Introduction," p. 4.

19. Ostergard, "The Nation as Event," p. 110.

20. Ibid., p. 127.

all-embracing view of nature, language and history based on a fundamentalist Christian interpretation of world history" that nevertheless had immense appeal in Denmark as a more modern religious substitute for the Lutheran orthodoxies of old. In its transformation of the traditional Lutheran past, it bore striking resemblances to the writings at that time of Ralph Waldo Emerson, one of the most important figures of American intellectual history in the nineteenth century. Both Grundtvig and Emerson, as Troels Norager writes, were engaged in a mission of "religious reform as a way of translating traditional religion into different [Danish and American] forms of 'civil religion.'"[21]

Grundtvig was significantly responsible for the nineteenth-century elevation of "the people" as the ultimate source of authority in Denmark, in effect taking the place of the Lutheran God of old – one might say that "the people" became the new God of the Danes. Grundtvig himself was ambivalent about democracy – partly because he was skeptical about the wisdom of the common people – but by the end of the nineteenth century democratic political institutions had displaced the absolute, divinely bestowed authority of the Danish king. Grundtvig was not himself a revivalist but he inspired many other Danes who were revivalists and drew upon his teachings and worked to translate them, according to their own thinking, into newly democratic political and economic institutions.

Translating old Norse, Danish and other Nordic documents and newly dramatizing central events of Danish and Nordic history, as Ostergard comments, Grundtvig "took it upon himself to reestablish what he took to be the original 'Nordic' mind or 'spirit'" that would be a core element of the new national identity of Denmark.[22] The result, as Ostergard considers, constituted "Grundtvig's independent interpretation of the Lutheran heritage" of Denmark. It established the basis for a new powerful nationalism that was another main change in Danish identity in the nineteenth century. In contrast to the efforts of the "somewhat gloomy, German Pietism" that also sought to

21. Norager, "Crisis of Religion and Nineteenth-Century Spiritual Reform," p. 285.

22. Ostergard, "The Nation as Event," p. 116.

reform Danish Lutheran orthodoxy, Grundtvig offered a more "optimistic tone" that appealed in the second half of the nineteenth century to a spreading belief that human "progress" was rapidly transforming the human condition for the better. [23] God seemingly had assigned a larger role to actions by human beings themselves in the reaching of a new heaven on earth. As with the social gospel movement in the United States, there were strong secularizing elements present in all this – a Christian God was not necessarily essential to the whole human-directed enterprise – that would later become more evident. Indeed, in the twentieth century, as examined in previous chapters, the new national religion of Denmark would become a Grundtvigian "secular Lutheranism" that took the form of Danish social democracy.

For international audiences, his Danish contemporary Soren Kierkegaard would eclipse Grundtvig in fame and influence in the twentieth century. Matias Mol Dalsgaard finds that this greater worldwide regard for Kierkegaard reflects the limits of Grundtvig's role as the creator of a specifically Danish identity, while Kierkegaard had "no interest" in national identities and addressed questions of universal religious concern. Yet Dalsgaard considers that both must be understood as products of the Danish Lutheran heritage. Following after Luther, they "both vehemently criticize notions of Christianity that reduce faith to a quiet thing. Both attack the Christianity of safety – that is, versions of Christianity in which the living and passionate nature of faith comes under the yoke of a rationalized or institutionalized notion of grace or justification" – in this respect they both are in fact "good Lutherans." Indeed, as Dalsgaard comments, "Grundtvig and Kierkegaard have in common what I label 'Danish Protestantism.' Dogmatically, both Grundtvig and Kierkegaard operate within the framework of Lutheran theology," although they both emphasize elements "within this framework, in style and thought, [... of] individual and spiritual freedom"[24] Grundtvig's reform of Lutheranism

23. Ibid., p. 129.

24. Dalsgaard, "Community and Individuality," pp. 306, 302.

would become the normative foundation of the Danish social democratic state of the twentieth century; Kierkegaard's modern version of Lutheran religion would become a central work of twentieth-century philosophy and theology. The fundamentally Lutheran sources in both cases are only coming to be recognized more clearly today, both as products of the Danish Second Reformation.

Lutheran Roots of Nordic Welfare Systems

In their 2001 edited book, *Nordic Welfare States in the European Context*, Kautto et al. ask whether the Nordic welfare states are "distinct" relative to other welfare states in Europe. They conclude that yes, while not in every respect, "the Nordic countries as a group tend to be different from other groups of Western European countries in key dimensions of policy and welfare." While there has been some convergence in Europe among national welfare systems, "a 'Nordic model' in welfare or living conditions seems to persist." The chapters included in the book, reporting on studies of various European welfare states, "reveal systematic similarities among the Nordic countries; they display a lower level of income inequality, and the relative poverty rates among typically vulnerable groups [...] appear to be lower than in other countries." The Nordic countries appear to be different from much of Europe in the extent to which they are "continuing to solve care needs by [directly] providing publicly run care services." In another difference, "when analyzing the degree of patterning of unemployment related benefits and assistance, it was possible to identify a distinct overall configuration of policies in the Nordic countries."[25]

Like most students of European welfare states, Kautto et al. attribute little of the significant differences they identify among European welfare states to the influence of the historically dominant religion of each European nation. Writing in 2009, however, Yale political scientist Sigrun Kahl finds that the character of state welfare systems in

25. Kautto et al., *Nordic Welfare States in the European Context*, pp. 263, 264, 265.

Europe closely reflects whether a nation has a Catholic, Lutheran or Calvinist/Reformed heritage. The religious past still "works its way into politics by shaping a country's political tradition, and religiously rooted ideas become part of the accepted spectrum of plausible policy options." This may be the case, Kahn explains, even when the explicit religious influence is no longer present. Instead it is now commonly "indirect" and thus "the religious factor may remain virtually unnoticed" by the national architects of welfare systems, and the actual major "impact of religion may be hard to detect" – especially when the automatic presumption of most welfare state architects is that their efforts have little to do with religion. But taking a deeper look, Kahl finds that "in the domain of poor relief [social assistance] there exist important institutional similarities and systematic differences between countries that are driven by the institutionalized (and secularized) principles of Catholic, Lutheran and Calvinist social doctrines" of their national histories, including both the First Reformation and the Second Reformation in the Lutheran North.[26]

A Catholic model was common to "medieval charity" across Europe. The First Reformation, however, was "the 'critical juncture' in [changing] how welfare states addressed poverty." The largest tension between Catholics and Protestants was over the principle of "feeding one's poor brothers" as essentially a right of the poor to private support versus public institutions "requiring the paupers to work for their own bread." Catholic welfare systems thus emphasized the unconditional obligations of society to the poor, while Calvinist/Reformed countries were insistent that any able-bodied poor must be willing to work as a requirement for social assistance. The Lutheran countries of Europe occupied a middle ground: "Lutheran countries such as Germany, Denmark and Sweden, have sought to balance feeding the poor with a strong socialized obligation to work." Although such different ways of thinking first emerged more than 400 years ago in the wake of the Reformation, their staying power has been such that

26. Kahl, "Religious Doctrines and Poor Relief," p. 267.

"these institutionalized social doctrines have also affected the organizing principles of modern social assistance and the timing of its introduction" in nineteenth- and twentieth-century Europe.[27]

In Catholic countries, as explained previously, welfare typically took the form of "alms giving." The Catholic rich gave to the poor, who were regarded as more deserving in the eyes of God; as their part of the bargain, the poor who were favored by God were expected to pray for the rich. For Luther, however, this was all rejected as yet another form of salvation by good works, alms giving belonging to the same category as indulgences, by which the rich also sought (if more directly) to purchase a heavenly destination. As Kahl writes, for Luther "all human works were sins, as long as the person performing them was a sinner. [...] Generous donations [to the poor] could not prevent sinners from eternal damnation, and the poor [themselves] were not justified by living in poverty."[28]

In the Lutheran world, as Kahl thus explains, "the concept of work changed in two respects. First, Luther raised the status of work immensely by construing it as an intrinsically positive activity that was pleasing to God." Hence, "the Lutheran approach promoted a culture in which 'daily work had its own value and gave social status' independently of its material rewards." It was expected of all people in society and – while it could not bring about salvation – "the poor peasant's work was worth as much as that of the wealthy artisan." Summing up the Lutheran approach to social assistance, "to be included in society, the poor have to work. Once they do, they have a right to a minimum standard of living; if they cannot work or there is no work, they should still be supported." Lutheran (and Calvinist/Reformed) areas of Europe aggressively stamped out begging; in Catholic areas the approach was very different – indeed, the presence of beggars afforded a greater opportunity for the rich to take an action pleasing to God.[29]

Such different Lutheran and Catholic ways of thinking retained their influence in the centuries after the Reformation. In Lutheran

27. bid., p. 268.
28. Ibid., p. 271.
29. Ibid., pp. 271, 272.

Prussia, municipalities were required in 1808 to establish "communal authorities on a uniform basis" to improve the provision of assistance to the poor. Kahl reports that at the end of the nineteenth century in Germany "the share of the population in Lutheran cities that received public relief was much higher than in the Catholic and mixed denominational cities." In 1892, 6.7 percent of the population of Lutheran Berlin received public assistance and other German Lutheran cities had similar rates. In Catholic Cologne, however, 3.8 percent received such public assistance and in Catholic Munich it was a mere 1.2 percent.[30] In such Catholic areas, care for the poor continued to be seen as properly an act of private charity undertaken with the assistance and guidance of the church, rather than a public responsibility. Such religious differences in European welfare attitudes and systems – now shaped in Nordic Lutheran countries from the Second Reformation onward – persisted into the twentieth century.

A Comparison: A Calvinist "Second Reformation" in America

Among the areas of difference between the Lutheran and the Calvinist ethic, none is greater than the understanding of the relationship between church and state. While the Lutheran ethic tended towards a theocratic blending of the two, Calvinists took a much more positive view of religious leadership throughout every area of society, and they also took an adversarial attitude towards any state that sought to defy the basic demands of Calvinist religion. Carlos Eire thus explains that "Calvinists became formidable agents of change and social, political and economic transformation" on Calvinist terms. Calvinists thus commonly represented a "formidable challenge to those in power."[31] Calvin himself said that "the king who in ruling over his realm does not serve God's glory exercises not kingly rule but brigandage."[32] Indeed, as Eire writes of Calvinist history, "everywhere they estab-

30. Ibid., p. 274.
31. Eire, *Reformations*, p. 701.
32. Quoted in ibid., p. 701.

lished communities, Calvinists would be activists, working as agents of the divine, trying to shape localities and whole nations according to their vision, challenging the authority of anyone who disagreed – no matter how exalted their status – [and thus] spreading their activism as widely as possible."[33] Although the United States always had a much greater pluralism of religion than the Nordic world, the influence of Calvinism in shaping American history was so great that it is appropriate to speak of America as a "Puritan [Calvinist] nation."

As in the Nordic world, American historians and social scientists have typically interpreted the modernization of the United States in secular terms, as due to forces such as economic industrialization and the advance of science and technology. As is also the case in the Nordic world, however, new voices have been appearing since the 1990s that put a greater emphasis on religion. Until his death in 2013, Robert Fogel was an economist at the University of Chicago who undertook pioneering studies in economic history that led to his winning a Nobel Prize in economics in 1993 (shared with another economic historian, Douglass North). In 2000, he authored a new interpretation of the history of the American nation from the eighteenth century to the end of the twentieth century. As he now argued, particularly surprisingly for an economist, the history of the United States had been driven as much – or more – by religion as by economics (the two are of course often interconnected). Indeed, as Fogel argued, there had been four religious "Great Awakenings" (mass revival movements that reached widely across American society) that had each been a decisive factor in shaping American political and economic history.[34]

The first American Great Awakening occurred in the mid eighteenth century, around the same time that new religious currents were first beginning to challenge Lutheran orthodoxy in the Nordic world. In the United States, however, it was a Calvinist orthodoxy that was challenged. As Fogel reports, "until 1790, about 80 percent of Americans (90 percent of the free population) were of British descent and were attached primarily to the dissenting British churches" that were

33. Ibid., p. 701.

34. Fogel, *The Fourth Great Awakening & the Future of Egalitarianism.*

either Calvinist outright or had strong ties to Calvinism. These included Congregationalists (American Puritans), Presbyterians (the Scottish branch of Calvinism), Baptists, Quakers and Methodists. The first American Great Awakening was characterized, as Fogel writes, by "the justification of public, emotional, revival meetings, the emphasis on 'new birth' (conversion) as the central object of the revivals, the emergence of the ethic of benevolence as an aspect of new birth, and the modification of the Calvinist doctrine of predestination, which held that only those designated by God before birth would be saved." Seeking to recover the impetus of the Reformation of the sixteenth century, American revivalists 200 years later again "called on people to trust their own experience and not depend on the authority of church officials"– frequently orthodox American Calvinists who all too often had lost touch with the original Calvinist religion.[35]

As early as the first Great Awakening, "revivalist leaders accused orthodox [Calvinist] leaders of corrupting the church." As in the Nordic world in the nineteenth century, such religious developments proved to have a great influence on American history. Indeed, Fogel argues that the first American Great Awakening "provided much of the popular ideological foundation for the [American] Revolution by questioning the legitimacy of established authority, eroding colonial boundaries and promoting popular discontent." Ironically, as he notes, even in the late eighteenth century the strong Christian forces that were advancing the movement for American independence were partially disguised when the American founding fathers typically justified their actions in the 1770s and 1780s in an Enlightenment rhetoric "of natural rights rather than divine revelation."[36]

Christian religion in the United States even in the late eighteenth century was taking "secularized" forms that maximized its impact at a time of increased questioning of traditional Christian authority, and when appeals to science were becoming a leading source of public legitimacy.[37] This also occurred in Europe with the events of the French Revolution, described by Alexis de Tocqueville in the 1850s as

35. Ibid., p. 20.
36. Ibid., p. 20.
37. Becker, *The Heavenly City of the Eighteenth-century Philosophers*.

having been propelled by beliefs that sought the "whole regeneration of the human race" and thus were of "a species of religion" that in its functioning in many respects had the character "of a religious revolution" – indeed of a new type of Christian religious revolution, now disguised in the secularized Enlightenment language of a French "civil religion."[38]

Fogel dates the second American Great Awakening from 1800 to 1850. Its messages were similar to but further amplified those of the first Great Awakening. Its impact on American public life was if anything even more explosive. As Fogel writes, reviving earlier Puritan aspirations in the seventeenth century that New England should be a beacon for building a new world, Puritan Calvinist "leaders of the Second Great Awakening [...] preached that the American mission was to build God's kingdom on earth. Belief in the imminence of the millennium promoted a zealous quest not only for personal salvation but also social perfection." Although the religious justifications were now Calvinist, rather than Lutheran, the result of American revivalism was similar to the Nordic world: "An array of reform movements sought to make America a fit place for the Second Coming of Christ."[39] Systems of mass public education were introduced partly in order to ensure that every person could read the Bible, resulting in a literacy rate in the American northern states in 1840 of more than 90 percent, then the highest in the world. Fogel finds the roots of the American movement for the abolition of slavery, the movement for women's suffrage and the temperance movement – all to become major forces in American history – in the second Great Awakening, in combination with the first Great Awakening together comprising an American Second Reformation.

The moral crusade against slavery of the second Great Awakening as it was manifested in the nineteenth century lead eventually to the election of President Abraham Lincoln in 1860, precipitating a terri-

38. de Tocqueville, *The Old Regime and the French Revolution*, pp. 12, 13, 11.

39. Fogel, *The Fourth Great Awakening & the Future of Egalitarianism*, p. 21.

ble civil war between the north and the south. As Fogel observes, the abolition of slavery in the United States resulted from the initial efforts of "militant evangelical reformers who were also deeply involved in the temperance and women's rights movements." Indeed, "American abolitionism began as a theological rather than a political movement." Much like activists for women's rights in the Nordic countries, American abolitionists drew on the basic Christian message that all human beings are created equally in the image of God – now including black slaves. Fogel writes that, "convinced that they were divinely inspired, they [the abolitionists] rejected out of hand the proposition that material gain or any other worldly consideration could justify the degree of [evil] domination that slavery gave to one group [of human beings] over another."[40] Though significantly shaped by Calvinist influences, the second Reformation was at least as important for American history in the nineteenth century as the Lutheran reform movement was for Nordic history in the same period. In both cases it was in major part the religious power of a second Reformation that broke down an old order, opening the way for the radical political and economic developments of the late nineteenth and twentieth centuries in the Nordic world and in the United States.

Conclusion

The Nordic social democratic religion of the welfare state succeeded politically with help from multiple sectors of Nordic society. In the nineteenth century, it was the revival movements that brought to the Nordic world the winds of religious individualism, democratic principles of governance and support for a much expanded women's role in society; at the same time, they helped to undermine the authority of the monopolistic Lutheran state churches. Early twentieth-century social democrats who sought the Nordic version of a "socialist

40. Ibid., p. 105.

paradise on earth" carried on these trends but in new forms. The rise of Nordic social democracy – perhaps because it retained so much of historic Lutheranism – owed much to a political alliance of convenience forged by social democrats with the liberal and other Nordic heirs to revivalism.

As secular trends advanced across the Nordic world over the course of the twentieth century, Nordic public awareness of the importance of the nineteenth-century second Reformation for the rise of social democracy dwindled. Indeed, many secular social democrats came to believe that their movement represented a triumph of irreligious modernity over the unhappy history of bias, ignorance, illusion, mass emotion, and other failings of traditional Christianity. They would thus have been surprised to discover that much of their own political and economic agenda, and the cultural norms on which it was based, actually first took shape in the nineteenth century among Christian true believers.

If they could have seen the future, many Nordic nineteenth-century revivalists would have been equally surprised to discover that in their eagerness and fervor for Christian revival they had actually done much to open the doors, not to the expected Kingdom of God on Earth, but to the displacement of traditional Christian religion by a new, secularized religion of Nordic social democracy. It is admittedly not a new story. Martin Luther and John Calvin would have also been surprised – horrified might be a better word – to hear that the first Reformation did so much to open the way to the Enlightenment, modern ideas, the industrial revolution, and eventually a decline of traditional Christian belief across Europe. Both the first Reformation and the second Reformation had their greatest long-term impacts not as the realization of a positive agenda of social and religious reform that they had affirmatively sought to advance themselves, but through indirect and unintended consequences. Most importantly, both the first and second Reformations worked in practice to undermine an old order that otherwise would have posed an obstacle to radical social, political and economic change – the longstanding authority and power of the Roman Catholic Church in the case of the first Reformation, and then the centuries-old Lutheran orthodoxy of the state churches in the Nordic countries in the case of the second Reformation.

CHAPTER 9

From Lutheran God to Economic God

Besides the Second Reformation, another challenge to Lutheran orthodoxy in the Nordic countries came from a very different source: the rise of science in the seventeenth century and its rapidly expanding scope from the Enlightenment onwards. The discoveries of science often seemed to undermine the main beliefs of Christianity. As a result of the geological and paleontological discoveries of the eighteenth and nineteenth centuries, for example, it appeared that the traditional biblical account of "the Creation" must be mythical and that the Book of Genesis therefore must be given a "metaphorical" interpretation. Darwinism was particularly corrosive for many aspects of Christianity, including again the belief that the earth was created around 6,000 years ago much as it exists now. For the growing numbers of people newly feeling such concerns, the goal was not a revivalist aspiration to restore an earlier and truer Christianity but to update Lutheranism (and Christian religion in general) in light of the rapid spread of scientific knowledge and other modern realities. Rather than a "Second Reformation," large numbers of people also eventually abandoned traditional Christianity altogether – even as they unconsciously retained much more of their Christian heritage than they were aware of.

Luther's theology of salvation, moreover, appeared increasingly problematic to eighteenth- and nineteenth-century eyes. If salvation was by faith alone, and the presence of this faith in any given human being was in God's hands alone, as Luther had said, it meant that God predestines some people for salvation and others for damnation, entirely independent of their individual thoughts and actions in this world. This was becoming more and more difficult to accept for many modern minds.[1] If Christianity emphasizes the fundamental distinction between good and evil, how could it be that God would not reward those of his followers who had dedicated their lives to advancing the good in the world?

In a sixteenth-century world that often seemed fundamentally corrupted as a result of the Fall in the Garden and in which all were therefore grave sinners – as was Luther's message – this theology of human impotence in the face of God's total omnipotence might have seemed less objectionable. But in the eighteenth century people were beginning to have hope that there would be increasing human progress in the world, depending significantly on the choices and ethical behavior of the Christian devout and other human beings. Perhaps all that could still be said empirically was that grave sinfulness is a pervasive element of human existence (a difficult argument to criticize then and now). If a newly scientific perspective suggested that this was not due to a Fall in a distant Garden, however, this raised a fundamental question: where did "sin" originate, and why had it seemingly always been such a central presence in human affairs? New answers would become necessary for many modern men and women. The result would be a host of "secular" religions that claimed a scientific authority, even as they offered answers to age-old religious question such as the origins of human sinfulness – and for this and other reasons should still be included as their own special subcategory within the overall category of all "religion."

German sociologist Franz-Xavior Kaufman writes that after the Reformation "the Roman church lost its universality, and the idea of universality moved from church to natural law and human rights. But this did not mean that it lost its Christian character. The idea of universal human rights has ripened in the realm of Christian brotherhood and as a consequence of the belief that all men were created

1. The American psychologist Erik Erickson thus eventually sought to understand Luther, not as a matter of the content of his writings, or the intrinsic merits of his theology, but as the product of psychological forces that shaped him in his early life. Erickson, *Young Man Luther*.

equal by God." Similarly, "the occidental form of constitutional law is deeply influenced by Christian ideas, as well as the prevailing morality even in so-called secularized societies. But this law and morality have by and large become separated from organized religion" in its explicit forms.[2]

The comprehensive study of religion in the modern age, as it would seem, should thus extend well beyond the traditional teachings and institutions of Christianity. The transformation from a more traditional Lutheranism of the nineteenth century to a newly secularized Lutheranism of the twentieth century – as then embodied in Nordic social democracy – offers an important case study of such modern religious developments. As another German sociologist Gottfried Kuenzlen put it in 1997,

> The declining public importance of religion, especially in its institutionalized forms, signifies only one aspect of the modern development [of religion]. If you study the actual process of the genesis and history of the modern age in its different steps and branches, if you search for the basic ideas, world views and actions motivated by them, you can see that the loss of the social importance of the historical religion did not lead to the loss of the questions which were answered by it in a way obligatory for everyone. [...] The actual history of the modern age has also got its own secular history of religion. It is the history of the secular promise of salvation and of the hopes for redemption in this world. Our present situation is not simply the result of a process of secularization, which formed a secular order. The secular society gave up the old confession of faith but not the whole of faith. The genesis and victory [of modern ideas] took place in the spirit of a new faith. For that reason the secular society has got its own history of faith.[3]

2. Kaufmann, "Religion and Modernization in Europe," p. 93.

3. Kuenzlen, "Religion and Modernization in Europe," p. 98.

The External Environment and the Sources of Sin

The cause of evil in the world is one of those central questions of human existence to which Kuenzlen referred, questions for which some kind of answer will always be demanded by thoughtful people. Indeed, from the Enlightenment onward, increasing numbers concluded that the true source of evil in the world lay in the external circumstances in which a person lived. The character of a human being, as it now became characteristic of the modern age to believe, was formed by his or her experiences in life, starting from birth (or even in the womb). For the Enlightenment, therefore, it was bad experiences in bad environments that produced bad people. The most important part of the external environment in which a person lived, moreover, was its material state. Indeed, growing numbers believed it must be dire poverty and other severe material deprivation that caused so many people to behave in such socially and individually reprehensible – "sinful" in traditional Christian terms – ways to others. This would explain why, as Luther, Calvin and others had said, but others saw in an altered modern light, the characteristic state of human existence had always been a pervasive corruption of human nature and presence of sin. Money (or its lack), as this economic "theology" is sometimes expressed, is "the root of all evil."

Carlos Eire reports that in "1500 it is estimated that nearly one quarter of the population [of Christian Europe] lacked enough food to eat or secure shelter, and that vast numbers of urban and agricultural laborers lived on the margins, always on the edge of ruin or starvation. A crippling injury, a debilitating disease, or one dismal harvest was often all it took to turn an entire family into paupers."[4] Such circumstances were then taken for granted with little hope for any radical change for the foreseeable future. For many in 1500, their main hopes were focused on a heavenly destination in a world to come. But this began to change dramatically in the eighteenth century as sci-

4. Eire, *Reformations*, p. 704.

entific knowledge and economic progress accelerated. Indeed, the idea spread that human beings might by their own actions be able to take control over their economic future.

If this were true, and severe economic deprivation such as existed in Europe in 1500 was in fact the source of sin in the world, a radical theological implication followed logically: that human salvation might be in the hands of a new priesthood – the economists of the world – who would replace the Roman Catholic and other traditional priesthoods of history. Economic salvation by the performance of good works would now consist of discovering the laws of economics and putting them to human use to build a far more abundant material world in which all of humanity could eventually expect to live. Karl Marx, for example, prophesied the emergence of a "new man" in a new human condition in which all economic scarcity had been abolished. The traditional Christian God was no longer necessary; creating this new heaven on earth would depend on human thoughts and actions that would be sufficient in and of themselves to abolish all economic deprivation and thus also sin in the world.

The principal responsibility would rest in the political decision-making process, in the modern era increasingly conducted by the nation state. Secular governments would thus become the new state churches of the various forms of "economic religion."[5] As noted above, Karen Anderson wrote in one instance that the Swedish social democratic state might appropriately be seen as a "church as nation."[6] The Swedish god would no longer be a Lutheran God but an economic god – as was the case by the middle of the twentieth century for all five "nation-states as churches" of the Nordic social democratic world. As matters turned out, however, the economic god retained surprisingly many similarities to the Lutheran God. As one might say, the secularized Lutheranism that emerged as the religion of the Nordic countries in the twentieth century placed its faith in a new economically based but still a modern "Lutheran god."

5. I have previously developed such themes in Nelson, *Reaching for Heaven on Earth*; Nelson, *Economics as Religion*; and Nelson, *The New Holy Wars*.

6. Anderson, "The Church as Nation?"

Multiple Denominations of Economic Religion

The specific manner by which rapid economic progress might be best achieved – and with it a secular economic salvation – could be seen in a variety of different ways. Although the workings of economic systems have been studied from the days of the ancient Greeks, the contemporary discipline of economics emerged in the eighteenth century as part of a wider revolution in the economic thought of the Enlightenment. In developing the truths of an "economic theology" of social democracy in the first half of the twentieth century, the Nordic countries were relative latecomers to economic religion. Hence, they could draw from the various available understandings of the correct path of economic salvation that at earlier dates had already gained many followers elsewhere in Europe.[7]

A DIVINE HARMONY – When Adam Smith wrote in 1776 about *The Wealth of Nations*, he meant material wealth. Smith differed from most later prophets of economic progress, however, in that his fundamental goal was not to achieve total material abundance. Smith was a pivotal figure in the transition from traditional Christian religion to secular religion. His strategy was not to abandon the Christian God of old but to dress it in a new Enlightenment vocabulary of "nature." A leading American economist, Jacob Viner, thus wrote that in Smith's *The Theory of Moral Sentiments* there "is an unqualified doctrine of a harmonious order of nature, under divine guidance, which promotes the welfare of man through the operation of his individual propensities." In *The Wealth of Nations*, which came 25 years later, Smith was less forthcoming about this divine presence, but the underlying moral philosophy ("theology" really), as Viner thought, was little altered.[8] Smith himself did not say so explicitly but it has been increasingly understood by recent scholars that for Smith the "invisible hand" is in reality a disguised way of speaking about the hand of God.

7. This section draws on Nelson, *Reaching for Heaven on Earth*, and more recently on Nelson, "The Secular Religions of Economic Progress."

8. Viner quoted in Alvey, "The Secret Natural Theological Foundation of Adam Smith's Work,", p. 335. See also Waterman, "Economics as Theology"; and Oslington, *Adam Smith as Theologian*.

The Wealth of Nations set a pattern that would be widely followed in the modern age, speaking about God without saying so directly and explicitly. Rather, the Christian God – in the Nordic case the Lutheran God in particular– did not disappear from the world but increasingly appeared instead in the new disguise of an economic god. Smith's implicit God, however, was not Lutheran but Calvinist.

In a 2011 edited book of essays on *Adam Smith as Theologian*, the Australian economist and editor Paul Oslington wrote that its purpose is "to understand theological influences on Adam Smith's work and its theological content."[9] Rather than studying the *Wealth of Nations* from the customary economic perspective, a deeper understanding of Smith required contributions from multiple disciplines including economists, philosophers, theologians and intellectual historians. From this wider perspective, as Oslington explained, there has been a growing recognition of the "providential aspects of Smith's work [as] identified by many [recent] scholars." At the core, as he concludes, is "the invisible hand [that is] [...] the special providential hand of God, which works to maintain the stability of the [economic] system."[10] In another essay in the book on "Christian Freedom in Political Economy: The Legacy of John Calvin in the Thought of Adam Smith," Joe Blosser writes that "Calvin and Smith hold that Providence means that God both creates the world and continues to love and govern it." For both of them, "God's hand works indirectly, secretly, and indivisibly through natural causes and human actions," as seen in the workings of the invisible hand in the free market.[11]

The term "natural" recurs throughout Smith's writings as a moral standard to be sought in economic matters and in society in general. Besides the large Calvinist influence, *The Wealth of Nations* was also strongly influenced by natural law theology, which had long been prominent in the history of the Roman Catholic Church. In Smith, it was combined with a Calvinist sense of the human condition as deeply corrupted. Although most human beings were frail and fool-

9. Oslington, "Introduction," p. 1.
10. Oslington, "Divine Action, Providence and Adam Smith's Invisible Hand," p. 70.
11. Blosser, "Christian Freedom in Political Economy," p. 48.

ish beings who pursued their own interests without regard to the benefit of the wider community, God had fortunately arranged things so that society could still thrive in a happy natural harmony as its economic welfare broadly advanced. In Smith's eighteenth-century economic religion, it was not material advancement itself that saved the world, but the divine harmony of the market that reflected the true design for human actions according to the laws of "nature." Smith could thus be seen – and many did see him – as the new Newton of human society, having discovered the scientific laws of its fundamental natural workings, much as Newton had revealed God's natural design for the solar system. With this great advance of knowledge, it would finally be possible to live more successfully according to the natural laws that God had always intended for the world.

Smith was writing for a society in which Christian values and ways of thinking suffused every area of society, but tensions between religion and science were growing. Over the next two hundred years, the success of these Christian values and ways of thinking would increasingly depend on separating them from traditional religion, instead presenting them implicitly in various forms of "Christianized" secular religion. In the Nordic world, however, it was not the legacy of John Calvin but of Martin Luther that was reenacted in newly secular terms. By Luther's own standards this would have been rank heresy, but it was still a Christian, indeed a Lutheran, heresy.

MAXIMIZING HUMAN HAPPINESS – Jeremy Bentham, whose life overlapped significantly with that of Smith, developed a very different version of economic religion that departed importantly from Calvinism. Whereas Smith adapted Christian natural law traditions to a secular outward appearance, Bentham famously described the idea of natural law as "nonsense on stilts." As a utilitarian, his supreme goal was the maximization of happiness for the individual and for society as a whole – something that Calvin would have regarded as impossible due to the fundamental corruption of human beings and their existence. In defining ultimate objectives in such strictly human terms, Bentham took a large step – larger than Smith – towards outright atheism. Following Newton and the rise of the natural sciences, Bentham saw utilitarian economic theories – however farfetched they seem to us today – as achieving a new and genuinely scientific understanding of the earthly sources of human happiness. By putting the new economic and other social sciences to work, rapid progress in society, a large part necessarily in the economic realm, would soon yield much greater overall happiness in the world – and thus Bentham's understanding of heaven on earth.[12] If no longer Calvinist, it was still in essence religious; for Bentham, the perfection of utilitarian economic science would show the path to a new perfection of the human condition.

Bentham was among the most successful advocates of new government policies of the modern age; his utilitarian economics and accompanying moral philosophy provided the grounds for a host of social reforms in nineteenth-century England. If Smith was an advocate of individual market freedoms, Bentham utilitarianism was a precursor to socialism and thus also to social democracy in the Nordic world. Human economic knowledge was to be applied as the foundation for a new science of positive governance that would maximize human happiness (in essence human welfare) in the world. Thus, although they were both British, Smith (from Calvinist Scotland) thus more closely reflected a Calvinist ethic, while Bentham was closer to an Anglican ethic (which has often been described as resembling a Lutheran ethic). Smith wrote about a world in which a calling from God could be found in the pursuit of self-interest in the market; Bentham wrote about a world in which a calling from God would have to be found in scientifically advancing the happiness of fellow human beings and especially of the poor, who needed the most help of all. Minus the scientific source of world understanding, this was a vision prescribed by Luther himself who saw a calling as advancing the Golden Rule for the benefit of the whole community.

12. See Nelson, *Reaching for Heaven on Earth*, pp. 106–114.

THE SCIENTIFIC MANAGEMENT OF PRODUCTION – Important intellectual roots of Nordic social democracy can be also found in France, later transmitted in part via the progressive movement in the United States that was in its heyday from 1890 to 1920. Rather than a way of maximizing happiness, French positivists of the first half of the nineteenth century such as Claude Henri Saint-Simon and Auguste Comte taught that physical and social science would soon achieve a comprehensive scientific understanding of the workings of material production. As such scientific knowledge was perfected, a more perfect economic management of whole societies would increasingly become practically feasible.

There was an element of Smith here, in that the systematic application of science to the production side of society would reduce the frictions and strains that had been due to past human misunderstandings of the true material workings of the economy. A perfect society would have to be an efficiently run society in which no sands were thrown into the gears of industrial production out of sheer scientific ignorance. Compared with Bentham and Smith, there was also a more explicitly religious side to French positivism, which acknowledged its roots in traditional Jewish and Christian religions, as when positivists wrote of their new scientific "temples of Newton."[13] Based on the application of modern science to all social questions, Saint Simon himself prophesied a new earthly kingdom in which scientific socialism would become a new "religious doctrine [that] shall be presented in all the generality of which it is susceptible" and "will regulate alike the action of the temporal and that of the spiritual power." When the truly scientific organization and management of the full social and economic system is realized, for Saint Simon it would mean that "the golden age of mankind is not behind us, [but rather] is in the future perfection of the social order [and that] our children will arrive there one day." As he was dying, Saint-Simon explained that "religion cannot disappear from the face of the earth; it can only undergo transfor-

13. Ibid., pp. 114–122. See Jones, "Religion and the Origins of Socialism."

mation." The positivist faithful would soon announce that in the perfectly organized society to come, "Saint-Simon will be chief of religion, the Pope."[14]

But French positivism was ultimately closer to Bentham than to Smith. For both, there is the idea that human beings can perfect the scientific understanding of society; that this scientific understanding will allow them to assert their mastery of natural and human environments; that government can put the new scientific understanding of society to work for the perfection of the human condition; that the traditional deities of religion are historic fictions; and that the ultimate realities of society are to be found in the material – economic – elements. The new high priests of French positivism would be its economists and engineers, as would also be the case for American progressives at the beginning of the twentieth century, and then the social democrats who provided the intellectual leadership and reached top government positions in the nations of the Nordic world from the 1930s onward.

PROGRESSIVE UTOPIANISM – A fourth vision of economic salvation that emerged in the nineteenth, and then played a large role in the history of the twentieth century – including in the Nordic countries – was that of progressive utopianism. Though idiosyncratic in many ways, Karl Marx was among the first to advance this vision. Living most of his adult years in the second half of the nineteenth century, Marx was witness to the astonishing surge of material productivity that began earlier in the century but really took off in the second half, as physics, chemistry and other natural scientific knowledge would increasingly be applied to give human beings comprehensive technological powers to put the natural world to use for human purposes. This included, most extraordinarily, the physics of electricity discovered in the 1860s by the Scotsman James Clerk Maxwell.

The continuing rapid technical and economic advances meant that by the end of the twentieth century, an ordinary person in a developed

14. Quoted in Talmon, *Political Messianism*, p. 71. See also Manuel and Manuel, *Utopian Thought in the Western World*.

nation of the world lived more than twice as long as in 1870, and had a material standard of living above that of a member of a royal family as recently as the seventeenth century. It was a truly revolutionary development in human history (even as the recognition of this is now dulled by familiarity), chronicled and at least partly inspired by economists. Nowhere on earth did this revolution have greater practical consequences than in the Nordic countries, bringing heat and light to the former cold and darkness of the frozen North over much of the year. It is perhaps partly for this reason that the citizens of the Nordic countries were especially likely to see virtually God-like powers at work in modern scientific and economic progress.

Marxism is a prototypical economic religion but with its own rather idiosyncratic vision of the economic path of human salvation. The decisive feature of the human condition for Marx is the class struggle which arose with the rise of organized agriculture and civilization, thus yielding surplus production and a fierce class competition for the resulting material possessions above those necessary for mere survival. From that point on, members of society were bound to fight fiercely and constantly with one another for control of such material outputs. As a direct consequence of the class struggle, human beings became "alienated" from themselves – the Marxist version of "original sin" as found in Christianity. With the explosion of economic growth coming into view in the second half of the nineteenth century, however, it now appeared that not only dire poverty but all material shortages might fairly soon be abolished, ending the historic material basis for the class struggle, alienation and thus all the many past ills of society.

Among the many forms of economic religion, Marxism was also distinctive in that Marx saw a culmination of class struggle in apocalyptic terms, amounting to a secularization of the biblical Book of Revelation and the ultimate arrival of God's kingdom on earth following terrible wars and destruction as the final stage of history. Astonishingly in retrospect, many hundreds of millions of people around the world believed this outwardly secularized but in its essence only modestly disguised biblical account (among the Nordic countries having its greatest influence in Finland). As a new form of disguised Christianity, Marxism fostered a host of religious revolutions in numerous countries across the world, making it the most powerful religious force of twentieth-century history. Among economic religions, it was Adam Smith and Karl Marx who borrowed most directly from original Christian sources, probably the reason that their historic impacts were greater in the modern age than those of any other economists (or indeed any other economic thinkers – Sigmund Freud, for example, a non-economic competitor for this level of influence).

A leading contemporary American philosopher, Alasdair MacIntyre, thus declares that "Marxism shares in good measure both the content and the functions of Christianity as an interpretation of human existence, and it does so because it is the historical successor of Christianity" (or it seemed so for many until 1991).[15] Making much the same point, a contemporary Israeli historian Igal Halfin concluded in 2000, based on extensive archival research, that the "eschatological" elements of Russian communism, borrowed from Christianity, were decisive influences in determining the very categories of thought that shaped the former Soviet Union's government and economy in its first decade or two after the Bolshevik revolution in 1917. As Halfin reports, "Marxists would doubtless have renounced notions such as good, evil, messiah, and salvation as baseless religious superstitions that had nothing to do with the revolutionary experience. Yet, these concepts, translated into a secular key, continued to animate Communist discourse" in Russia for many years. Most Russian communists were nevertheless altogether blind to the reality of the close "affinity" of Russian communism "with Christian messianism."[16] Yet, as described by Halfin, the parallels are obvious to us today:

15. MacIntyre, *Marxism and Christianity*, p. 6.

16. Ibid., p. 39.

> The Marxist concept of universal History was essentially inspired by the Judeo-Christian bracketing of historical time between the Fall of Adam and the Apocalypse. The Original Expropriation, at the beginning of time, represented a rupture in the timeless primitive Communism, which inaugurated History and set humanity on a course of self-alienation. The universal Revolution, an abrupt and absolute event, was to return humanity to itself in a fiery cataclysm. [...] Imbuing time with a historical teleology that gave meaning to events, Marxist eschatology described [human] history as moral progression from the darkness of class society to the light of Communism.[17]

The secular Marxist apocalyptic version of Christianity played a significant role in the development of Nordic social democratic thinking in the first two decades of the twentieth century. It never succeeded, however, in becoming the basis for Nordic national identities. By the 1920s and 1930s and onward, leading social democrats increasingly came to think in less violent and more peaceful terms than those of class warfare. Heaven on earth would instead be reached gradually and by democratic parliamentary processes guided by the application of social scientific methods. Luther had condemned any attempts by the masses to overthrow existing authority by revolutionary means. In this and other respects, the approaches of Nordic social democrats would draw on the Lutheran heritage of the Nordic nations, a key factor in the growing political success of Nordic social democracy from the 1930s..

Instead of Marx, the leading economic prophet for Nordic social democrats was the Englishman John Maynard Keynes – the most important professional economist of the first half of the twentieth century. Keynes also preached a form of the progressive utopianism characteristic of that period. In 1930 in "Economic Possibilities for

17. Ibid., p. 40.

our Grandchildren," Keynes wrote that continued rapid economic growth would soon "lead us out of the tunnel of economic necessity into daylight." It will all come about, he explains, as a result of "the greatest change that has ever occurred in the material environment for human beings in the aggregate." After this happens, and once relieved of the terrible pressures of severe economic deprivation, we will finally be "able to rid ourselves of many of the pseudo-moral principles which have hag-ridden us" and blighted so many lives since human beings emerged on earth.[18]

Keynes differed from Marx, however, in that his language was much less stridently prophetic and he saw economic progress as occurring incrementally and by means of the manipulation of the market mechanism as guided by democratic politics. Keynes was no great admirer of the workings of the market but he regarded it as temporarily useful – indeed, essential to the rapid economic progress that would be the path of human salvation. Unlike Adam Smith, however, Keynes was not willing to leave the market to its own devices; rather, modern economic science would reveal the laws of market processes that could then be expertly employed to manage the market for human purposes (such as maintaining full employment). Nevertheless, despite these significant differences, Keynes' underlying religious vision was surprisingly similar to that of Marx in its utopian hopes for the fairly near future – showing the pervasive worldwide impact of progressive economic worship from 1850 to 1950.

Nordic Social Democracy as Keynesian Religion

Social democracy in the Nordic world is thus not alone in translating the main tenets of Christian religion – as derived from Lutheranism in its specific case – to the form of a secular religion of economic salvation on earth. Indeed, as indicated above, it was characteristic of the modern age in general to create new forms of outwardly secular

18. Keynes, "Economic Possibilities for Our Grandchildren" (1930), in Keynes, *Essays in Persuasion*, pp. 366–372.

religion that nevertheless drew on Christianity as their main sources of inspiration.[19] Marxism, socialism, capitalism and other modern secular religions all saw economic progress as the salvation of the world, even as they often disagreed radically – and sometimes fought terrible wars over these disagreements – as to the correct means of achieving economic salvation. Owing partly to their geographic isolation and long economic stagnation until the end of the nineteenth century, the Nordic countries' social democracy was among the last to emerge of the leading economic religions of the modern age. It thus drew significantly, as explained above, on its predecessors among earlier European economic religions, and then especially on Keynesian economic religion as it came into full fruition in the 1930s.

In his magisterial history (translated into English in 2011) *The Age of Social Democracy: Norway and Sweden in the Twentieth Century*, Norwegian historian Francis Sejersted examines in close detail the fundamentals of social democratic thought and their development in Norway and Sweden.[20] As he observes, social democracy in the Nordic world was also a "liberation project" for human beings on earth. The processes of liberation were "closely linked to scientific rationality, or the demythologizing of the world," including prominently the discarding of some of the false religious myths of the past. Applying scientific knowledge, social democracy represented a "struggle to build the ideal society," at the center of which would be a national project of "modernization" that would consist at its heart of "technical and economic progress," thus freeing people "from poverty and the oppressiveness of work" and releasing them to live much better and happier lives – all of these being core precepts of the Keynesian gospel as well.[21]

By radically improving the external material environments in which people lived, combined with intensive processes of education, it seemed it would be possible in the Nordic world to "mold individuals to fit the new society." As levels of material abundance rapidly

19. Glover, *Biblical Origins of Modern Secular Culture*.
20. See also Misgeld, Molin, and Amark, eds., *Creating Social Democracy*.
21. Sejersted, *The Age of Social Democracy*, p. 2.

increased, the future citizens of Nordic social democracies would increasingly be "morally mature, healthy, productive, and reproductive." Although the Nordic social democratic state is often thought to put its greatest emphasis on achieving social equality, Sejersted explains that in Sweden "it is striking to see how much the social democrats were preoccupied with production problems at the expense, to a certain degree, of the traditional preoccupation of the Socialists with problems of redistribution."[22] In the United States, the early twentieth-century American progressivism that was so influential in that period has been labelled by historians the "gospel of efficiency."[23] In a similar vein, the implementation of social democracy in Sweden was characterized, as Sejersted writes, by a deep "concern for industrial efficiency," the means by which Swedes would be released from severe material shortages and other historic economic deprivations.[24] Its roots can be traced back to Saint Simon, Comte and other French socialists of the first half of the nineteenth century, but it was now presented in the technical language of twentieth-century professional economics and other social sciences.

Hence, as Sejersted observes, for social democrats the production "engineer became in a special sense the representative of modern society."[25] When technical questions involved the organization of the whole society and economy rather than its specific production processes, however, the Nordic social democrats looked to economists, sociologists, psychologists and other social scientists – the new "social engineers," as one might call them, of Nordic societies. Sejersted thus writes:

> On the [whole] societal level the [industrial production] engineer had to compete with other experts who, by acquiring the ideals of the engineer, had developed aspirations to become the generalists of the planned economy – experts such as economists, doctors and architects. The man who expressed

22. Ibid., pp. 2, 45.
23. Waldo, *The Administrative State*.
24. Sejersted, *The Age of Social Democracy*, p. 45.
25. Ibid., pp. 46, 47.

> this new social political ideology most clearly was the Swedish economist Gunnar Myrdal. He presented his vision of technocracy in an article in 1932. This new ideology was "intellectual and coolly rationalistic," in contrast to the old sociopolitical ideology [of traditional socialism], which, he says, was sentimental. The romance of the new [social democratic] ideology was that of the [social scientific] engineer.[26]

In 1954, the Swedish social minister Gunnar Strang thus declared that "the motive of social policy has shifted [...]. Now, when conditions for new social reforms are to be discussed, it is the problem of production and effectiveness, the question of making the common cake larger, that comes to the fore." This would involve, for example, the nationally "planned economic management of the input factor 'labor.'" With the strong support of social democratic governments, the Swedish economy was characterized by an "unusually high number of international industrial corporations," including internationally flourishing steel and ship building industries (the latter reaching a production peak in the 1960s).[27] Much as Keynes had said, before a society of full equality and other core long-term social ideals could be realized, it would first be necessary to achieve a high level of material prosperity in a nation such as Sweden. In its Nordic version as grounded in a Lutheran ethic, however, the state would have an even larger direct role in advancing economic progress than in the Keynesian strategy of using and guiding private market mechanisms.

Given the central place of economic progress, it should not be surprising that economists such as Myrdal (often collaborating with his wife Alva Myrdal, a sociologist) in Sweden and Ragnar Frisch in Norway were assigned leading expert roles in advising and participating in Nordic governments. In 1969 Frisch was awarded the Nobel Prize in its first year (shared with Jan Tinbergen of the Netherlands), and Myrdal received the Prize soon thereafter, in 1974 (shared with

26. Ibid., p. 47.

27. Ibid., pp. 45, 221, 218.

Friedrich Hayek). Myrdal began his career as a theoretical economist but soon became actively involved in the social democratic cause in Sweden, both as a prolific writer on political and economic subjects and as a direct participant in government. He was a social democratic member of parliament from 1935 to 1938 and then from 1944 to 1947 (when he also served as Minister of Trade and Commerce), as well as the General Secretary of the United Nations Economic Commission for Europe from 1947 to 1957. Bertil Ohlin was another Swedish economist who won the Nobel Prize (in 1977, shared with the Englishman James Meade) and also participated actively in Swedish politics as a leader of the Liberal Party from 1944 to 1967. Another Swedish economist, Dag Hammarskjold, was a leading member of the "Stockholm school" of economics that achieved wide public influence and flourished in Sweden in the 1930s. He became chairman of the Board of Governors of the Bank of Sweden from 1941 to 1948 and then Secretary General of the United Nations from 1953 to 1961 (when he perished in a plane crash in Zambia).[28]

The Swedish establishment of the Nobel Prize in economics in 1968 was symbolic of the great post-World War II hopes invested in economics in the Nordic countries.[29] Sejersted thus comments that "there is scarcely any doubt that it was the social sciences, particularly the economists in the Keynesian tradition, who became the generalists and reform technocrats par excellence in the new Social Democratic society" of Sweden – as was also the case, to a similar extent, for social science experts in the other Nordic countries. As it assumed governing responsibilities from the 1930s onwards in Sweden, "the Social Democratic regime consequently completed the slow transformation from cultural humanism to economics as the society's dominant perspective." In the "golden age" of social democracy from the 1950s to the 1970s, "economic, political, and welfare policies became more important than cultural policies; economic growth, industrialization, and equalization more important than symbolic pro-

28. Hannson, "The Stockholm School and the Development of Dynamic Method," pp. 171–173.

29. Offer and Soderberg, *The Nobel Factor*.

duction and identity politics."[30] Nordic social democrats were to be hard-nosed economic realists, not devotees of secular religious fantasies such as a looming world order based on principles such as "from each according to his ability, to each according to his need."

Much as the prominent American economist Richard Ely had earlier argued in the late nineteenth century, the older garden-variety socialism had been a religious cause that implicitly assumed that good intentions alone could bring heaven to earth. Although he was equally utopian in a very different way, Marx himself had been severely critical of what he characterized as such conventional "utopian socialists" of his own time. The Nordic social democrats from the 1930s onwards now took what they regarded as a genuinely scientific view; the "progress" leading to the perfection of Nordic society would have to be informed by the continuing systematic application over many years of the expertise of economists, other social scientists, production engineers and other professional men of affairs.

Economic Religion and Nordic Social Solidarity

The Danish sociologist Gosta Esping-Anderson writes that the Swedish welfare state was built on the four basic "principles of universalism, egalitarianism, 'decommodification,' and efficiency."[31] As long as economic and technological progress was seen as the true path to such a new heaven on earth, it encouraged a powerful sense of personal commitment in Sweden and elsewhere in the Nordic world to serve the cause of progress. In practice, this often meant a willingness to accept short-term sacrifices in order to achieve longer-term economic gains – a shared national commitment to "pay the price of progress" when it was necessary This was a moral duty of each Swedish citizen that was justified by the transcendent goal of the perfection of the human condition on earth by economic means. In general, a devoutly believed religion can play an important practical role in any

30. Ibid., p. 212.

31. Esping-Anderson, "The Making of a Social Democratic State," p. 36.

political and economic system in working to counter what economists call the "free-rider" effect, the private incentive for self-interested individuals to maximize their own wellbeing, even when this may come at the expense of wider gains for the whole society.

In Sweden, for example, the social solidarity as encouraged by the social democratic version of economic progress made it possible for the government to plan and execute the movement of significant numbers of people from one geographic area to another as part of the overall objective of maximizing the efficiency of the Swedish economy. Many other nations are unlike Sweden in that large numbers of people strongly resist changes that will harm them individually, no matter how great the benefit for society as a whole, and their resistance often succeeds. But in Sweden, as the chief economist of the Swedish Employers Association explained, government is guided by "the moral thing to do – that when [a geographic] area no longer has great economic potential we then arrange a mobility-promoting labor market policy that makes it easier [but still necessary] for people to move away," counting on the willingness of fellow Swedes to accept this, however much they may consider themselves damaged individually by government actions.[32]

Sejersted similarly observes that with government actions blessed by the reigning economic religion in Sweden, it was possible to rearrange the population, to "direct labor power 'ruthlessly.'" In Sweden in the 1960s the government plans and actions "downgraded and to a large extent depopulated the sizeable areas of the Swedish periphery that were no longer economically efficient."[33] Unlike many other countries, in social democratic Sweden the religious values of the modern project of economic transformation held sway over most other values. Sweden still had a state church but its unifying faith was no longer the Lutheranism of old but a social democratic economic religion, the new source of Swedish national identity that nevertheless amounted in key respects to a disguised Lutheranism.

32. K. O. Faxen quoted in Sejersted, *The Age of Social Democracy*, p. 222.

33. Ibid., 222, 223.

Social Democracy, American Style

Historians and other European commentators on the history of the nineteenth and twentieth centuries have often expressed surprise that, unlike in the Nordic countries and many other European nations, Marxism and old-fashioned socialism never gained much traction in the United States. This is true, however, only in the following sense: the United States rejected the European class-based Marxism and socialism of the late nineteenth century and first decades of the twentieth century, a viewpoint that looked to the revolutionary transformation of society by means of class warfare. Such a vision could never have had any real attraction in the United States, given the foundational American belief that democratic processes guided by constitutional rules are the only legitimate means of long-term fundamental political change, a core tenet of the American civil religion dating back to the adoption of the American constitution in the late eighteenth century.

It was also significant that the United States was settled in the second half of the nineteenth century and early twentieth century by many millions of immigrants – including large numbers from the Nordic countries – who had freely chosen to come to find a new home, not to create a revolution against existing authority. Despite common initial hardships, many of these immigrants and their families, moreover, thrived in their newly adopted nation.[34] They and their heirs were not as much antagonistic to the basic political and economic institutions of the United States as often deeply thankful.

In another respect, however, that is perhaps surprising to Europeans and many others, the United States was actually another "socialist" country. It was not, however, the socialism of class conflict but of the scientific management of society based on expert scientific knowledge for human progress – much like the vision of social democracy that triumphed in the Nordic world from the 1930s onwards. In the

34. This included in my case two Finnish grandparents on my mother's side and four Swedish great grandparents on my father's side.

United States such similar views came earlier (perhaps because class warfare was never an option) under the name of "progressivism," as it emerged in "the progressive era," typically dated from 1890 to 1920. In its practical results, it also reflected a more powerful influence of the Calvinist ethic. In Calvinist America, compared with the Lutheran Nordic countries, there was in general a more skeptical view of the proper role of the state that limited the possibilities for a complete progressive triumph. Social democracy in the Nordic countries could step into the shoes of the old Lutheran state churches in the twentieth century, but there was no similar opportunity in the United States.

Owing to the large practical obstacles to the formation of successful new political parties within the constitutional arrangements of the American political system, and despite the growing acceptance of progressive political principles, there would not be any new American progressive party – with the major short-term exception of 1912, when former President Theodore Roosevelt attempted to win back the Presidency by running under the banner of his own newly formed "Progressive Party," competing against the incumbent Republican president William Howard Taft and his Democratic challenger Woodrow Wilson (Wilson, of course, won, owing to the now divided opposition). In the United States, rather than forming a new party for the purpose, progressive ideas were mainly formulated and implemented within the two existing Democratic and Republican parties.

Key American industries were never nationalized outright but a comprehensive "progressive" system of national regulatory control over railroads at first and then other forms of transportation, banking, communications, electric power and other key industries de facto established a near equivalent. Until the American deregulation movement achieved many successes in the late 1970s and early 1980s – the American versions of the outright privatization movements then occurring elsewhere around the world – it was not possible to change an airline, railroad or truck route or the fare for such a route in the United States without the approval of the national government (as was the responsibility of the U.S. Interstate Commerce Commission and the Civil Aeronautics Board). While the ownership of such industries thus remained nominally private, for most practical purposes they had been nationalized in the United States as well. In American progressivism, similar to Nordic social democracy, it was expected that the national government will serve as the leading instrument for the scientific planning and management of American society. To a greater degree, however, such planning was expected to be implemented in the United States through the state manipulation of "the market mechanism."[35]

In the first half of the twentieth century, until the cataclysm of Nazism and World War II, the Nordic countries looked mostly to Germany for leadership in key areas of intellectual and other activity. The direct intellectual and policy links of the Nordic countries with the United States were not strong, although there were some connections. University of Helsinki professor of political history Pauli Kettunen thus writes that a key influence in the development of Nordic social democratic thinking in the interwar period was a commitment to "the objectives of economic and technological rationalization" in many areas of society such as "the development of labour protection." He explains further that "the American ideology of *Safety First*, with its connections to scientific management, had a remarkable influence in Finland, as elsewhere in Europe in the 1920s and 1930s, not only on the safety activities of enterprises, but also on the practice of factory inspection," all this part of a spread within the labor movement of a broader "ideology of [technical] rationalization."[36]

In the United States, a leading American political scientist and student of public administration, Dwight Waldo, would write in 1948 that in the progressive era in the United States "students and reformers of all kinds fell to making human relations and governmental practices scientific. [...] This faith in science and the efficiency of the scientific method thoroughly permeates our literature on public administration" of the first half of the twentieth century.[37] It would

35. Nelson, *Reaching for Heaven on Earth*, Ch. 6.

36. Kettunen, "The Nordic Welfare State in Finland," pp. 230-231.

37. Waldo, *The Administrative State*, p. 21.

similarly permeate the literature of Nordic social democratic governancefrom the 1930s to the 1980s.

A Digression: The American Case of the National Lands

If I may be permitted a digression, having worked as a staff economist in the Office of the Secretary of the U.S. Department of the Interior from 1975 to 1993, as I did, I have spent much of my professional career as an economist studying the American national system for the management of its "public lands."[38] This is an unusual case study of American direct national ownership of a means of production that further illustrates the presence of large traditional socialist elements of thinking even in America's supposedly "capitalist" system. Although not well-known in Europe (and among surprisingly large numbers of Americans in the Eastern parts of the nation as well), the American national ("federal" as Americans say) government today still owns almost 30 percent of the total land area of the United States, most of it in the American West. In that region national ownership overall is almost 50 percent of all land holdings (California today remains 45 percent nationally owned land).[39]

Throughout most of the nineteenth century, the goal of the national government had been to dispose of its immense land holdings to private ownership – and to a lesser extent to state government ownership.[40] That all changed radically from 1890 to 1920 in the American progressive era, however, when American land policy shifted to retaining the large remaining "public lands" in national government ownership so as to be managed according to the goals and principles of scientific management. The U. S. Forest Service, for example, was created in 1905 to manage what is now about 190 million acres of American land (almost 10 percent of the total U.S. land area) for sci-

38. "The Office of Policy Analysis in the Department of the Interior."

39. See Nelson, "The Public Lands."

40. Nelson, *Private Rights and Public Lands*.

entific management purposes; the National Park Service was created in 1916; and the national government began to retain ownership of its large remaining subsurface mineral rights in this period. Unlike other parts of the American economic system, it was uniquely feasible in this case to establish a system of outright national ownership of a key means of production – constituting an American "land socialism," as one might say – because in the West many of the most valuable forests and other rural lands were still in national government ownership in 1890, at the beginning of the progressive era.[41]

The public lands, one might say, were from the progressive era onward a small domain of democratic socialism within the vast expanses of the entire American economic system. In 1905, U.S. Secretary of Agriculture James Wilson – harking back to the French positivists – declared that the "performance of the resources of the [national forest] reserves is therefore indispensable to continued prosperity, and the policy of this department for their protection and use will invariably be guided by this fact." In making management decisions – here harking back to Jeremy Bentham's utilitarianism – in managing the lands "the question will always be decided from the standpoint of the greatest good of the greatest number in the long run," as the national government would now work scientifically to determine how to do this.[42] The national common ownership of forests and other Western "public lands" is today still widely seen as a symbol of American national unity, not of class strife, much as social democrats would seek to advance the "social solidarity" of all "the people" of the Nordic countries.

The American historian of national land policy Samuel Hays emphasizes the critical role played by scientific values in the national land and resource policies of the progressive era and the decades to follow. Much as Nordic social democrats would argue a few decades later, the American "progressive conservation" movement of the early twentieth century was above all:

41. Nelson, "Mythology Instead of Analysis."

42. Quoted in Pinchot, *Breaking New Ground*, p. 261.

> a scientific movement, and its role in history arises from the implications of science and technology in modern society. Conservation leaders sprang from such fields as hydrology, forestry, agrostology, geology, and anthropology. Vigorously active in professional circles in the national capital, these leaders brought the ideals and practices of their crafts into federal resource policy. Loyalty to these professional ideals, not close association with the grass-roots public, set the tone of the Theodore Roosevelt conservation movement. Its essence was rational planning to promote efficient development and use of all natural resources. The idea of efficiency drew these federal scientists from one resources task to another, from specific programs to comprehensive concepts. It molded the policies which they proposed, their administrative techniques, and their relations with Congress and the public. It is from the vantage point of applied science, rather than of democratic protest, that one must understand the historic role of the [progressive] conservation movement.[43]

American and Nordic Economics

Going well beyond the public lands, the American progressive movement provided much of the blueprint for the development of the American welfare and regulatory state over the course of the twentieth century. After World War II, as America became a leading nation on the international stage, such American developments became more important to the whole world. In the post-war years, for example, as Nordic countries looked to the application of economics and other social sciences as foundational elements of social democratic faith, this worked to increase the connections between American progressives and Nordic social democrats. The Swedish economist Bo Sandelin writes that "after the Stockholm [economic] school [of

43. Hays, *Conservation and the Gospel of Efficiency*, p. 2.

the 1930s] there are only stray signs of anything that could be called a Swedish way of economic thinking." Rather, after World War II, "Swedish economists, with a few notable exceptions, have taken the Anglo-American mainstream economics as an ideal, and become a part of it."[44]

The origins and early development of American economics itself lay in the progressive era, including the founding of the American Economic Association in 1885. In those years older American universities such as Harvard, Yale and Princeton were being transformed from their Christian religious origins into the training grounds for the many engineers, economists and other professional experts who would be needed to administer the emerging American administrative state – organized on specialist disciplinary lines such as economics, political science, engineering, business, forestry, etc. that still characterize these universities today. Funded in significant part by John D. Rockefeller, the University of Chicago was newly established in 1890 as a progressive-era university with the goal to advance the basis of scientific knowledge to guide the rapid economic progress of American society (other brand new universities organized for similar secular purposes were Cornell in 1865 and Johns Hopkins in 1876). As can now be seen in retrospect, this was not actually a rejection of any religious foundation for the American university but a change in the form of the religion. Instead of institutions of Christian religion, American universities now became institutions of secular progressive religion – as they remain in essence today.

The large influence of American economics in the Nordic countries was partly due to this early progressive transformation of its university systems at the beginning of the twentieth century.[45] By the end of World War II, the United States had moved into an international leadership position in the economic and other social sciences (also partly because a number of leading European social scientists had moved to the United States in the 1930s and 1940s). After the first

44. Sandelin, "Beyond the Stockholm School," p. 214.

45. Nelson, "The Economics Profession and the Making of Public Policy."

Nobel Prize in economics was awarded in 1969, for example, from then until 2000 economists who were based at, or had worked significant amounts of time at, the University of Chicago won 13 out of the 45 total Nobel Prizes in economics awarded by the Swedish judges in this period. Overall, 9 of the 16 Nobel economics winners from 1969 through 1980 were American, a trend that continued from 1981 to 2000 when 17 out of the total 29 Nobel economics winners were American.

Although there were close similarities between progressivism and Nordic social democracy, it is also true that there are significant differences between the American progressive state and the Nordic social democratic state. This is not because the methods and results of American social science have been significantly different from the results of Nordic social science (they are today parts of the same professional economic community). Rather, it reflects the differences between the Calvinist ethic with its powerful historic influence on the politics and economics of the United States, versus the Lutheran ethic which has done so much to shape Nordic social democracy. The Calvinist ethic inhibited the willingness of Americans to place their full trust in the government to scientifically manage all of American society, whereas such a high level of trust came more easily to the countries of the Nordic world with their history of a Lutheran ethic and Lutheran state churches.

Conclusion

The blind spot of both American progressivism and Nordic social democracy was their neglect of questions of the foundations for moral values in society. Indeed, the social sciences on which both were significantly based often made strong claims that they were "value-free." In the glory years of Nordic social democracy, there was little discussion or seeming interest among leading Nordic social democrats in exploring the underlying value foundations of the Nordic governing systems. Rather, as in the United States, the leading subjects of public discussion in the golden years of Nordic social democracy from the 1940s to the 1980s involved practical questions of how best to implement the scientific management of Nordic society. What technical policies and actions would work to stimulate more rapid economic growth in the Nordic countries? How might any tensions between the pursuit of maximal economic growth and maximal economic equality best be resolved? What government actions would be required to maintain full employment? What was the best system of taxation that would raise the large revenues needed to sustain the Nordic welfare state without creating adverse incentives for work effort? And so on; there were many more like these.

It is not actually the case, however, as was suggested by many Nordic (and American) economists themselves, that such economic discussions involved only technical matters and were thus value-free. Rather, there were always powerful underlying value assumptions at work at the very core of economics and other social sciences. It was just that such foundational values were regarded by social scientists as so obviously correct that American progressives and Nordic social democrats saw little if any reason to justify them – or often even to recognize explicitly their existence. They were like the air in the atmosphere, a background presence that could automatically be taken for granted.

In recent years, however, there has been a developing recognition within the Nordic world (and in the United States) that such long-standing social democratic assumptions of a normative character perhaps cannot be so unquestioningly assumed. Environmentalism would emerge in the 1960s as a secular religion that often frontally challenged the idea of the necessarily redeeming benefits of science, technology and the whole enterprise of human economic progress. In the United States, new forms of Christian fundamentalism, some of them also skeptical of the modern project, attracted millions of new followers. As explored in this book, a new body of Nordic scholarship has increasingly recognized that the values of social democracy were actually in significant part a transformation of the old Lutheran values – now refashioned to a superficially scientific dress. Once this is more widely recognized, the future intellectual boundaries for Nordic public discussion of the Nordic social democratic project will have to be enlarged.

CHAPTER 10

Nordic Paths to Modernity: Four Variations on a Theme

In their Introduction to a 2010 edited book collection on *Religion and the Political Imagination*, Columbia University professor Ira Katznelson and Cambridge University professor Gareth Stedman Jones write that:

> Until quite recently, a rather simple story prevailed. "Secularization" purported to describe a universal transition from a traditional religious picture of the world to a rational conception. Every society was thought to be caught up in this global trajectory, even if each progressed along it at different speeds. In this approach, the division and differentiation of church and state into separate spheres was identified with a progressive separation of politics from religion, an overall shift from a religious to a rational and scientific mentality, and a waning acceptance of religious authority. This perspective has, for some time, lost its capacity to persuade. And yet, something profound did happen. How should it be understood, studied and analysed?[1]

Katznelson and Jones further state that "history has played a joke upon once-vibrant expectations that religion would wane as modern life advanced."[2] Among the past illusions was that the expected processes of secularization would follow a common path across the world. Instead, as matters have turned out, the working out of the tensions between traditional religion and scientific knowledge and

1. Katznelson and Jones, "Introduction: Multiple Secularities," p. 1.

2. Ibid., p. 2.

other modern developments have been different in the United States from Europe, different in the Islamic world from both Europe and the United States, and different in Asia from elsewhere. The processes of modernization (or not) involve a set of case-specific stories. Even within Europe, modernization within France has been very different from that in Italy, and in both these countries has been very different from in the Nordic world. There is, however, enough in common among the Nordic countries that we might speak of a Nordic pattern of modernization that is distinguishable from that of the rest of Europe. But even the five Nordic countries had their significant historical difference as they transitioned first from the nineteenth century to the twentieth century, and now to the twenty-first century.

The Nordic processes of modernization are of special interest because these countries are today widely seen around the world as the leading examples of nations that have been successful in creating modern societies that behave "rationally." It seemingly follows that they must also have been the most successful in putting old-fashioned ideas, religions, customs, governing arrangements, economic institutions and other heritages of a pre-modern past behind them. The modern age began in the Enlightenment and thus the "modern" might be said to begin with the incorporation into the culture, governance and other workings of a nation of Enlightenment thinking and values. In this sense, the processes of modernization moved more rapidly at first in much of the rest of Europe than in the Nordic countries.[3] The creation of the American nation in the late 1700s was itself in significant part an Enlightenment project (although also owing much to Calvinism), well before any similarly powerful Enlightenment influences were being felt in the Nordic world. But once the Nordic world fully embarked on a process of modernization towards the end of the nineteenth century, it moved faster than any other part of the world – at least until the development of the countries of the Asian "tigers" late in the twentieth century.

3. Wittrock, "Modernity: One, None, or Many?"

Modernization could move so fast in the Nordic countries partly because it provoked less resistance than in many other places. The Norwegian historian Francis Sejersted writes that "on some issues the Social Democrats' policy was unambiguous. First, it was modernist, in the sense that they thought and argued from scientific norms of rationality and argumentation." From the 1930s on, "wherever it dealt with the conflict between traditionalists and modernists," the social democratic "movement stood on the side of modernity."[4] Sejersted characterizes Nordic modernism in terms of four main characteristics. One critical element is the development of democratic governance and the defense of individual rights, including the right to select the government leadership by electoral means. Equally important, as discussed in the previous chapter, is the process of "economic development through technological progress," which would free the members of society from severe economic scarcity – here expressing a basic tenet of faith that is a defining feature of all economic religion. Another core tenet of Nordic modernism is that "modernization implies a consolidation of the nation state" that provides the institutional "framework within which to construct the new society." Yet, even as there was a new national focus, there must also be room for diversity: "modernization implies a differentiation process, that is a move from a [traditional] homogeneous society with a common worldview to a society divided into many functionally distinct entities with their own systems of values and customary forms of communication."[5] In the heyday of social democracy in the Nordic world, admittedly, the social solidarity of the nation state – the heir to the Lutheran state church – frequently took precedence over any deep encouragement of local cultural pluralism.

While these general features were common to all the Nordic countries, the exact route of modernization differed among them. As noted in Chapter 2, the 2012 edited book collection, *Nordic Paths to Modernity*, includes a number of illuminating chapters concerning

4. Sejersted, *The Age of Social Democracy*, p. 130.

5. Sejersted, *The Age of Social Democracy*, pp. 2–3.

the historical paths followed by each Nordic nation to reach its own version of modernism within the broader context of the triumph of social democracy after World War II. It was, broadly speaking, a process of eroding Lutheran state church orthodoxies over the course of the nineteenth century under the influence of pietist, revivalist, free church and other new religious currents entering into the life of Nordic societies. As traditional Lutheran church authority waned, the Nordic states took on many of the former social responsibilities of the Lutheran church as they had existed at the beginning of the nineteenth century. Nineteenth-century modernization also meant a transition from eighteenth-century royal absolutism to government in the name of "the people" as put into practice by democratic means.

Modernization in Norway

In *Nordic Paths to Modernity*, Oslo University College professor Rune Slagstad states that "one feature of Norwegian reformism since the early nineteenth century [...] has been its basis in science: it has been a scientific reformism." He traces three stages of the Norwegian scientific modernization project, the first being "the 'civil servants' state [that] was established as part of the revolution of 1814 [transferring Norway from Denmark to become part of Sweden] and its dual transformation of both political and academic institutions." Although advocating radical changes, it was not a science regime as we would understand it today but actually a "legal knowledge regime" in which "the avant-garde of the new state were the lawyers" – including in the 1830s "two young lawyers, Frederick Stang and Anton Martin Schweigaard, who were to become the regime's principle strategists." Both of them regarded "capitalism as also a civilizing force," in addition to its increasingly recognized ability to expand greatly the material wealth of Nordic societies.[6]

6. Slagstad, "The Metamorphoses of Norwegian Reformism," pp. 144, 145, 147.

Such leading advocates of Norwegian modernization in the nineteenth century were representative of (classical) liberal trends that worked to undermine the European heritage of monarchy and entrenched traditional Lutheran religion.[7] Indeed, it was not only the Nordic world – the nineteenth century was the heyday of related forms of liberal thought in many other places around the world, most notably in England. A second key step for Norwegian modernization, as Slagstad relates, challenged "the cultivated bourgeoisie's hegemony," a process that "culminated in 1884 with the change of regime and the defeat of the civil service state elite with the introduction of parliamentary democracy based on the competing political parties." In its thinking, this represented "a compromise between [...] Franco-British rationalism and German idealism." A new related agreement on the directions of "reform reached by the [Norwegian] elite also had a formative effect on the Liberal Party state's nation building." It combined elements of a newly reformist "liberal attitude on planning" with the thinking of emerging "elites of popular culture, the common ground [of the two] being their closeness to political democracy."[8]

This late nineteenth-century "democratic-pedagogical regime," although increasingly challenged by socialist ideas and working class influence, survived into the 1930s and the rise of social democracy in that decade. Slagstad finds the culmination of the third stage in Norwegian modernization "when the Labour Party gained control of the political center in 1945 [...] in coalition with the economists," following the expulsion of the Germans from Norway after five years of wartime occupation. Along lines described in the previous chapter, the new "knowledge regime" of the Labor Party state was "that of the social sciences." In other words, its new creed sought to build a "modern Norway [that] was to be created through the mobilization of positivist science, with the new social science professions as the avante-garde in social democratic policies of reform."[9]

7. See also Kurrild-Klitgaard, "Classical Liberalism and Modern Political Economy in Denmark."

8. Slagstad, "The Metamorphoses of Norwegian Reformism," pp. 147, 148.

9. Ibid., pp. 144, 158.

Although hope for the Marxist path to a "new man" was gone, Norwegian intellectuals remained optimistic that "on the basis of the new social sciences" it would still be possible to create "a new society – and, as the boldest [still] added, a new man," now to be formed by the full triumph of social democracy.[10] By the 1980s, however, this was increasingly appearing to be another utopian ideal. Slagstad suggests that, "following the decline of the social democratic regime" in that decade, signs of yet another stage of modernization – or perhaps even the arrival of a new post-modern era – "have become visible."[11] One such sign was the growing recognition that twentieth-century modernization had not cast religion aside but was better understood as a yet another new stage in the long history of religion. For Norwegian social democratic true believers, this was sometimes a bitter pill to swallow.

Denmark

Danish historian Uffe Ostergard in his contribution to *Nordic Paths to Modernity* finds that the Danish path in its broad contours was similar to that of Norway (not surprising since Norway was part of Denmark for four centuries). Ostergard writes that "the foundations were laid for the great reform process in the various parts of the multinational state [of Denmark] from 1784 to 1814." The reforms were "initiated primarily by representatives of the German speaking aristocratic elite within the composite state" of Denmark, as it then still included the duchies of Schleswig and Holstein that would be lost to Germany in 1864.[12] Unlike any other of the five Nordic countries, Denmark experienced a radical shrinkage of its boundaries, moving from a major European territorial power to a small nation state at the end of the nineteenth century. Uniquely among the Nordic countries, the traumas associated with this sharply declining power status among

10. Ibid., p. 161.
11. Ibid., p. 144.
12. Ostergard, "The Danish Path to Modernity," p. 51.

the states of Europe played a major part in the Danish processes of modernization in the nineteenth century.

Danish philosopher and historian Ove Korsgaard writes that, "looking back on the procession of events since the mid-1800s, the development of Danish identity and society has been propelled by political programs of three different [social] 'classes.'" The first of these, "the National Liberals[,] caused the shift that replaced the monarch with the people as the centre of the symbolic order." The National Liberals consisted of a cultural elite formed among the "bourgeoisie of higher civil servants (priests, lawyers, professors and doctors)." They combined the traditionally favorable attitude of nineteenth-century European liberals toward market freedoms with a more typically Nordic Lutheran view of "the importance of state institutions in matters of national integration." The disastrous war with Germany in 1864, however, brought their period of "cultural and political legitimacy" and political leadership to an end in Denmark.[13]

Korsgaard reports that "in the power vacuum that appeared, [...] popular Grundtvigianism was the only movement with any general appeal." Unlike the National Liberals, "the Grundtvigians regarded civil society, not the state, as the complement of the people." Setting the terms for Danish identity and governance into the twentieth century, the Grundtvigians would eventually be displaced by the social democrats. The key period of their ascendance was the 1920s, when they discarded more traditional class-based social thinking and accepted that "the nation was the basis for the realization of democracy and socialism" in Denmark. The full triumph of such thinking was achieved with the acceptance of the social democratic party platform in 1934 of "'Denmark for the People' (Danmark for Folket)."[14]

After 1864, as Ostergard similarly observes, bitterness over its large wartime losses of territory meant a new Danish "conscious demarcation from Germany and all things German, [out of which] the

13. Korsgaard, "The Danish Way to Establish the Nation in the Hearts of the People," pp. 157, 141, 157.

14. Ibid., p. 157.

modern, popular and democratic Denmark emerged." Denmark turned toward Great Britain to diminish the dominant German role of its past, introducing new intellectual and economic currents. Another important factor in Denmark, as Korsgaard also emphasizes, was the large influence in the mid and late nineteenth century of the "religious and social movements of the Grundtvigians and their opponents in the Pietist 'Inner Mission.'" Their combined effects introduced a new element of religious pluralism and otherwise worked to transform the sterile orthodoxies of the traditional Lutheran state church of Denmark, opening the way for democratic governance and other modern developments. In the early twentieth century Danish social democrats then began to adapt their thinking "to the unique agricultural-industrial conditions of Denmark and developed a strategy very different from the Marxist orthodoxy of the German [social democratic] mother party."[15] As disastrous events later in the twentieth century would demonstrate, the German social democrats should have heeded the example of their Danish neighbors.

Danish events culminated, Ostergard reports, in a new "consensus line [that] was first openly formulated in 1923, and later on adopted in slogans such as 'the people's cooperating rule' and, somewhat less clumsily, 'Denmark for the people.'" As in the other Nordic countries, it was part of a process that took several decades by which the Danish social democratic party "restructured its line from a class-based to a more all-embracing strategy," as it would be advanced by a democratically elected Danish national government of all the people.[16] Once again, a key to all this was a new faith in the objective methods of the social sciences – the means by which, rather than the word of God, the public interest of all Danes collectively could now scientifically and rationally be identified and implemented.

Writing in the *Scandinavian Journal of History*, Niels Christiansen and Klaus Petersen find, however, that it was not until "the end of the 1950s," enabled by the very rapid economic growth of the post-World

15. Ostergard, "The Danish Path to Modernity," pp. 57, 61.

16. Ibid., p. 61.

War II era, that the real "construction of the modern Danish welfare state started." Much as the Norwegian historian Francis Sejersted describes for Sweden and Norway, they write that in Denmark the most "influential agents were the Social Democratic-minded social engineers. For [a] long [time], research into social problems (e.g., unemployment) had been a part of social-policy making. But now the use of experts and scientific analysis was institutionalized in a more radical way." The National Institute of Social Research, established in Denmark in 1958, was responsible for much of this research and in this capacity "became a central agent in the social reforms of the 1960s and 1970s." In the 1960s Denmark looked to its governing body of professional experts to establish a system of "rational administration," a chief goal of social democratic leadership.[17]

As elsewhere in the Nordic world, the prominent role assigned to objective social science worked to promote a strong sense of social solidarity in Denmark. As Christiansen and Petersen explain, "the firm belief in the possibilities of a rational-scientific mind inherited from the 1930s [social democratic] cultural vanguard enabled it to present solutions to social problems as non-political science" – thus standing above the liabilities of typical conventional and conflict-ridden "politics." Many members of this early 1930s Danish vanguard of "social engineers" not only provided technical expertise after World War II but rose to top political and administrative positions in Denmark. They successfully asserted that the scientific management of government programs and activities would separate them from the private interest clashes, ideological crusades, petty squabbles and more other traditional political workings that in the past had worked to undermine public confidence in the Danish government to serve effectively the overall needs of Danish society. As Christiansen and Petersen write, the social democratic faithful now believed "in planning and rational solving of problems [that] made it easier for the political parties to form political compromises, and to legitimize the

17. Christiansen and Petersen, "The Dynamics of Social Solidarity," pp. 182, 187.

compromises as the best solutions" for all of Denmark.[18] The new Danish priesthood of social science established a new firmer "modern" basis of religious legitimacy for the Danish state – this very act by itself capable of improving the functioning of the state.

Sweden

In the nineteenth century in Sweden, as Bernd Henningsen had written in 1997 in *The Cultural Construction of Norden*, "the enlightened, absolute pragmatism of the upper strata of society, and not least the agrarian economic structure and the peripheral location in Europe, favoured an evolutionism which retained those familiar ideological constructs which could be integrated into the [new] national state paradigm" as it was emerging. In general, the nineteenth century was a period of rapid "political, economic, and social changes [that] took place in Scandinavia [and] that demanded a cultural identity that was different from [existing] dynastic power constructions – a newly constituted population of Swedes needed new channels for the transmission of meaning." As part of this modernizing path, moving beyond the stale Lutheran orthodoxy of old, the new "debate on (national) identity now involved multiple cultural elements: history, traditions, language, literature, and religion," all of which drove basic change. Henningsen finds that – much as in Denmark – "by 1864, the new construction was firmly embedded in the collective consciousness of the North."[19] Such modernizing trends in the Nordic world had the largest transformative effects first in Sweden, which for a century saw itself as "fortunate enough to hold the patent on modernity."[20]

Fifteen years later in *Nordic Paths to Modernity*, the Swedish social theorist Bjorn Wittrock further examines "The Making of Sweden" in its modern phase. Wittrock writes that "foreign observers of Sweden in the first half of the twentieth century tended to refer to the prevalence of a work-ethic, of a sense of duty and perseverance and, most

18. Ibid., p. 184.
19. Henningsen, "The Swedish Construction of Nordic Identity," pp. 96, 97.
20. Ostergard, "The Geopolitics of Nordic Identity," p. 62.

notably a personal demeanor characterized by restraint, not to say humility, across different social strata, including leading politicians."[21] Such national traits provided a critical boost to Swedish economic prospects that could not be attributed to specifically modernizing trends alone but reflected deeper cultural roots. The long history of Lutheranism in Sweden was being reworked into new forms to support the arrival of the social democratic welfare state in the twentieth century.

Wittrock observes that, as elsewhere in the Nordic world, the breakthrough of social democracy in Sweden occurred in the 1930s, commencing there a "formative period of the 'Swedish people's home' and 'the Swedish model,' from 1932–33 onwards." This marked the start "of a period of four and a half decades during which there was, except for a brief interlude in the summer of 1936, a Social Democratic prime minister."[22] The full implementation of the Swedish social democratic agenda did not take off until after World War II, however, which commenced a new "era of 'radical rationalism' and technocratic planning ideals" that may have reached its height in the 1960s and 1970s. As noted previously, this led to the first awarding in 1969 of a Nobel Prize in economics, suggesting that economics was the master discipline with a fully scientific standing and consequent ability to produce the technical knowledge to control the economic forces in society for human benefit – similar to the transforming consequences of physics, chemistry and other natural sciences that had made possible human control over the natural world. The new confidence in rational social scientific methods produced in Sweden a wide " belief among decision-makers and administrators that there were no or few problems they could not effectively tackle and solve" with the use of such professional expert tools.[23] It has become increasingly apparent in the last few decades, admittedly, that this Swedish belief itself was more religious than scientific in character – with new immigrant populations in Sweden proving remarkably resistant to

21. Wittrock, "The Making of Sweden," pp. 108, 107.

22. Wittrock, "The Making of Sweden," p. 103.

23. Ibid, p. 106.

conversion, perhaps because in actuality they were being asked to convert to a secularized and thus implicit Lutheranism.

As noted above, throughout the Nordic world, the end of World War II meant a turn to specialized expert knowledge that represented a step away from traditional German and other continental European influences and towards the Anglo-American world. Thus, in Sweden, as Wittrock writes, "the whole movement toward rationalistic planning techniques [...] emerged out of operations analysis and systems analysis in the military sector in the United States in the 1950s, and which were then subsequently exported across the whole range of Western nations under the umbrella of the OECD [Organization for Economic Co-operation and Development]; they carried labels such as programme budgeting, social indicators, and management by objectives," drawing on the social sciences for their expert methods and means of practical implementation. Over the long run, this social democratic turn to rational social science brought about a transformation in Swedish public life from a "traditional judicial orientation" that originated in the nineteenth century towards "both a more political and technocratic one," elevating the social sciences above the less "scientific" disciplines of the law, philosophy and the humanities that had once formed the core of Swedish university learning.[24]

Finland

In "Nordic and Finnish Modernity: A Comparison," another contribution to the *Nordic Paths to Modernity*, University of Helsinki sociologist Risto Alapuro writes in 2012 "how similar were the results in all the Nordic cases, despite a wide variety in the nature of external pressures to which each was subject in the emergence of modern politics." Drawing on the writings of historian Bo Strath, also at the University of Helsinki, Alapuro finds a common pattern in the Nordic countries

24. Ibid., pp. 97–98.

in the period between World War I and World War II in that the "social liberal parties based on middle classes and peasants and/or agrarian parties were able to cooperate with the Social Democrats" who had previously been unable to obtain political control on their own. Thus, "in the North liberalism merged with the state into an ideology of modernity, and later on, petty bourgeoisie and the small farmers, guided by a socially-oriented liberalism, merged with the workers, thereby creating the Nordic model of progressive politics" that led to the successes of social democracy from the 1930s onwards.[25]

In its specific path to modernism, Finland again followed the familiar Nordic model, even as it faced a number of circumstances that differed from the other Nordic countries.[26] One large difference, for example, was that, following the Russian military victory over Sweden, Finland after 1809 was a Grand Duchy of Russia until the Bolshevik Revolution in 1917 opened the way for Finland to declare its national independence in December of that year.[27] While Russia acceded to the Finnish demand for independence (perhaps influenced somewhat by the fact that Lenin had spent much of his time in 1906 and 1907 hiding in Finland, before fleeing Russia altogether), it nevertheless continued to intervene actively in Finnish political affairs, thus helping to precipitate a divisive and destructive – if short – civil war in early 1918 between the Finnish "Reds" (associated with Russia) and the "Whites" (won by the latter partly with German assistance). As a legacy of this bitter conflict, Finland experienced greater internal tensions during the interwar period than other Nordic countries, requiring conciliatory steps by the social democrats (who had associated themselves with the losing Red side) who only slowly won back a place at the center of political life by the 1930s. The trauma of the Winter War against Russia in late 1939 and early 1940, the later "continuation war" in which Finland was allied with Germany against the Soviet Union from 1941 to 1944 and then the large post-war repa-

25. Alapuro, "Nordic and Finnish Modernity," pp. 194, 192.
26. Klinge, *A Brief History of Finland*; Klinge, *Let Us Be Finns*.
27. Jussila, Hentila and Nevakivi, *From Grand Duchy to a Modern State*.

rations imposed by the Soviet Union – part of the post-war pattern of "Finlandization" in Soviet-Finnish relations (including the presence until the 1970s of the only significant communist party in the Nordic countries) – was another example of Finnish exceptionalism.[28]

Also unlike the other Nordic countries, the dominant figure in Finnish politics in the post-war period, President Urho Kekkonen, was not a social democrat, even as he exercised quasi-monarchical powers in Finland that in other Nordic countries were exercised by prime ministers and democratic Parliaments. The Finnish language itself also made Finland unique in this respect. Finally, Finland was also slower to take off economically, not taking on the character of a fully modern and prosperous economy until a decade or two after the other Nordic countries. Yet despite all these significant differences, the remarkable fact is that Finland nevertheless in the larger picture continued to be so fundamentally Nordic in its social, political and economic character throughout the late nineteenth and twentieth centuries and the processes of Finnish modernization. This lends further support for the idea that there exists, as Alapuro describes it, a "Nordic pattern of social democracy as a continuation or a transformation of Lutheranism and parish political culture, and of [the] social liberalism [of the late nineteenth and early twentieth centuries], and of the concomitant model of containing tensions between freedom and equality" in a specifically Lutheran and Nordic way.[29] In the Nordic world, as Finnish historian Henrik Stenius explains, one must look back to "the Post-Reformation centuries" and the Lutheran state churches of those years that created a religious heritage that remains powerful even today, in both the core values and the institutional forms of all the "modern" Nordic societies.[30]

It was thus critical in Nordic history, as Stenius also writes in 2012 in *Nordic Paths to Modernity*, that in the Nordic countries "the Reformation was a state-driven project, not a protest from below." With a single Lutheran state church headed by the King, "the laws and

28. Zetterberg, *Finland After 1917*.
29. Ibid., p. 193.
30. Stenius, "Paradoxes of the Finnish Political Culture," p. 214.

the norms of the [Nordic] state were the same as those of the church. The moral and legal codes were identical, not giving much space for alternative religious or political conduct," thus limiting internal conflict and establishing a basis for a common "Nordic culture of convergence, consensus and conformity." In the nineteenth and twentieth centuries, the older God of Lutheranism was being replaced in the Nordic world by a new economic god of human progress whose laws were discovered by the natural and social sciences. Nevertheless, the Nordic and Lutheran patterns established centuries ago in the post-Reformation centuries otherwise persisted with remarkable fidelity, even as the Nordic states were widely coming to be seen in other places around the world as the leading national examples of shedding the past in order to enter the modern world. Much as Wittrock noted with respect to Sweden, Stenius observes that in Finland in the twentieth century one was expected to "bide your time, and meanwhile be obedient, work hard, become educated and be nationalistic." He concludes that such expectations in part reflect a "universalistic figure of thought" found throughout the Nordic world that "is rooted in the conformist ideals of their pre-modern Lutheran societies."[31]

The path to modernity in Finland and other Nordic countries thus did not travel as large a distance in its basics from the original Lutheran culture and governance as is commonly thought. Instead, it represented a radical transformation in the outward forms for expressing much the same old Lutheran ideals – often only present unconsciously among Nordic social democratic true believers (who may be surprised now to hear the claim that they remain "implicit Lutherans"). It was a key to the success of Nordic social democracy that a good Nordic citizen be obedient to the scientific dictates of the social democratic state, much as he or she had once obeyed the commands of a Lutheran state priesthood. During the course of a person's education and in other Nordic settings, for example, professional experts would assess the various states of knowledge and talents of each

31. Ibid., pp. 215, 219.

individual citizen; the Nordic state would then aim to steer people of the Nordic nation to appropriate educational opportunities, work activities and other suitable roles in society, scientifically determined in order to maximize the use of their individual capabilities. In Finland, as University of Helsinki historian Pauli Kettunen explains, such thinking in the 1930s and 1940s became central to the social democratic "idea of society as a functional whole that must and can be steered by scientific knowledge," a growing conviction that had also been significantly strengthened "in particular by the experiences of World War II," which had demonstrated the remarkable resilience of the Finnish people and their state and helped to inspire confidence in its leadership.[32]

In 1961, a Finnish social democratic economist, Pekka Kuusi, published a book on *Social Policy for the 60s*, one that Kettunen ranks as "perhaps the most influential social science study ever published in Finland." Offering "a design for the Finnish welfare state," it was written "in the spirit of Gunnar Myrdal" and other leading Nordic social scientists. The economists had the most important expert role because the entire enterprise of social democracy depended on achieving high levels of economic abundance that would not only offer abundant material goods and services but also work to abolish economic tensions and thus to advance democracy, social equality and in general peace and social harmony. Thus, as Kettunen observes, Kuusi's was a prescription for a "growth-oriented society" whose economic successes would also shape the character of other features of Finnish society; it would be a Finnish nation in which "the 'social' no longer represented a counter-principle [opposed] to the 'economic,'" as many humanistic and other more traditional Finnish thinkers – along with others in the Nordic world – had long previously asserted.[33]

Grounded in economics, Kettunen sees Finland as having a governing system in which "the concrete modes in which the Finnish political system was shaped contributed to the conceiving of the plan-

32. Kettunen, "The Nordic Welfare State in Finland," p. 231.

33. Ibid., p. 231.

ning reason not as a political matter of making use of the state but as an *inherent property* of the state itself." In Finland, perhaps more than in other Nordic countries, one finds a "tight intertwining of the history of professional expertise and the administrative history of the nation-state." In the role of "civil servants as professional experts," their efforts were seen by fellow Finns as transferring "the issue in question from the sphere of interests into the sphere of [social] needs, and from the sphere of politics into the sphere of [technical] administration," reflecting the longstanding "close connection between professional expertise and the state."[34] In one Finnish case, the revision of national pension policy in 1961, Kettunen writes that "the crucial role of planning expertise emerges." The necessary social "compromise was very much a creation of the planning reason, the technocratic professional knowledge, and these experts had the self-awareness of being the representatives of the national common good."[35]

America's Path to Modernization: The Third Great Awakening

In some ways, the United States was the earliest nation to advance along a path of modernization, beginning with the adoption in the late eighteenth century of democratic government of "the people," a national constitution, the separation of church and state and other features of the American governing system. America had the advantage in this regard that it was mostly a blank slate – especially those large areas west of the original 13 eastern colonies that had barely been touched by European influences prior to American Independence (and which would only later become new states). Thus, it was possible in early America to create whole new forms of political and economic structures without having first to displace the existing products of a long national history. The national cataclysm of the Civil War from 1861 to 1865 also proved a decisive transformational moment

34. Ibid., p. 243.

35. Kettunen, "The Nordic Welfare State in Finland," p. 241.

in American history, destroying much of what had existed before and resulting in a great increase in the powers of the victorious national (union) government.

Another decisive transitional period in the broader modernization of the United States, as noted previously, was the progressive era from 1890 to 1920. Significant steps toward the realization of progressive goals were taken in those years, such as the creation of the Federal Reserve Bank in 1913, the retention of immense areas of national lands and resources in the western United States under the continuing ownership of the national government and the national granting of the right to vote to women in 1920. The periods of the most significant actual implementations of the progressive design, however, were the New Deal years under President Franklin Roosevelt in the mid 1930s, and then the Great Society years of President Lyndon Johnson in the 1960s. Roosevelt and Johnson brought consummate political skills to the implementation task, and were required to make many political compromises, but the overarching American vision nevertheless had already been set in the progressive era. To study the roots of American modernism as it developed over the course of the twentieth century, therefore, is to study American progressivism.

Like his interpretations of earlier key periods of American history, as discussed above, University of Chicago economist Robert Fogel understands the history of the progressive era – more so than most American historians at least until recently – in religious terms. Indeed, he regards American progressivism as the product of a third Great Awakening in American history dating from 1890 to 1930. Fogel observes that one camp of the third Great Awakening included Christian fundamentalists who "hewed closely to the urban reform programs of the Second Great Awakening," such as curbing the use of alcohol, advancing social equality and improving the living conditions of the poor. Such American religious reformers of the late nineteenth century, who saw their efforts as realizing a society based on true Christian principles, "were initially strong in all areas of the country."[36]

34. Ibid., p. 243.

35. Kettunen, "The Nordic Welfare State in Finland," p. 241.

36. Fogel, *The Fourth Great Awakening & the Future of Egalitarianism*, p. 23.

In the end, however, as Fogel writes, in the early twentieth century,

> the winning camp of the Third Great Awakening has come to be called *modernist* or *liberal*. Modernists applied scientific principles to the study of the Bible, on the assumption that it was a historical document written by men who were trying to understand God's will within the context of their own times and civilizations. Modernists also believed that evolutionary theory was consistent with biblical thought because the world was evolving, not only toward human beings as the highest form of life, but also toward ever more perfected human beings. In this view, the laws of nature were God's laws, and scientists were the ones who would discover and explain them. As theologians were needed to interpret the Bible, scientists were needed to interpret nature.
>
> The millennialist dream of the Second Great Awakening thus became transformed by the [progressive] modernists. Disciples of the Second Great Awakening had the wrong theory of how the millennium would arrive, the modernists believed. The new theory emphasized, instead of the Second Coming of Christ, a new, more secular optimism about perfecting American society. In place of divine revelation, now stood the revelations of science. Since most of the problems were not physical or biological but social, [in America] a new breed of social scientists was required who understood the problems of the cities and who knew how to reconstruct them in a way that would alleviate the social crises of the age.[37]

As such modernist views increasingly held sway in the United States in the twentieth century, the end result by the end of the twentieth century was that, as Fogel writes, "a secular class of experts on the natural and social worlds has usurped the monopoly that theologians once had" in interpreting the events of the world to the wider American public and in providing guiding rules for individual and collective

37. Ibid., pp. 23–24.

action. Yet, while the setting and language were new, the questions addressed and the core mission were as grounded in traditional American religious concerns as ever. Fogel writes that, as the third Great Awakening unfolded, "the modernists tended to emphasize the natural goodness of man, and sin was reinterpreted 'chiefly as error and limitation which education in morals and the example of Jesus could mitigate, or else as the product of [social and economic] under-privilege which social reform could correct.'" Thus, in the modernization process social "ethics replaced [the old Calvinist] theological doctrine as the foundation of the Christian Witness, and to many [American] modernists the Sermon on the Mount became the core of the Bible."[38]

Among the most influential of the American modernists of the third Great Awakening were the "Social Gospelers [who] insisted that the ethics of the Sermon on the Mount applied to economic and political institutions as much as to individuals." But progressive modernists soon translated the biblical messages into a new secular key that said little or nothing about God. As Fogel writes, "the victory of the [progressive] modernists [...] laid the basis for the [American] welfare state, providing both the ideological foundation and the political drive for the labor reforms of the 1930s, 1940s, and 1950s, for the civil rights reforms of the 1950s and 1960s, and for the feminist programs of the late 1960s and early 1970s."[39] The third Great Awakening, in short, took the old American Calvinist drive to create a model Christian society as an example for the world, and refashioned it into a new secular drive to create a new exemplary American heaven on earth along a path grounded in science, expertise, technology and economics. Underneath it all, however, a surprising amount of the old Calvinist heritage survived as would become apparent in American life from the 1960s onward.[40]

38. Ibid., p. 72, 119.
39. Ibid., p. 25.
40. Nelson, "Calvinism Without God."

Conclusion

The Nordic heyday of social democratic thinking and practice lasted from the 1950s to the 1970s. In those same years, however, doubts were already growing in the United States. Indeed, in the decades immediately after World War II, leading American political scientists such as David Truman, Robert Dahl and Charles Lindblom increasingly saw the American progressive design for governance as characterized by an excessive confidence in the technical powers of the social sciences, combined with a large overestimate of the capacity of the American political system to exclude private interest groups from significant political influence, whatever the rational planners might be saying.[41] For better or worse, as Theodore Lowi famously wrote in the late 1960s, rather than scientific management, interest group politics would be the driving force in American democratic governance for the foreseeable future.[42]

This became a full-fledged American neo-liberal assault on progressive principles from the 1970s to the 1990s, led by University of Chicago economists such as Milton Friedman (winner of the Nobel Prize in economics in 1976) and George Stigler (winner in 1982). Although the principles of social democracy similarly came under growing challenge from the 1980s onwards in the Nordic countries, the attacks there were never as strong as in the United States. The social solidarity of the Nordic countries – grounded in a Lutheran ethic, rather than the historically more individualistic Calvinist ethic in the United States – continued to provide a more congenial environment for the implementation of Nordic scientific management ideals.

41. Truman, *The Governmental Process*; Dahl and Lindblom, *Politics, Economics, and Welfare*; Lindblom, "The Science of 'Muddling Through'."

42. Lowi, *The End of Liberalism*.

CHAPTER 11

Temperance and Eugenics: Less Happy "Scientific" Outcomes

The path to the modern societies of the Nordic countries was not, however, without a few bumps along the road – developments within broader modernizing trends that are today widely seen as having gone wrong. Partly because they occurred in unexpected settings, such cases can serve usefully to illustrate the thinking and values that lay behind modernization and, in the Nordic world, the rise of social democracy. They also illuminate the complexity of the modernization process, including some of the less attractive sides of modernism itself, a matter perhaps of increasing Nordic interest in the twenty-first century, as the modernist vision of social democracy is being more widely contested. The two cases of particular interest examined below are the Nordic temperance movements that grew in part out of the religious revivalism of the nineteenth century, and the Nordic eugenics laws enacted in the 1930s providing for sterilizations with the objective of extending the practice of scientific management to reproductive matters that would supposedly improve the "quality" of the national gene pool.

Temperance and the Modern Project

As in its early adoption of women's suffrage in 1906, and not unrelatedly, Finland led the Nordic world in passing legislation for national prohibition of the production and sale of alcoholic beverages. In 1907, the new Finnish Parliament (now including women for the first time), enacted a law with large majorities to establish prohibition in Finland. It was never signed by the Czar, however, so never took legal effect.

Implementation of prohibition in Finland thus had to await Finnish independence in 1917, resulting in the adoption of a Finnish prohibition regime in 1919 that lasted until 1932. Although many states and localities in the United States had already adopted their own versions of prohibition much earlier, 1919 was also the year in which an amendment to the U.S. Constitution established a nationwide American regime of alcohol prohibition. Remarkably enough, the United States ended prohibition in 1933, just one year after Finland. Among western developed nations, the United States and Finland share a common history of having had two of the longest periods of time in which a strict nationwide prohibition on alcohol production and sale was in effect.

Martin Luther was famous for his hearty living, including generous consumption of at least wine and beer. For Luther, there was no doubt where the evils in society originated; the Fall in the Garden of Eden had resulted in a depraved state of human existence that reflected the pervasive consequences of original sin. For Luther, moreover, the devil was a constant presence in the world, tempting fellow Germans and others to violate God's commands. Luther would have rejected the idea that there could be another devil in the world – alcohol – as a main source of human evil, suffering and misbehavior. Indeed, it was not until belief in original sin, predestination and other main elements of traditional Christianity began to erode in the Enlightenment that new "secular" devils such as the "demon temptation" of alcohol began to emerge. As examined in Chapter 9 above, the most important of these explanations historically were economic; human beings so often behaved so badly because they were driven to it by the dire poverty and other severe material deprivations of the economic environment in which they had always lived in the past.

But there would be other new secular explanations as well, if in some cases complementary with the economic understandings. Indeed, for many people it would be the consumption of alcohol that came to be seen in the nineteenth century as the single most important factor in corrupting the morals of society and causing so many other bad things to happen. If alcohol could be removed from society, it would go far to eliminate the presence of sin in society – another new secular form of salvation. Again, it would be an outcome no longer dependent on God coming to earth Himself, but something that could be accomplished by the modern actions of human beings themselves. As the temperance movement illustrates, the modernization project was not so much a turn away from Christianity as the development of new – often disguised as "scientific" – ways of expressing longstanding Christian messages.

A leading Finnish sociologist at the University of Helsinki and expert on alcohol policy, Pekka Sulkunen, thus writes that "the temperance movements of North America and Western European countries were prime examples of the modern project." For the temperance movements in the nineteenth and twentieth centuries, "sobriety was only one element in a new total way of life steered by rationality and self-control. Its function was to ensure progress, merging the public and the private good."[1] Sulkunen comments further that in Finland and other European nations "the mission of temperance was far wider than just the control of addictive alcohol use. It was based on the belief that the abolition of drink from society would correct all evils, even those brought about by industrial poverty, political corruption and irresponsible citizenship."[2] For the true believers, the temperance movement was yet another utopian project in search of a new path that paralleled the traditional Christian millennial hope for the arrival of a new heaven on earth. In this sense, as Sulkunen and others have pointed out, it was quintessentially modern, and in the Nordic world one more earthly manifestation – although among the least successful ultimately in achieving its aims – of the Nordic modernization project.

1. Sulkunen, *The Saturated Society*, pp. 57, 65.

2. Ibid., p. 65.

The Case of Temperance in America

Sociologist Harry Levine, a leading American authority on the history of U.S. alcohol control policy, explains that in America too the "view of alcohol as the cause of many or even most social problems continued throughout the 19th century and into the 20th century." Among the wide-ranging problems of society for which the temperance movement saw alcohol as a main cause were "poverty, crime, broken families and orphaned children, personal failure and business collapse." The final national adoption of prohibition in the United States in 1919 was a product of the progressive era and its mission to build a new heaven on earth through the scientific management of society – now including strong government actions to eliminate the scourge of alcohol from American society. Historian Clark Warburton thus writes that "at the time of the adoption of the Eighteenth Amendment" in 1919 prohibiting production and sale of alcohol in the United States, "and the Congressional passage that year of the Volstead Act" to implement it, "it was predicted that these measures would usher in a new economic era" – the central goal of all those large numbers of Americans who worshipped economic growth ("progress"), now to be decisively advanced by American national alcohol policy.[3] Prohibition, in other words, will save the world – by a new modern path of alcohol control, rather than the traditional Christian way of a second coming of Christ to earth.

It may come as a surprise to many people, and as Levine writes, "it is worth repeating that this entire way of discussing alcohol is not more than 200 years old" both in the United States and elsewhere around the world. Indeed, "the 'liquor question' [...] did not exist in the 17th century or for most of the 18th century."[4] To the contrary, drinking was widely seen until the early nineteenth century in a generally positive light, individually and socially. James Madison, a great

3. Warburton, "Prohibition and Economic Welfare,", p. 89.

4. Levine, "The Alcohol Problem in America," pp. 109-110.

American patriot who was a main author of the U.S. constitution, and would go on to serve as President for two terms, reportedly drank a pint of whiskey a day.[5] Levine reports that in the United States:

> In the 17th and 18th centuries alcoholic beverages, and especially rum, were highly esteemed and universally valued and were in no way stigmatized or regarded as tainted or evil. All liquor was regarded as good and healthy; alcohol was tonic, medicine, stimulant and relaxant. It was drunk at all hours of the day and night, by men and women of all social classes, and it was routinely given to children. Legal regulations and Puritan ministers commonly referred to alcoholic drink as "the Good Creature of God." During the 18th century per capita consumption was higher than in the 19th century and higher than it is today, and drunkenness was common. New England's Puritan ministers praised alcohol but denounced drunkenness as a sinful and willful misuse of the "Good Creature." Most colonials, however, regarded drunkenness as unproblematic and unsurprising; drunkenness was seen as the natural, normal and harmless result of drinking. One historian concluded that in 1776, at the time of the War for Independence, alcohol drinking had such an important and esteemed place in American life that it would require a revolution to displace it.[6]

A revolution in American thinking about alcohol, however, did begin in the first half of the nineteenth century. More traditional forms of Christian religion were losing influence and newer "scientific" ways of understanding unfolding events in the world were gaining ground. For growing numbers of Americans, the real source of human depravity was no longer some – probably fictitious – event in a Middle Eastern Garden long ago but the very real presence of large-scale alcohol consumption occurring in their midst. Curtailing drinking became central to both individual moral improvement and broader social re-

5. Von Drehle, "The Demon Drink."

6. Levine, "The Alcohol Problem in America," p. 110.

form. Encouraged by temperance preachers, millions pledged themselves to a life of personal abstinence over the course of the nineteenth century.

Levine thus writes that "by the 1830s, the essentials of American temperance thought were worked out, and they remained the fundamental precepts throughout the century." A first basic precept was that drinking alcohol led to addiction; "though apparently harmless at first, the demand for it increased so that one became utterly enslaved – hooked," due to the temptations of this modern devil. A second basic temperance precept was that alcohol acted "to weaken the moral centres of the brain and reduce drinkers' control over their own behavior. [...] A significant portion of poverty and crime (usually about three-fourths) was attributed to the moral degradation caused by alcohol." Finally, the third basic precept was that "alcohol was a poison and weakened the entire constitution. [...] It directly caused a great many diseases and it prepared the body for many more."[7]

Such thinking set the stage for the rise of a temperance movement that would grow rapidly in numbers and influence in the United States over the remainder of the nineteenth century. This movement, as Levine observes, was characterized by a "very sympathetic and supportive attitude toward habitual drunkards who they regarded as addicts with a condition beyond the control of the will; often they called this condition a disease." In their helplessness, what they required was a modern "exorcism," which temperance leaders now hoped to provide. The focus in the nineteenth century was thus on helping individual people to escape from their own alcohol "addiction." This would require not only education and social support for the individual drinker but also wider improvements in the social environments that encouraged people to turn to alcohol for relief in the first place. In this sense, curbing alcohol abuse in the nineteenth century was not primarily a problem that could be resolved by passing laws against it. As Levine writes, "the nineteenth-century temperance movement saw

7. Ibid., p. 111.

prohibition being achieved as part of a broad moral reformation of American society, and not simply as the result of pressuring for specific laws."[8]

As noted in earlier chapters, in the progressive era from 1890 to 1920 Americans retained a powerful commitment to moral reform but now adopted new strategies to pursue this objective. Professional experts would apply technical methods in order to bring about the scientific management of American society that would be led by the state. As the external circumstances – especially the economic – of American life were gradually perfected in this fashion, progressives were confident that moral reform would be a predictable consequence. Thus, the goal of reform efforts should not be focused on the morals themselves but on the achievement of national scientific management and efficiency to raise the material state of American society. The national government, rather than state and local governments, would be best equipped to bring together the most knowledgeable professionals who would then be properly situated to bring all this about. Of particular importance, it was also time for the national government to act forcefully and expertly to control alcohol abuse. Indeed, removing alcohol from society might be a precondition for all the other forms of human social and economic progress that were sought.

The Anti-Saloon League played a critical role in the politics of American alcohol policy during the first two decades of the twentieth century. In 1913, it first endorsed the idea of a national constitutional amendment to completely prohibit the production and sale of alcoholic beverages, a strategy that fit the new progressive-era view that greater social control was needed in all areas of life, partly as a response to radical changes across American society associated with the rise of the large business corporation and other rapid economic transformations of that era. Levine thus comments that, as one element of the American progressive movement, "the prohibition crusade was justified in terms of the needs of a new complex, heterogeneous, class-stratified, industrial, efficiency-oriented society of the 20th century-

8. Ibid., p. 112.

tury." Although temperance in the nineteenth century had been a middle-class movement seeking to improve the lot of workers and others further down the income scale, solving the alcohol problem now became important to the welfare of the middle class itself. Levine writes that "the old middle class of small businessmen, the new middle class of professionals and technical experts, as well as representatives of the corporations, all shared the [progressive-era] concern with finding new ways of maintaining social, political, and economic order." The support of the corporate elite for national alcohol prohibition was particularly important to the political success in 1919 of the approval of a national constitutional prohibition amendment. Business leaders were motivated in part by a belief that American corporations "would receive substantial economic benefits from it; more sober and abstaining workers would mean greater efficiency" and thus more rapid economic progress.[9] So alcohol prohibition became for many a key element of the national strategy to achieve the goals of the American progressive "gospel of efficiency."

Unlike most major governing innovations of the progressive era, such as the U.S. Federal Reserve (created in 1913 to oversee U.S. banking), national alcohol prohibition had a short lifetime. It proved impossible to enforce a law so intrusive on individual behavior and in the face of massive citizen resistance. Despite the common modern assumption to the contrary, legislating utopia overnight is an unlikely prospect. The United States largely gave up the effort with the approval of a new constitutional amendment to repeal alcohol prohibition in 1933. Unlike Finland and other Nordic countries, it largely gave up on alcohol control policy at the national level altogether. The United States did not attempt, for example, to use very high taxes as a surrogate form of prohibition (remarkably, the cost in Finland in 2014 of 1.75 liters of ordinary vodka in a state liquor monopoly shop – "Alko" – was about $50, compared with little more than $10 for the same vodka at a private liquor store in Washington DC). Since the 1930s American alcohol policy has emphasized instead the helping of individual alcoholics

9. Ibid., p. 113.

through organizations such as Alcoholics Anonymous, and controlling the social damages that can be specifically attributed to excessive alcohol use (such as increasingly strict laws against drunken driving).

Alcoholics Anonymous is yet another example of the old adage that "the more things change, the more they stay the same." This applies perhaps nowhere more than to religion; as old religions fade, their place is taken by seemingly new religions that in actual fact offer the greatest changes only in their outward forms. In the United States in the second half of the twentieth century, groups of recovering alcoholics thus gathered together in mutual support systems organized by Alcoholics Anonymous in which they confessed their past alcohol sins and committed to reform their future lives – to be born again, alcohol-wise. Although the language and settings were new, it recalled the Christian revival meetings that had thrived in the United States – as in Finland and other Nordic countries – in the nineteenth century.

Ernest Kurtz, author of a leading history of Alcoholics Anonymous in the United States, recognizes the obvious religious parallels, even as they may not be recognized by most recovering alcoholics today. As he writes, "in its understanding of the conversion process [to sobriety], Alcoholics Anonymous unconsciously reflected a larger religious tradition that had been exemplified most strikingly in an earlier age of American 'Revivals.'" Old-fashioned Christian revivalism included four stages: personal conviction of one's own deep sinfulness, heartfelt repentance, surrender of excessive pride and personal reformation of one's own life. For the twentieth-century members of Alcoholics Anonymous, all this was newly characterized as "hitting bottom, surrender, ego reduction, and maintenance of humility," now described in the fashionable "therapeutic" language of the times. Nevertheless, Kurtz writes, "whether presented as 'serenity' or as attained adult life, the sobriety promised by Alcoholics Anonymous to its adherents was clearly [individual] *salvation*" in a new modern dress.[10]

10. Kurtz, *Not-God*, p. 183.

Temperance in Finland

The consumption in the early nineteenth century of remarkably large amounts of alcohol by contemporary standards was not limited to the United States. This high alcohol consumption was partly explained by wider economic developments; there had been significant improvements in distilling technology that lowered the cost of production of alcoholic beverages. There had also been significant improvements in the means of transportation, making cheap supplies of liquor more easily and widely available. With economic barriers thus sharply lowered, levels of drinking soared in the late eighteenth and early nineteenth centuries. In Sweden, one estimate puts the annual consumption of spirits there in 1830 at 50 liters per capita per year (about one liter per week) – meaning that a considerable number of people, since this was an average, were consuming much more.[11] In a 2000 report, part of a government-supported Study of the Nordic Alcohol Policy Systems, Pekka Sulkunen, Caroline Sutton, Christoffer Tigerstedt and Katariina Warpenius seemingly understate matters in reporting that in the early 1800s throughout the Nordic countries "there was widespread misuse of spirits" (based on today's understanding of proper use).[12] The negative public reaction to this helped to generate the impetus for the rise in the nineteenth century of Nordic temperance movements.

Surprisingly, as would later be the case in the twentieth century with respect to social science knowledge, Finland was significantly influenced by American temperance developments. Columbia University historian John Wuorinen reports that "the early phase of the Finnish temperance movement was [...] markedly influenced by the contemporary temperance work in other lands. [...] The first Finnish temperance tracts, which began to appear as early as 1843, were translations of American originals." Revivalist trends in religion, which provided much of the impetus for nineteenth-century temperance, were, even in those days, surprisingly international. This American

11. Clark, *Deliver Us From Evil*, p. 21.

12. Sulkunen, Sutton, Tigerstedt and Warpenius, *Broken Spirits*, p. 29.

influence proved to be lasting: "from that day on, American experience was drawn upon to give inspiration as well as guidance in the propaganda for temperance and ultimately for prohibition" in Finland.[13]

As in the United States, Finnish alcohol policy in the nineteenth century had ambitions extending well beyond simply reducing the levels of alcohol consumed or the extent of drunkenness. Perhaps to an even greater extent than in the United States, limits on Finnish alcohol consumption came to be seen as a panacea for all the problems of society. Representatives of the early Finnish workers' movement, for example, were actively involved in the development of the temperance movement. Indeed, the twentieth-century Finnish trade union movement evolved to a significant degree out of the temperance movement in the late nineteenth century. Both the temperance movement and trade unions were committed to improving the overall well-being of Finnish workers, and reduced alcohol consumption was for both of them a critical part of this larger agenda.

In Sweden as well, as Pekka Sulkunen and Katariina Warpenius write, "temperance socialists" described "their ideals about enlightened modern working-class life" in terms of "cleanliness, orderliness, temperance and self-respect, even a sense of superiority" in their social achievements. In such early socialist understandings, "unregulated sexuality, gambling and immediate satisfaction implied also unregulated and conflict-ridden social relationships, whereas individual abstinence [from alcohol] represented a wider belief in progress and civilization, through '*bildning*,' self-education of the working class."[14] In these early years, alcohol control was seen as a more important immediate factor for achieving socialist goals than could be expected any time soon from class struggle. By the first decade of the twentieth century, however, Nordic trade unionists and social democrats were moving to shed such close temperance ties, partly because they were becoming uncomfortable with the close associations with religious revivalism and other "conservative" temperance overtones, even as socialism was become increasingly secular in character.

13. Wuorinen, "Finland's Prohibition Experiment," p. 216.

14. Sulkunen and Warpenius, "Reforming the Self and the Other," p. 432.

Sulkunen and Warpenius explain that in countries where people "drank alcohol primarily in the form of strong spirits," and where strong temperance movements developed, "these cultures were largely Protestant." In other parts of the world where Protestantism had few adherents, even those such as Poland and Russia where "alcohol consumption [also] took the form of heavy spirits, […] [the] temperance movements were of little importance."[15] Sulkunen and Warpenius observe that "what determined temperance cultures was the Protestant ethic as it was expressed through control of one's appetites and individual self-control and discipline with respect to the use of alcohol."[16] As discussed above, over much of Europe the Protestant ethic is more accurately described as a Calvinist ethic. Until the nineteenth century, Calvinism had little presence in Finland. As discussed in Chapter 8, however, this began to change in the nineteenth century with the spread of revivalism both within and outside the Lutheran state church. In the last few decades of the nineteenth century in Finland, because the temperance movement functioned outside the traditional Lutheran state church, its diversion of religious energies was another contributing factor to the declining role of the traditional Lutheran church in Finnish society.

Some of the same practices that distinguished revivalist church life carried over to the temperance movement. Irma Sulkunen, Seija-Leena Nevala-Nurmi and Pirjo Markkola explain that in the nineteenth century in Finland "the development of a civil society […] was closely interwoven with the building of the nation-state, [and] was initiated and took shape precisely through dynamic activity at the grassroots level." Local organizations often proved to be a breeding ground of modernization in which "new conceptions of citizenship were formulated, and the demand for increased democratic rights and a concomitant new model of citizenship were adopted." As Sulkunen and her co-authors write, "in Finland, as in most Protestant countries, this phase of popular organization was preceded by powerful religious revivals in which both sexes participated side by side on an equal footing."[17]

15. Sulkunen et al., *Broken Spirits*, pp. 18, 19.
16. Ibid, p. 19.
17. Sulkunen, Nevala-Nurmi and Markkola, *Suffrage, Gender and Citizenship*, p. 98.

Indeed, the most important of the new popular organizations in the late nineteenth century was the Finnish temperance movement; in 1900, for example, a petition demanding prohibition was presented to the Parliament, signed by 140,000 individuals – fully five percent of the population of Finland at the time. Also in 1900, about half of the members of the temperance movement in Finland were women, making temperance a major factor in the rapidly growing role of women in Finnish political life and society more generally.[18]

The temperance movement thus proved an important spawning ground for various later social reform movements in Finland. Temperance leaders regarded state action as important to the success of their cause, leading them to become strong advocates for governance by parliamentary democracy, where they saw their best chances of practical success in implementing their ideas. Given the large role of women in the temperance movement, the connection to the women's suffrage movement was particularly close, with many women actively participating in both causes. The high point in this wider social role for the temperance movement was the first decade of the twentieth century when, as noted previously, Finland became in 1906 the first nation in Europe to enact women's suffrage and its parliament in 1907 became the first in Europe to vote for alcohol prohibition (although it was never approved by the Czar).

After Finnish prohibition was finally adopted in 1919, the difficulty of enforcing it and its manifest failure to solve the main social and economic problems of the nation led to growing opposition. The ending of prohibition in Finland in 1932 occurred in a period that also witnessed the rise of social democratic principles as a basis for Nordic governance (as in the United States in 1933 it coincided with the assumption of the Presidency by Franklin Roosevelt). Rather than alcohol consumption, social democrats were more concerned with reworking the basic social and economic structures of society. While abandoning efforts at outright prohibition, Nordic social democratic

18. Ibid., pp. 88, 98.

governments did, however, continue aggressively to attempt to suppress alcohol consumption through taxes and other means – to a degree that is almost unique in the western world. In this respect at least, the Lutheran state church tradition perhaps encouraged such attempts at comprehensive government control over the actions of the citizenry that would not have been possible in most other European nations.

Eugenics and the Modern Project

Besides the movement for total alcohol prohibition, another unhappy side of the modern project in the Nordic world – seen today in a much more negative light than the failures of alcohol prohibition – was the eugenics movement of the first half of the twentieth century . It is today surprising to learn the extent to which leading medical professionals, biologists, psychologists and other professional experts and intellectual leaders more generally of the first half of the twentieth century advocated eugenics. In Sweden, as Bo Strath comments, "the discourse on modernity, enlightenment and welfare informed by a Darwinian development language in several academic disciplines, perhaps did not determine, but facilitated the sterilizations." Compulsory sterilization was seen as part of the modern progressive project that social democracy was working to advance. Strath thus explains that "it was indeed the visions to create a new and better society that motivated the sterilizations."[19]

Again, as with prohibition, there was a close connection between a historically Protestant religion of a nation and the likelihood of an active eugenics program. In this case, the greater general skepticism of the Roman Catholic Church with respect to modernizing trends served it well. Indeed, the leading nations in the world in eugenics activism were the United States and, in Europe, specifically the Lutheran countries of Germany and the Nordic world. The Norwegian historian and philosopher Nils Roll-Hansen writes that "while steriliza-

19. Strath, "The Normative Foundations of the Scandinavian Welfare States in Historical Perspective," p. 48.

tion laws were introduced in several states in the United States during the first wave of mainline eugenics around World War I, no European government introduced such laws in this period. Only with the wave of reform eugenics were such laws introduced in Europe, mainly in countries with a Lutheran state church."[20] In the Nordic cases, many of the leading advocates of eugenics policies in the 1930s were social democrats. It was thought to be an important element in the progressive objective of establishing the scientific management of society.

Eugenics in America

Once again, American developments had an important influence on the Nordic countries, if often transmitted first to Germany and from there to the Nordic world. The American Madison Grant was an influential figure in the early twentieth century history of the United States. He came from the upper strata of American society, tracing his ancestry on his father's side to Richard Treat, dean of Pitminster Church in England, one of the first Puritans to arrive in New England in 1630. Grant was a close friend of Theodore Roosevelt and travelled in the same New York social circles, including membership in the elite (and politically influential) Boone and Crockett Club founded by Roosevelt. A Yale graduate born to wealth, Grant was a founder of the Bronx Zoo in 1895 and became a leading figure in American environmental history.

Yet most of Grant's activities have been expunged from the public records of the American causes he served. He also became one of the leading American advocates of a eugenics crusade to save the world, and especially the 'superior' races – and at the very top stood the Nordic race. Christianity taught that human beings were unique among the species in the world in that they were all created "in the image of God." Social Darwinists such as Grant, however, rejected such unscientific thinking. If human beings were one more animal species, as

20. Roll-Hansen, "Conclusion," p. 262.

Darwin had seemingly shown, Grant considered that genuinely scientific policies applicable to nonhuman animals logically might be applied as well in matters involving the future of the human species. Just as cattle were bred for certain favorable traits, it seemed persuasive to Grant – and to surprisingly many other leading American progressives of the time – that the scientific case was also strong for the deliberate breeding of human beings to advance the natural qualities and evolutionary fitness of the entire future human species.

Grant's best known statement of this "scientific racism" was his 1916 book, *The Passing of the Great Race*. The American journalist Carey McWilliams wrote in 1940 that as "the bible of the Nordics, the book had an enormous influence [...] [It] contains the frankest and most clear-cut statement of the racist ideology ever published" in the United States.[21] The book proposes, as Grant explains in the opening sentence, "to elucidate the meaning of history in terms of race."[22] Past accounts of history had typically emphasized the roles of kings, popes, scientists, philosophers and other prominent individuals; other accounts such as Marxism and Herbert Spencer's social Darwinism emphasized the interactions of economic groupings of people; and still other historical theories emphasized the influence of religion and other ideas. But after Darwin it seemed that the natural workings of evolution would also have be recognized as a central factor. As his biographer Jonathan Spiro writes, Grant in fact focused his entire theory of human history on the fundamental role of inherited characteristics and evolution, thereby producing a "history of mankind [that] is actually a tale of the evolution, migration, and confrontation of races."[23] Indeed, grounded as it was in the transmission of favorable survival traits by processes of human reproduction, Grant and others would claim that such a racial understanding of history was the most consistent with the new Darwinist evolutionary understanding.

Observed from America, Grant sees the history of Europe as shaped by three races, the "Nordics" of northern Europe, the "Alpines" of east-

21. See Spiro, *Defending the Master Race*, p. 154.

22. Grant, *The Passing of the Great Race*, p. 1.

23. Spiro, *Defending the Master Race*, p. 145.

ern and central Europe, and the "Mediterraneans" of southern and southwestern Europe. The Nordics, according to Grant, are the "Master Race." The colder climate and harsher living conditions in the north, he theorizes, imposed a more ruthless selection process of survival of the fittest, resulting in a superior Nordic race extending from Germany northward and westward in Europe. The original settlers of the United States, Grant finds, were also Nordics, although more recent waves of immigration of other racial groups from Europe are now threatening the racial purity of the American nation. The Nordics are not only physically bigger and stronger but, as Grant argues, are also superior in "moral, intellectual, and spiritual aspects [that] are [as] persistent as physical characteristics [among races], and are transmitted unchanged from generation to generation." Grant writes that "in the Europe of today the amount of Nordic blood in each nation is a very fair measure of its strength in war and standing in civilization."[24] The spread of intense nationalist feelings in Europe in the nineteenth century had often been grounded in similar feelings of national superiority but now this sense of superiority was given a new racial – rather than a religious, cultural or economic – cast.

For Grant the evolutionary scientific realities were to be become the basis for new government policies. As explained in *The Passing of the Great Race*, his "reform" agenda includes three main steps. First, birth control measures should be widely instituted and promoted especially among racially inferior races and less fit individuals. Second, laws should be passed to prohibit marriages between different races because "to bring halfbreeds into the world" will dilute the evolutionary success of the strongest race and thus must be "regarded as a social and racial crime of the first magnitude." The most ambitious effort will be a widespread eugenics campaign in which at a minimum "the least desirable [...] ten per cent of the [American] community" will be identified and sterilized, thus serving to restrict "the perpetuation of the [...] remaining least valuable types" and to maintain and even boost the inherited natural qualities of the population of the United States.[25]

24. See ibid., pp. 148-149.

25. See ibid., p. 156.

Although today such writings would be regarded as deplorable or worse, such beliefs remarkably were not only held by Grant but were widely shared at the time within American society. As Spiro remarks in his comprehensive study of the eugenics movement in the United States, Grant sees eugenics as offering a "rational, efficient, and scientific remedy" for the ills of American society. Genetic management would thus be a key part of the overall progressive project of the comprehensive "scientific management" of the nation.[26] Indeed, many progressives of the time were among the strongest supporters of eugenics, seeing it as an unflinching application of the best – the Darwinist – science available.[27] Those who opposed eugenics were said to be cultural conservatives who were exhibiting pre-scientific habits of thought.

The use of eugenics would thus admittedly have to overcome the hurdle, as Spiro explains Grant's thinking, of the presence of many "well-meaning humanitarians, [who have] [...] fallen under the spell of Christianity with its unfortunate and wholly unscientific bias in favor of 'the weaker elements.'" Grant suggests that we "can now see that social workers and their ilk have done 'more injury to the race than black death or small pox.'" Grant considers that the old-fashioned sentimentalists are simply unwilling to face the new Darwinist scientific realities – that, as he writes, "nature cares not for the individual. [...] She is concerned only with the perpetuation of the species or type." In a world ultimately governed by the biological laws of natural evolution, the collective maximization of human progress according to the scientific "laws of nature require[s] the obliteration of the unfit, and human life is valuable only when it is of use to the community or race."[28] An active eugenics program thus becomes an important expression of a nation's genuine commitment to the maximum progress of the human race – now along an evolutionary path to heaven on earth.[29] The ending of free immigration into the United States in the early 1920s was motivated in significant part by the de-

26. Ibid., p. 151.
27. Leonard, *Illiberal Reformers.*
28. Spiro, *Defending the Master Race*, p. 151.
29. Nelson, *Reaching for Heaven on Earth*, Ch. 4.

sire to curb the entry of what were seen as inferior groups from eastern and southern Europe.

With his family wealth, wide range of social contacts and political skills, Grant was no marginal figure in American life but a person of wide influence who had a great deal of success in influencing government policies and actions. More than 25 American states passed laws against miscegenation, prohibiting marriage and other sexual relations between whites and blacks, and in some cases also extending these limitations to American Indians and Asians. Even more states passed eugenics laws establishing programs of sterilization of the mentally ill and otherwise "defective." Around 60,000 Americans were eventually sterilized with some states even continuing the practice into the 1960s. In upholding one such program in Virginia, Justice Oliver Wendell Holmes (widely considered among the great justices of U.S. Supreme Court history) in 1927 famously wrote for himself and seven Justices (there was one dissenter) that "it is better for all the world, if instead of waiting to execute degenerate offspring for crime, or to let them starve for their imbecility, society can prevent those who are manifestly unfit from continuing their kind." Holmes infamously concluded his opinion with the phrase, "three generations of imbeciles are enough."[30]

In summary, as Jackson Lears recently explained, Grant "found himself drawn to the potent phrase 'survival of the fittest,' which pervaded elite circles by the early twentieth century. [...] It was only a short step, for Grant, from culling inferior elk to culling inferior humans. Breeding was all." Lears writes that Grant's book *The Passing of the Great Race* "was widely praised," including an admiring letter to Grant from former President Theodore Roosevelt – who himself had long exhibited a "love of war" as a way of identifying those with superior qualities. In the United States, a "racial hysteria [...] bubbled barely beneath the surface of American popular culture in the 1910s and 1920s," justified as the ruthless application of the most advanced scientific thinking to achieve the perfection of the human race, neces-

30. *Buck v. Bell*, 274 U.S. 200 (1927).

sarily along an evolutionary path that could be well served by effective government eugenics policies.[31] It was yet one more form of modern utopianism, another example of the modern tendency to seek a secular salvation here on earth by (so it was then said) direct human action guided by science.

From America to Germany

Madison Grant's most important follower, at least in terms of historical impact, was not an American but a German (originally Austrian). While probably with some exaggeration, Adolf Hitler wrote to Grant that his book, *The Passing of the Great Race*, "is my Bible." Moreover, as Spiro writes, Hitler's "closest advisors were avid fans of Madison Grant and accepted all the major tenets of his scientific racism." More broadly, "Nazi racial thinkers often pointed to Madison Grant and his disciples as the inspiration for their work." Themes common to Grant and the Nazis were "the primacy of race, the worship of modern science, the subordination of the individual to the state, millennialism, the need for positive and negative eugenics and animal husbandry."[32]

These were all core elements of Hitler's manifesto, *Mein Kampf*, dictated to Rudolf Hess while he was in Landsberg prison in 1924 and which includes a long section on "People and Race." Hitler's argument there is grounded in an explicitly Darwinist framework of thought. It assumes "one of the most striking principles of Nature's rule: the inner separation of the various species of all earth's living creatures." It is not only other species but human beings themselves whose existence, morals and everything else of importance are to be understood in Darwinist terms. Among humans no less than other species, the central principle is that "the stronger must rule" as part of a "ruthless selection method" that is a scientific law of the biological world. Within the human species, its members are not only differentiated individually but also according to the race to which they belong. Presenting himself as applying Darwinist principles without any

31. Lears, "The Usefulness of Cranks," pp. 37, 41.

32. Spiro, *Defending the Master Race*, p. 357.

false sentimentality for the human situation, Hitler argues that "nature does not desire the mating of a weaker species with stronger individuals. Even less does she desire the mating of a higher race with a lower race." Such behavior would frustrate the evolutionary improvement of any species and no less the human species as a whole. As Hitler puts it, "if this were allowed to happen over thousands of years, the efforts of natural selection would be for nothing" in terms of the rapid overall progress of the human species.[33] At a time when the secular worship of progress had become the most powerful religious force in Europe, and however horrific his subsequent actions, Hitler was fitting into the tenor of the times, then, in making the claim that he could reveal the actual scientific path of human progress. His early German followers saw Hitler as virtually a new messiah who would lead them to an earthly salvation.[34]

Scientific racism, at least superficially grounded in Darwinism, it is necessary to make clear, did not in itself produce the Hitler of *Mein Kampf* and the Nazi party. It was a necessary condition but much less than a sufficient one. Hitler, even as he claimed to be following a strict scientific analysis, frequently strayed far from any scientific application of Darwinist principles. He also introduced strong moral appeals into the Nazi message, surprisingly often drawn from Christian teachings – an essential part of its attraction for millions of Germans. In *Hitler's Ethic*, American historian Richard Weikart thus writes that "it is admittedly true that Hitler himself – if not all his Nazi followers – would have ranked as a cultural conservative." Weikart observes that "many Germans cheered when Hitler promised to clean up the moral depravity of the urban areas and return to the legendary, pristine purity of the village community. His fulminations against prostitution, homosexuality, abortion, and birth control resonated with those Germans who rejected the loose moral standards of the twentieth century" – standards that were encouraged by the moral relativism that had being spreading rapidly in the early twentieth century.[35] But Hit-

33. Hitler, *Mein Kampf*, pp. 246, 247.
34. Redles, *Hitler's Millennial Reich*.
35. Weikart, *Hitler's Ethic*, p. 19.

ler defended his old-fashioned moral principles in brand new evolutionary terms – abortion and birth control, for example, were now immoral because they impeded the rapid population growth of the superior Aryan race and thus the evolutionary progress of the human species. National socialism as developed by Hitler and other Nazis was a bastardized blend of Darwinism, Christianity and other elements of German history.[36]

Eugenics in Finland

Eugenics in Finland, as in the United States, arose as one element of the general application of the ideas of scientific management of society that were being widely advocated in progressive circles in the early twentieth century. In a 2005 article on "From Race Hygiene to Sterilization in Finland," Finnish researcher Marjatta Hietala relates that in Finland "at the turn of the [twentieth] century, especially in [the field of] medicine, innovation, progress, and scientific advance came to be highly valued. Experts became important in the task of changing society." She explains that "the monolithic Lutheran state religion" had long encouraged Finnish habits of deference to a state church – which now in the twentieth century was replaced by a new scientific state church. Encouraged by the new scientific priesthoods in Finland "people trusted experts and professionals. Training and trained people enjoyed high esteem and one of the most valued groups was the medico-legal experts" who were responsible for implementing the necessary scientific practices to maintain the future health and vitality of the Finnish population.[37]

Given its high prestige, it was of particular importance that the Finnish medical establishment was the source of some of the leading advocates in Finland of using eugenics as a scientific tool for advancing general public health. Hietala observes that in Finland "during the 1910s [...] the most active supporters of eugenics and sterilization

36. Redles, *Hitler's Millennial Reich*; Steigmann-Gall, *The Holy Reich*.

37. Hietala, "From Race Hygiene to Sterilization," p. 198.

were the chief mental officers of the mental asylums, the directors of reformatories, and those responsible for child welfare."[38] In lecturing before the Ekonomiska Samfundet i Finland in 1912, for example, Professor Albert Palmer argued that "it would be fortunate for society if reproduction by idiots, alcoholics and other degenerate people could be prevented."[39] The means of accomplishing this objective would be their sterilization – by compulsion if necessary – that would prevent their giving birth to new people with the same hereditary defects. As Hietala further reports:

> The idea of sterilization was discussed publicly at the 6th Nordic Conference on the Welfare of the Handicapped in Helsinki in 1912. On that occasion the Danish professor Keller, director of the Bregninge Institute for Idiots, suggested using sterilization in the care of criminals and "morons." At the same meeting Dr. Albert Borkman, then the medical superintendent of the Pitkanieme Central Institution, suggested the adoption of sterilization "for preventing the ever increasing incidence of mental illnesses, feeblemindedness and mental degeneracy." According to him this measure should be applied to common criminals, "idiots," genuine epileptics, those long-term mentally ill people who had been discharged from an institution and, finally, to alcoholics who had been treated in institutions at least twice. The director of the Perttula Reformatory, Edwin Holman, had reached the same conclusions. According to him society should be allowed the right and power to prevent the continuation of a degenerate line and he considered sterilization as one effective measure.[40]

There was little likelihood of the implementation of any such sterilization policy in the Finland of 1912. The power of the various "conservative" forces in society, ranging from the Lutheran church, to liberal parties that were heavily committed to the maintenance of individual private freedoms, to agrarian parties grounded in the tra-

38. Ibid., pp. 202, 206.
39. Quoted in ibid., p. 203.
40. Ibid., p. 204.

ditional values of the countryside, was too great. Such thinking nevertheless continued to percolate in Finland for the next 20 years. In 1923, Harry Federley assumed the chair in genetics at the University of Helsinki. As a highly regarded Finnish researcher, he had a wide range of international connections, especially German and Swedish. Hietala reports that "as early as 1926, Federley suggested that because marriage counseling and propaganda had proven ineffective, special segregation or sterilization measures should be considered for those with an 'inferior' genetic inheritance." To be effective, it would be necessary to adopt a law allowing compulsory sterilization, even recognizing that it would be resisted by many as "alien to the western concept of justice." Advocates for eugenic measures found that, while their ideas appealed to many in the scientific community, "it was discovered that eugenic theories were unappealing to educated people with a background in the humanities."[41]

Before World War II, the Finnish advocates of eugenics as a key component of the modernization project drew heavily on foreign sources – mainly German – for their arguments. Hietala reports, for example, that the members of the medical school of the University of Helsinki "had strong ties" to their German counterparts. In 1935, more than 75 percent of the medical textbooks used at the University of Helsinki were written in German. In the medical as well as many other fields in the early twentieth century, there was "an increase in the number of high level personnel well-grounded in science and technology [who] would help to build Finland into a modern state. Like their counterparts in Germany, members of the Finnish government believed that scientific achievement was a necessary ingredient in building up the *Kulturstaat*."[42]

Indeed, the arguments for eugenics in Finland often sounded little different from those being made in Germany (and the United States). Federley, as Hietala comments, "suggested that the Nordic element was more dominant among the Swedish-speaking Finns. The purest form of the Nordic type could be found in the Aland islands."

41. Ibid., pp. 215, 209.

42. Ibid., pp. 201, 202.

In language similar to that of the American racial historian Madison Grant, it was said that in Finland "the East Baltic race [...] differed from the Nordic one mainly because of it lower height, its more square facial features, and the shape of the nose." The argument was made that there was a genetic disposition not only for such physical features but also for varying levels of "cultural development" among different racial groups living in different regions of Finland and which further "manifested themselves in the general state of health and hygienic conditions" there. As Hietala observes, by the 1930s "Finnish speakers reacted with considerable equanimity to these race classifications," which had spread by then from the leading proponents, originally found most frequently among Swedish-speaking Finns.[43]

Few if any German scientists would have imagined or supported the lengths to which Hitler would eventually take racial Darwinism in the 1940s with the Holocaust. But there was widespread support among German scientists in the 1920s and 1930s for the idea of scientifically managing the future human gene pool, and in particular for advancing by deliberate human efforts the prospects for the Nordic race, drawing on evolutionary biological and medical research of long standing. Robert Proctor in *Racial Hygiene: Medicine Under The Nazis* thus finds that German "physicians played an active role in both the theory and the practice of each phase of the Nazi program of racial hygiene and racial destruction."[44] In his book *Hitler's Professors*, written shortly after the end of World War II on the basis of the vast Nazi archives then newly available, Max Weinrich paints an even bleaker – if perhaps somewhat exaggerated – picture, that "the whole ruling class of Germany was committed to the execution of this crime" of racial scientific management. It was not a group of ill-educated and ignorant Nazi losers in society but eminently respectable "German scholarship [that] provided the ideas and techniques which led to and justified this unparalleled slaughter" – although the Final Solution of the 1940s had not itself been advocated in such circles. Nevertheless,

43. Ibid., p. 200.
44. Proctor, *Racial Hygiene*, p. 222.

those involved in the effort to develop and spread racist ideas in Germany "were to a large extent people of long and high standing, university professors and academy members, some of them world famous, authors with familiar names."[45] For many years Finnish medical and other expert professionals looked to such German authorities for world leadership in applying the knowledge of evolutionary science in order to improve the human species and Finnish society.

Eugenics and Social Democracy

In the United States the implementation of eugenics practices began earlier – occurring almost entirely at the state level of government – than in the Nordic countries. Indeed, it was not until the rise of the Nordic social democratic parties in the 1930s that some Nordic countries moved legally to put eugenics into practice. Many social democrats prided themselves on their commitment to scientific solutions and sought to distance themselves from supposedly "old-fashioned" ideas and moral principles of the past. The Marxist influence on social democracy also encouraged an attitude of ruthlessness in applying "scientific" economic knowledge to overthrow the old class order – including by violent means if necessary.

Among the Nordic countries, Sweden showed the strongest commitment to scientific management of the national gene pool. The first Sterilization Act in Sweden, introduced into the Parliament by a social democratic government, took effect in early 1935. As Gunnar Broberg and Mattias Tyden write, in Sweden "eugenics was incorporated into the social policy developed by the Social Democrats from the 1930s on."[46] The policy included circumstances in which sterilization might be compulsory, such as for the mentally deficient. Indeed, the 1936 Commission on Population in Sweden declared that "sterilization of hereditarily sick or inferior human beings is [...] a justified measure, beneficial to the individual as well as society."[47] From 1935

45. Max Weinrich, *Hitler's Professors*, quoted in Proctor, *Racial Hygiene*, p. 222.

46. Broberg and Tyden, "Eugenics in Sweden," p. 104.

47. Quoted in ibid., p. 106.

to 1941, there were 1,113 officially recorded sterilizations in Sweden for reasons of mental retardation, about half of the total number of sterilizations (and many others were not officially recorded).[48] In the case of such mentally incompetent people, one can assume that sterilization must have frequently involved a significant element of compulsion.

Broberg and Tyden report that in Sweden by the mid to late 1930s "the right of the state to enforce sterilization was no longer questioned" among social democratic and other top opinion leaders. The 1936 "commission argued that compulsory sterilization in the future might be considered among the 'psychologically inferior, though not formally legally incompetent, with asocial disposition,'" besides the more obviously mentally unfit.[49] In 1941 a proposed bill calling for investigations of still more aggressive sterilization measures was endorsed by 33 Social Democrats, 7 Agrarians, 2 Liberals and 1 Conservative.

Although they altogether rejected any idea of the "Nordic race" as a superior people in the world, or other racial interpretations of history, Gunnar and Alva Myrdal, reflecting the widely held views among social democrats in the 1930s, were advocates for sterilization and other eugenics measures. Broberg and Tyden thus comment that "clearly, Alva and Gunnar Myrdal spoke about sterilization, and about 'desirable parents' and 'unfit,' in the same manner as most debaters of the time." They "put sterilization in the context of social reforms" such as Swedish social democrats were moving rapidly to advance on a comprehensive basis across every area of society, seeing "sterilization of the deficient as an inevitable consequence of, as they put it in *Kris i befolkningsfragen*, 'the great sociological process of adjustment' to modern industrial society." Broberg and Tyden explain further that "the Myrdals regarded forced sterilization as a part of population policy and [...] advocated 'quite ruthless sterilization policies' for the mentally retarded."[50] As Sweden rapidly modernized, it would be necessary to dispense with many outmoded ideas and sentiments that

48. Ibid., p. 112.

49. Ibid., pp. 106, 107.

50. Ibid., pp. 105, 104.

reflected the ignorance and biases of a pre-scientific time, but still lingered for many people.

Finnish eugenics policy was influenced in the 1930s by such Swedish and other Nordic sources. In 1934 a series of widely publicized lectures were given in Helsinki as part of an official "Crime Prevention Week," many of them concerning possible eugenics measures, reflecting the view widely held then in Finnish expert circles that eugenics measures would be critical to future crime reduction in Finland. As Marjatta Hietala reports, "the structure of these lectures was very similar. They presented the results of the most recent research in the Nordic countries and in Germany – research and statistics from Germany were greatly trusted by the Finnish people." As a result of these and other such discussions in Finland, "by 1934 the professionals concerned with the welfare of the mentally ill and retarded, as well as those responsible for municipal poor relief had been abundantly informed about the [need for an] act on sterilization and warned about the deterioration of the racial quality of the nation."[51]

Dr. Rakel Jalas served as the vice-chair and then the chair of the Morality Committee of the Finnish Women's National Federation, seeking in this capacity to promote not only a national sterilization policy but also the introduction of castration of men who had been involved in sexual crimes. As Hietala writes, like many others in Finland at the time, "her basic ideology was social-Darwinism: no longer does society free itself from weak individuals by the [traditional slow evolutionary] method of natural selection." Instead, it would now be desirable to accelerate and improve upon the workings of the survival of the fittest in nature with appropriate state policy actions; in other words, "society must resort to multifarious measures and mainly to those which aim at preventing the birth of weak individuals."[52] Another element of this agenda was the development of better methods of birth control and the encouragement of their use among those members of society who were less successful and thus would inhibit the improvement of the national gene pool.

51. Hietala, "From Race Hygiene to Sterilization," p. 227.

52. Ibid., p. 245.

In this climate of expert opinion, the Finnish Parliament in 1934 enacted the Sterilization Act that then took effect in 1935. Although social democrats were not in the governing coalition, they had won 78 seats (37 percent, easily the highest percentage of any party) in the 1933 parliamentary elections, and the vote on the Sterilization Act was close to unanimous (only 14 out of 200 members voted against it).[53] Hietala attributes this broad support to "the esteem that professional experts such as doctors held in Finland. People were accustomed to relying on expert opinions." And the majority of the medical practitioners in Finland were advocates for sterilization. As a result, in the mid 1930s "there was [...] hardly any public debate on these issues at all" in Finland – it was enough for most Finns that there was seemingly a German and Nordic scientific consensus.[54]

The Finnish Sterilization Act explicitly allowed for compulsory sterilization, for example, of "idiots" (those with a mental age of less than six), "imbeciles" (a mental age between six and fourteen), and the insane, such as schizophrenics or manic depressives. In order to carry out a compulsory sterilization, an application had to be approved by the National Board of Health. Compared with the potential numbers, Finland was less zealous than some other countries, moving cautiously to implement the Act. Between 1935 and 1955, the Board of Health approved 1,461 sterilizations that were carried out on a compulsory basis (another 461 sterilizations were voluntarily requested for medical or other reasons). Of the total sterilizations of all kinds approved by the Board of Health, 59 percent were of people considered to be mentally retarded, 15 percent were schizophrenics, and 5 percent were said to be psychopaths. Women represented 85 percent of the total number of those sterilized. Epileptics represented the largest group seeking voluntary sterilizations. It was not until 1970 that the original 1930s Sterilization Act was repealed in Finland.[55]

Looking back over the history of eugenics in the Nordic world, however, the worst potential consequences of the eugenics movement

53. Ibid., p. 250.
54. Ibid., p. 244.
55. Ibid., pp. 235, 236.

were avoided. The numbers sterilized were small relative to the numbers of people who might have qualified, according to the thinking of leading eugenics advocates. This outcome does not seem to have been mainly a product of more rigorous scientific research that discredited the theories of eugenics (although some such research was being produced showing that, for example, many cultural and other human features were not hereditary). If human beings were simply another form of animal, however, the idea of breeding humans for certain traits was as scientifically logical as the idea of breeding dogs and cattle. It would seem that many Nordic government officials and others in leadership positions somehow did not actually believe – maybe only at an emotional level – that human beings were just like other animals, whatever Darwin had said. Conceivably there was something to the idea that all human beings were made "in the image of God." Nordic actions in practice, as one might say, were thus seemingly guided in some significant degree by an older traditional Lutheran ethic that had somehow survived in the Nordic world in the twentieth century despite the assaults of scientific modernism.

Conclusion

The Nordic countries have been characterized by a higher degree of social control over the actions of their citizens than perhaps any other nations in the world. There have of course been many dictatorial and other oppressive regimes in other nations that have imprisoned and otherwise harshly treated political opponents. But they have not attempted to regulate the details of individual behavior outside political realms to the same extent as in the Nordic world. The former Soviet Union, for example, never attempted to regulate consumption of alcohol with the same stringency as the Nordic countries. Highway speed limits today in the Nordic countries are some of the slowest in the world, and are actually enforced. It is possible to maintain a high degree of government control over wide areas of society only because most Nordic citizens comply willingly with government rules. They see it as part of their social obligation to the nation, a statement of their social solidarity.

This Nordic tradition of deference to authority originated as a deference to the Lutheran state church headed by the king. In the Nordic world in the twentieth century, however, the Lutheran state church role was largely replaced by scientific authority. The actions of the Nordic state were legitimate because they were believed to be grounded in scientific knowledge as interpreted and applied by leading professional experts (one might say the new "priests" of Nordic society). But the scientific method has achieved its greatest successes in understanding the workings of the natural world, and thus in providing a technical basis of knowledge that has enabled the human mastery of nature for immense human material benefit. When it comes to the human workings of society, or the wellsprings of individual behavior, however, there is no reason to believe that a body of technical experts will be able to provide definitive answers in a parallel way. Social science is not like physical science; it may not even be a science at all. Mistakes – even large mistakes – will be made, and it will be more difficult to correct these mistakes if they are defended by expert professionals who claim in the name of the progressive advancement of modern society to be acting solely in defense of the comprehensive application of scientific knowledge.

Two of the greatest modern mistakes of the twentieth century in Finland were alcohol prohibition and eugenics. As Hietala observes, "the nearest analogy to the Finn's eagerness to employ sterilization can be found in their ready acceptance of the Prohibition Act in 1919. [...] Both of these laws were passed without any significant opposition. [...] Both of these acts had a similar objective: the strengthening of the new nation's existence" by assertion of tight social controls over individual actions.[56] Alcohol consumption was believed to be threatening

56. Ibid., p. 247.

the cohesiveness and prospects for the future success of the Finnish economy and society; it was similar to the perceived national threat posed by growing numbers of "inferior" offspring of the many sexually active "unfit." The Nordic historic experiences of temperance and eugenics offer one more warning that actions described by leading scientists as necessary to the scientific management of society may raise critical issues outside the competence of "science" alone.

Dealing with such revealed limitations of science will be a key element in the rethinking of the social democratic project, as it commenced in the Nordic world in the 1980s. The Nordic history of the twentieth century raises a fundamental question, thus far unanswered: if not in economics and science, what is the source of the core human values of the Nordic world that necessarily transcend economics and science?

CHAPTER 12

Implicit Lutheranism: The Religion of Nordic Social Democracy

As discussed in previous chapters, Nordic scholars have been acknowledging more frequently in recent years that strong value assumptions underlie the Nordic welfare state. In 2005, for example, an edited book collection appeared on *Normative Foundations of the Welfare State: The Nordic Experience*. The Norwegian editors, Nanna Kildal and Stein Kuhnle, write that "the current external and internal challenges to the moral structures of welfare states have given normative analyses and normative theory in welfare research a more important role than has so far been the case" in the Nordic countries. They recall that in the past "normative analyses did not swell the ranks of welfare research publications during the Nordic 'golden age' of public welfare expansion" from the 1950s to the 1970s. In more recent years, however, "publications on welfare issues have been increasingly raising questions about the norms and values that are embedded in welfare policies." This was becoming more urgent in the twenty-first century because in the "assessment of several minor and larger, more or less incremental or casual, [proposed] welfare reforms during recent decades, studies of the more or less hidden governing values and principles in welfare policies are crucial for any interpretations, justifications or rejections" of new welfare initiatives.[1]

As Kildal and Kuhnle acknowledge, in the past key values underlying Nordic social democracy and the welfare state were thus often "hidden." In part, these values may have simply seemed so obvious, and were so taken for granted, that the designers of the Nordic social

1. Kildal and Kuhnle, "Introduction," pp. 2-3.

democratic states felt little need to identify them explicitly, let alone to debate them publicly. It was in a way like Christianity in medieval Europe, when Christian assumptions pervaded society and were simply taken without further discussion as fundamental truths of the world by the great majority of people. In the twentieth century, the individual and social values underlying social democracy were similarly taken widely in the Nordic world as fundamental truths requiring little or no further identification or justification. As examined in Chapter 9, the most important value assumption was a modern faith in the transcendent power of economic progress to remake the world for the better, taking the place of the transcendent saving powers of the traditional Lutheran God.

Here again, however, times have been changing. The late British Anglican vicar Edward Bailey launched a movement in the 1970s to study what he labelled as "implicit religion" – a term he preferred to the more familiar "secular religion" that he saw as actually an oxymoron. As interest spread in his efforts, he founded the Centre for the Study of Implicit Religion and Contemporary Spirituality in 1995, began publishing the journal *Implicit Religion* in 1998, and held annual meetings in England for many years where international scholars with related interests assembled.[2] Partly due to Bailey's efforts, there is now a chair in implicit religion at Cambridge University. He wrote in 2012 that there is much to be gained by recognizing the presence of actual religions in modern life whose tenets are mainly expressed in hidden and thus implicit ways. Hence, as Bailey states, we may advance significantly our understanding of modern society if we "apply something of what we now know about [traditional] religious life, to ordinary secular life," where actual religion is often still powerfully present in newly implicit ways.[3]

Yet the strong tradition in the social sciences in the twentieth century of aiming for "value-free" analysis has proven a significant obstacle to careful research on the implicit religious foundations of the

2. See Bailey, "Implicit Religion: A Bibliographical Introduction,"; Bailey, *Implicit Religion in Contemporary Society*; Bailey, *Implicit Religion*; Bailey, "Implicit Religion" (2009); and Bailey, "Implicit Religion" (2010).

3. Bailey, "'Implicit Religion?': What Might That Be?," p. 196.

Nordic welfare state. To study the founding sources and evolution of such foundational implicit beliefs is to engage in a form of theological analysis.[4] With the exceptions of some anthropologists, psychologists and a few sociologists, social scientists typically have lacked experience in the study of how the values of a society are formed, changed and maintained.[5] When they do take up value questions, they typically seek to identify the substantive content of "given" values, and to correlate such existing values statistically with certain socioeconomic outcomes. They generally tread cautiously, however, in addressing anything relating to the value dynamics of a given society, as to the manner that new beliefs develop in actual human minds. The obstacles have been further magnified when the values are found in modern developed nations and are derived from implicit religions that outwardly deny being forms of religion. For much of the twentieth century, social science did not take religion seriously, believing that the role of religion in modern society was fading and might well disappear altogether in the longer – or maybe even shorter – run.

In the *Normative Foundations of the Welfare State*, except in a chapter by Bo Strath, the subject of the possible large importance of religion thus seldom comes up. It is mostly taken for granted that the key values underlying the welfare state are secular values such as "equality" and "universalism," which are not derived from religion. Remarkably in light of the central role of Lutheran religion in shaping Nordic culture, governance and religion for many centuries, the historical fact of this pervasive Lutheran presence is barely recognized in the book (again, with the Strath chapter excepted). There are no entries for "Martin Luther" or "Lutheranism" in what is generally a comprehensive and detailed index.

4. See Nelson, "What is 'Economic Theology'."

5. A recent major exception is Deirdre McCloskey. See McCloskey, *The Bourgeois Virtues*; McCloskey, *Bourgeois Dignity*; and McCloskey, *Bourgeois Equality*.

A Case Study in Nordic Implicit Lutheranism

In another example of the continuing blind spot of surprisingly many Nordic social scientists when it comes to religion, it was still possible in 2013 for three Norwegian political scientists, Nik Brandal, Oivind Bratberg and Dag Einar Thorsen, to write an intellectual history of Nordic social democracy, beginning with developments in the nineteenth century, and include only a brief mention of Nordic religion and essentially nothing about the influence of Lutheranism itself. Ironically, their book, *The Nordic Model of Social Democracy*, is best seen as itself a strong religious statement, in this case of an implicit Lutheranism that is the actual religion of twentieth-century social democracy (or one could also speak of this faith as a "secular religion" which in common usage – whether the term is an oxymoron or not – has come to have almost the same meaning as "implicit religion").[5] Indeed, the neglect of traditional Lutheranism as an important contributor to the rise of social democracy is likely deliberate (if unconscious), a way effectively of saying that social democracy is a modern belief system that has left behind the old ignorance, biases and other failings of traditional Lutheranism. Since the religion of social democracy seeks the secular salvation of the world in "progress," it strengthens the faith to assert that the forward march of progress extends to matters of foundational belief as well – that social democracy is based on the newly objective, scientific values of the modern age.

Brandal et al. do acknowledge that, although they now disavow such thinking themselves, there was often a large element of "socialist utopianism" in the early history of social democracy.[6] This was partly a reflection of the significant Marxist influence in the early twentieth century. The class struggle was said by many social democrats to be leading to a perfect world under a state of true communism; it would be heaven on earth, a secularization of longstanding Christian millennial hopes and expectations. Indeed, Luther in his own

5. Brandal, Bratberg and Thorsen, *The Nordic Model of Social Democracy*. 6. Ibid., pp. 107, 180.

6. Ibid., pp. 107, 180.

time had been firmly convinced that he was living in the last days before Christ's coming to earth. Four hundred years later, Marxism created its own millennial expectations among the communist faithful, who were equally as hopeful with respect to the near-term prospects of a new heaven on earth.

Marxism was far from unique, however, in promising a path to a new heaven on earth, as described above in Chapter 9. Nordic social democracy was one of a number of "economic religions" of the twentieth century that expected the perfection of human existence not so very far in the future (John Maynard Keynes once optimistically said it might be as few as 100 years). They often differed on the actual best means of achieving the necessary rapid economic progress – the capitalist or socialist route, for example – but they were all sure that any abolition of economic scarcity would mean a radical transformation in the human condition for the better. Such a transformation would go far beyond the material conditions of human existence to drastically increase overall happiness, raise ethical behavior, ensure justice and advance other nonmaterial – and ultimately more important – aspects of society.

As they express this faith, Brandel et al. thus write that for both left and right "ends of the political spectrum, it is imperative that the economy, by historical necessity, constitutes the driving force behind societal developments" towards a much better future. Social democrats agreed on the central social importance of economic progress but differed from some other social movements as to whether such progress was historically inevitable. Rather, they believed that "democratically elected authorities could and should regulate the economy, in order to create an improved society and a better world."[7] The patient skillful practice of economic democracy would be an essential element in eventually arriving at a future Nordic heaven on earth.

In the early twenty-first century, admittedly it is no longer fashionable to profess outright "utopian" expectations explicitly; for true believers today, it is required that they express their highest hopes in

7. Brandal, Bratberg and Thorsen, *The Nordic Model of Social Democracy*, p. 183.

more cautious language. Brandel et al. thus warn that, given the chastening lessons of the horrors of European history of the first half of the twentieth century, Nordic social democrats today should be careful to avoid the earlier mistakes, when many people tended "to err on the side of naivete rather than cynicism" – and thus eventually endangered their own credibility.[8]

An Implicit Utopianism

Instead of the explicit utopianism of the early twentieth century, Brandal et al. recommend that social democrats today should present themselves as "moderate optimists who – in spite of everything – believe that it is possible to work systematically for a better world in gradual steps, thinking through how the world works at the moment, and how it gradually could be improved and better organized" over perhaps a long time. It nevertheless remains fundamental that "the social democratic perception of the world is one of continuous progress," even if there is no longer a well-defined specific end state to the progressive advance of history. Yet, writing in 2013, Brandel et al. find that since World War II, empirically, there is "no doubt that the world is a better place [...] as a result of systematic and consistent work for a better future." We can expect to continue to advance "basic values that point out the direction in which we ought to be headed. The repeated insistence on democracy and decent living conditions for all regardless of status and background is perhaps the clearest example" of such basic social democratic values whose pursuit will – unfortunately more slowly than was once expected – transform the world.[9]

As Brandel et al. sum up their 2013 social democratic vision for the future, "war, dictatorship, poverty and hunger are evils which will continue to be sources of human misery for the foreseeable future. But the struggle against these evils has merely just begun." Here they agree with Martin Luther, who also saw the world filled with evil forces. For Brandal et al., however, it will not be a Christian God who will come to

8. Ibid., p. 122.

9. Ibid., pp. 122-123.

earth to save us from sin. Rather, the Nordic world itself offers inspiring examples of the success of a modern "progressive movement" in realizing such goals of curbing sinfulness in the world through patient economic advancement. As they elaborate, "progressive ideas have been met with fierce resistance and great obstacles before." But there is no reason to abandon hope now; "the development of welfare states and democratic citizenship rights in Northern Europe in the years after the Second World War" – the years of Nordic social democratic political dominance – offer "a powerful reminder that people can through peaceful [democratic] means change their own lives and the world for the better, even under quite unfavorable circumstances.[10]

Brandal et al. consider that an important task for social democrats today is thus to spread the progressive word of these past Nordic successes to create a new basis for fundamental improvement in the human condition throughout the rest of the world. We should all have a confident faith that the continuing advancement of economic growth and other progressive forces will eventually triumph everywhere. Indeed, the encouragement and support for such a global progressive faith will itself be a necessary element in the long-term success of the progressive cause. Without this faith, it would be impossible to sustain on a worldwide basis the same kind of solidarity that has been so critical to the Nordic successes of social democracy. Indeed, at times Brandel et al. come surprisingly close to suggesting that the progressive heaven on earth will be attained "by faith alone." Without deep faith in its values and methods, the social democratic cause is hopeless; with faith, the future is assured. This is another way in which the progressive god of the twentieth century still resembles the God of Martin Luther 500 years ago.

As a key element of their implicit religion, Brandel et al. thus see it as the mission of social democracy to spread its values and truths around the world, offering the Nordic countries as an inspiring example. As they write, social democracy is "an *international* movement because it believes that its most basic ideas and demands are of a uni-

10. Ibid., pp. 123, 116.

versal nature," like Christianity before it. As a result, its "values therefore ought to be equally appreciated across the globe," far beyond the Nordic countries themselves. This reflects the social democratic conviction "that solidarity across borders, and between different people and cultures, is a necessary precondition for the development of a better and more peaceful world." Although the final goal is a true international community and solidarity of all peoples everywhere – where divisions among nations can be abolished – the practical realities today mean that social democrats have "accepted and adopted the nation state as a useful and indeed necessary arena for the exercise [and spread] of democracy in the modern world."[11]

The long-term objective is nevertheless supranational and intergovernmental cooperation among all nations – something like a radically improved and transformed United Nations. History has shown that nationalism all too easily leads to gross excesses that have been among the leading evils of modern history. At this point it becomes apparent that, despite their disavowals, an implicit utopianism actually lies behind the hopes of Brandal et al. for what would be the arrival of a future new heaven on earth.

Here again, the Nordic social democratic mission to save the whole world is heir to the Lutheran heritage of the Nordic countries. Indeed, not only Lutheranism but all of Christianity believes that its message offers universal truths that must be spread across the whole earth. The goal in Christianity is not to save the nation state but collectively all the people of the world. It shares this missionary goal with Islam – another Abrahamic religion – but otherwise this has not been typical of the major religions of history. China, for example, has never exhibited such a powerful drive to perfect the rest of the world in a Chinese mold. In the modern age, the missionary tradition of Christianity would be absorbed by new implicit forms of Christianity such as Marxism, socialism and capitalism – and in the Nordic countries by an implicit Lutheranism as preached in the new state church of social democracy. As Brandel et al. now proclaim, "the goal of implement-

11. Ibid., p. 109.

ing human rights as a practical reality across the globe is a logical continuation of the struggle fought by social democrats in Western countries, who have never believed that only some people deserve to enjoy the fruits of liberty, while others should remain in servitude."[12] The triumph of social democracy, in other words, will do what earlier Christians traditionally saw as happening one day – that Christ will come to earth again to save us all from our sins.

Social Democracy: The New Lutheran State Church

In the modern age, a new secular source of state legitimacy came about: revolutionary triumph in society, as characterized most importantly by the French Revolution and the Russian Revolution. It was closer to a Lutheran model of political legitimacy in that the very existence of state power and its successful exercise now justified the state itself. The success of a secular revolution thus was not to be seen as a matter of crass private or other selfish interests prevailing by conquest. Rather, as in both the French and Russian revolutions, the struggle was portrayed in radical utopian terms. Luther had said that Princes were chosen by God, however difficult this idea might be to comprehend in practice. Revolutionary triumph for the revolutionaries themselves meant that they must be creating a new state chosen by their secular god to advance the forces of good in the world, taking large steps towards heaven on earth under divine inspiration. Luther himself felt that way about his own role in freeing Christianity from Roman corruption and in setting the Reformation in motion.

The question of how this could be confidently predicted, however, was essentially mystical. Indeed, it would have to reflect the workings of some powerful hidden force for good – some kind of an implicit god. In Marxism, for example, this divine guidance was somehow mysteriously provided by the laws of economic history, a secular replace-

12. Ibid., p. 112.

ment for the Christian God. Earlier there had been Christian faith in God; for Marxists there would now be faith in History. For Luther, it was also a matter of faith that a Christian God had intended that the Princes and their governance would serve a Lutheran God's purposes, as social democrats would later come to have faith in the god of Economic Progress in the Nordic countries. As noted previously, political scientist Karen Anderson would thus write that in the case of the Swedish social democratic welfare state in the twentieth century, it represented a modern form of "church as nation."[13]

Since they give almost no attention to this interpretation in their 2013 book, one can assume that Brandal et al. would be skeptical about any such characterization of the Nordic social democratic state. Yet their own descriptions of the workings of Nordic social democracy offer close parallels to the traditional Lutheran state church of history. The Nordic welfare state, as they emphasize, is based on a high level of "social cohesion." Its success "does not require homogeneity" of "ethnic or cultural" groups in society, "but it does depend on a shared sense of community" of some powerful kind.[14] Brandal et al. rule out the Calvinist vision of a community like that described by Adam Smith, of individuals held together in the mutual pursuit of their own interests that nevertheless works as if guided by a powerful "invisible hand" (the implicit God of Smith) for the common good. In the Nordic world, rather than the Calvinist autonomy of the individual and skepticism of state authority, one finds the Lutheran strong sense of a common social identity that brings the citizens of the social democratic states together to form a single national community. For social democrats, its new faith in a new modern god of Science and Economics fulfills the requirement for a shared body of fundamental beliefs about the world that, as Brandal et al. say, must go beyond mere "cultural" features of the society. That is to say, it must represent a deeper – in essence a religious – form of collectively shared truth among the citizens of the Nordic nations.

13. Anderson, "The Church as Nation?," p. 229.

14. Brandal, Bratberg and Thorsen, *The Nordic Model of Social Democracy*, pp. 159, 174, 151, 174.

The overall guiding ethos of the social democratic state church, as Brandel et al. describe it, is one of "universality" and "proportionality." Universality means that the state is concerned, as the Lutheran ethic prescribes, with ensuring the welfare of all its citizens, rich and poor alike. In the Nordic welfare state this means that the state recognizes, for example, a basic moral obligation to "take care of the non-productive members of society" through a wide-ranging provision of social services "through kindergartens, schools, retirement homes, and [other] social benefits" such as health care, recreational facilities and higher education – necessary elements of a good life for all the citizens of the state. In the Lutheran ethic, a calling affirms the biblical Golden Rule, as it is here transposed into a secular setting. At the same time, the principle of proportionality, also found in the Lutheran ethic, means that "the broadest shoulders should carry the heavier burden."[15] Nordic generosity does not extend to tolerance of slackers, as would in fact endanger the very existence of the social democratic state.

University of Helsinki historian Bo Strath has been among those scholars who have been most explicit about the central role of Lutheranism in the rise of the social democratic state. Strath writes in 2005 that "there was in Scandinavia a tension between corporatist/collectivist and individualist ideas of social organization," a tension that could be traced as far back as tensions in the thinking of Martin Luther (and earlier Christians as well). In the nineteenth century, "the Lutheran and popular chain in political culture merged and formed a parish community, which later in the nineteenth century became the nucleus of the secular communes." Strath explains that in the Nordic countries in the twentieth century, it was a tension that newly "provoked political pragmatism. A good illustration is the transformation of the Lutheran state churches in the direction of *folk* churches by the social democrats in the 1930s."[16]

15. Ibid., pp. 146, 163, 146.

16. Strath, "The Normative Foundations of the Scandinavian Welfare States in Historical Perspective," pp. 45, 43.

For Strath, this transformation in the first decades of the twentieth century pragmatically blended traditional Lutheran, new liberal and older agrarian elements of Nordic society with working-class viewpoints to evolve into what can be described as "social democracy as a continuation/transformation of Lutheranism and parochial political culture." This was in contrast to the sharp "divorce between church and state in Catholic countries like France and Italy." It also differed from Germany, where historically "the Lutheran churches [...] fulfilled little of the potential" to advance individual liberties that was "inherent in Luther's thoughts," as would be reflected in the more authoritarian character of the German Lutheran state church in the late nineteenth and early twentieth centuries.[17]

Perhaps the fullest acknowledgment of this relationship is offered by the Danish historian Uffe Ostergard in a 2011 article, "Lutheranism, Nationalism and the Universal Welfare State." As Ostergard writes, in the traditional Nordic Lutheran state church "as the Christian authority, the king was not only responsible for his subjects' secular well being but also for the salvation of their souls. He could not leave this to the church but had to, together with the church, take part in the upbringing of the population to become true Christian people" – much as the Nordic social democratic state today assumes the educational responsibility of bringing up the citizenry in its fundamental beliefs and values. Similarly, in earlier times the Nordic "state and the church became completely interwoven through what without exaggeration might be termed a Lutheran royal church similar to the princely led churches [of Germany] and the Anglican Church" in England.[18]

The administrative structure of the traditional Lutheran state church had the King at the highest level responsible for all areas of faith and governance across the Nordic nation, leaving the actual administration not only of religious but many secular matters to the Lu-

17. Ibid., pp. 47, 44.

18. Østergåard, "Lutheranism, Nationalism and the Universal Welfare State, " pp. 87, 89.

theran clergy of the local parish, and thus bypassing any large intermediate role for the noble land-owning class that in any case had always been weak in the Nordic countries. Besides religious education, the local Lutheran church was directly responsible for the administration of general education, poor relief, the regulation of marriage and other family affairs, the keeping of population and other records and other such practical affairs of state.

This form of governmental organization has been maintained with remarkable fidelity into the administration of the Nordic social democratic state in the twentieth century, as it has occupied the former position of the Lutheran state church. As Ostergard writes, the historic "relationship between church and state in the Nordic countries is of great importance in explaining the fact that it is precisely in the Nordic countries that a [national] welfare state with universal rights" has been created in which the manner of exercise of these rights has been "administered locally through the municipalities [that have] come into being" for this purpose. In other words, "in order to understand the origins of these locally administered but centrally governed societies and their importance for the institutions of the universal welfare state we have to investigate the Reformation as a revolution from above in Denmark-Norway-Iceland and Sweden-Finland in the first third of the sixteenth century," whose organizational and other consequences are still with us today.[19]

In his teachings, Luther had, as Ostergard comments, put a great "emphasis [...] on the parishioners' role and the direct relationship between each individual and God." Unlike in the Roman Catholic Church, each individual should read the Bible, attend church where sermons would be preached (not as authoritative truth but to stimulate further thought), meet in religious discussion groups with other church members and otherwise develop the basis of knowledge necessary to form his or her own religious understanding and find his or her own path to a true faith in God. Luther might have violated

19. Ibid., p. 86.

20. Ibid., p. 89.

this teaching himself in practice in his sense of having been divinely chosen to reform Christianity and in his commitment to absolute state authority, but in principle for Luther no human being could prescribe religious truth for all – at least no-one but Jesus. As a result, unlike the Catholic world, in traditional Nordic Lutheran societies the local "clergymen did not occupy a privileged position as a social, holy class but were rather technical experts in the organization of church services and the details of the Holy Scriptures. Their role was to be preachers, not intermediaries between the public and God," leaving the individual "parishioners much more latitude and they became the principle institution in the Church."[20]

In the social democratic state church of the twentieth century, the relationship of citizenry and state followed the traditional Lutheran model. The new "technical experts" would be drawn from the social sciences, and they would teach the scientifically correct path of economic progress that would bring about the salvation of the world. The social democratic commitment to democracy in the twentieth century drew directly upon the legacy of the large role historically played by the parishioners in the governance of the Lutheran parish. As Ostergard comments, "the strong position of the parishioners is illustrated by the fact that right from the start (in principle, at least), they were supposed to choose the clergymen while the church was expected to select candidates to be appointed as bishops."[21]

While Luther early on taught church democracy in principle, this conflicted with his message not much later of the authority of the Lutheran Prince over the Lutheran state church. This was perhaps Luther's greatest contradiction of all and may have been the reason why Lutheranism never spread across the world as Calvinism did. The distinguished British political historian Quentin Skinner wrote in 1978 that "the political theories of the early Lutherans played a vital role in helping to legitimate the emerging absolutism monarchies of northern Europe." As a real-world institution, the Lutheran church had no

21. Ibid., p. 89.

power independent of its royal sponsor and defender. As a result, there was no easy way to interpret Luther as saying anything other than that "even tyrants rule by divine right, and that even when they do manifest wrong it must still be blasphemous to oppose them."[22] This legacy of Luther would not be finally overcome until the Second Reformation in the Nordic world in the nineteenth century, setting the stage for a "reformed" (and eventually secularized) Lutheranism that provided the foundations for mid-twentieth-century social democracy.

Skinner explains that such autocratic elements of Luther's thought and action were rejected much earlier by Calvinism, most importantly for the history of the world by English Puritans and their fellow North American Puritans.[23] Calvinism from the beginning was more consistent in putting into practice the powerful democratizing implications and commitment to take the necessary steps to better the world according to God's expectations. Writing about the great worldwide historic significance of Calvinism, Ernst Troeltsch, a leading German theologian and close friend of Max Weber, explained in 1912 that:

> The great ideas of the separation of Church and State, toleration of different Church societies alongside of one another, the principle of Voluntaryism in the formation of these Church-bodies, the (at first, no doubt, only relative) liberty of conviction and opinion in all matters of world-view and religion. Here are the roots of the old liberal theory of the inviolability of the inner personal life by the State, which was subsequently extended to more outward things; here is brought about the end of the medieval idea of civilisation, and coercive Church-and-State civilisation gives place to individual civilisation free of Church direction. The idea is at first religious. Later, it becomes secularized.... But its real foundations are laid in the English Puritan Revolution. The momentum of its religious impulse opened the way for modern freedom.[24]

22. Skinner, *The Foundations of Modern Political Thought: Volume 2, The Age of Reformation*, p. 73.

23. See Woodberry, "The Missionary Roots of Liberal Democracy."

24. Troeltsch, *Protestantism and Progress*, pp. 125-126.

Ostergard thus observes that in studying the consequences of the Protestant Reformation for "national identity, church and welfare schemes and state and nation building," it is important "to distinguish between Protestantism in general and Lutheranism in particular." Ostergard considers that Max Weber's writings on the role of the Protestant ethic in the development of capitalism and other matters are "exemplary" and have "been tremendously fruitful" but it will be important to keep in mind that, as this book has similarly argued, "the Protestantism that Weber studied was Calvinism" and that the Nordic implications of the Protestant ethic will be different because its citizens, as "Lutherans, [...] think differently from Calvinists." That is to say, rather than a Calvinist ethic, the Nordic countries have been guided over the course of their history by a Lutheran ethic.

In summary, Ostergard concludes that "Luther's teachings laid the ground for the modern understanding of society, which in the very long run resulted in mass democracy and the welfare state" – which in the Nordic countries was found in its social democratic version. It is therefore wrong to think that the main explanation for the development of Nordic social democracy is as "a translator of an international socialism" to the particular circumstances of the Nordic world. Given the fading in the twentieth century of traditional Christianity, however, it was necessary to translate the language and institutions of traditional Lutheranism into newly disguised "modern" forms, since a new way of expressing old religious truths could now succeed only in implicit forms. In Denmark, therefore, one finds its "welfare state is a result of secularized Lutheranism in national garment."[25]

Conclusion

The fact that Nordic social democratic religion could only be expressed implicitly has held back the level of Nordic discussion of the full political and moral philosophy – the theology – of social democracy.

25. Ibid., pp. 89, 93.

This fact may be one reason why the Nordic countries have found it difficult to deal with immigration from Muslim countries and to understand the exact sources of the resulting cultural tensions. The Nordic elites have taken it for granted that the "secular values" of social democracy are universally valid. It has thus been disconcerting to find that Muslim minorities have not easily assimilated to these values, even those second-generation Muslims born and educated in the Nordic countries themselves (a few of whom have turned to radical Islamic beliefs that their elders would have spurned). But such problems might become more comprehensible if social democracy is understood to be an implicit and thus disguised Lutheranism. Perhaps to ask a believing Muslim to assimilate to Nordic social democracy and its core beliefs is really to ask this person to convert from Islam to Lutheranism.

EPILOGUE

Since 1980: The Nordic Crisis of Social Democracy

The United States has been experiencing a crisis of faith with respect to its own political and economic institutions that began well before the economic crisis of 2008 and the Presidential election of 2016. In polls, the percentage of Americans who say they have confidence in government to do the right thing has declined precipitously since the 1960s – partly the result of foreign debacles such as the Vietnam and Iraq wars but also of the polarization and gridlock that has increasingly afflicted domestic policy making since the 1990s. In 2005, a leading American journalist, Robert Kaiser (former managing editor of the *Washington Post* from 1991 to 1998, and associate editor and senior correspondent of the *Post* from 1998 to 2014), decided to look outside the United States to find a country that was doing better. The idea was to make an intensive visit and study over the course of a few weeks to try to discover the secrets of its national success, perhaps thereby providing some good role models from which the United States might learn something useful. Among all the countries in the world, Kaiser picked Finland as the most interesting and promising country that "worked."[1] He described his findings in a series of newspaper articles and blog posts that appeared in the *Washington Post* and on the internet between May 2005 and August 2005. If it had not been Finland, it might well have been another Nordic country, so his observations are relevant to other Nordic countries as well.

1. Kaiser is not alone in offering Finland as a potentially useful model for the United States. Anu Partanen was born in Finland and moved to the United States to be with her husband. Based on her experiences there, she authored a 2016 book explaining how Americans should learn from Finland to improve their own country. See Anu Partanen, *The Nordic Theory of Everything*.

A View from America

As he wrote in the introduction to this series, in 2005 "Finland just might be the world's most interesting country that Americans know least about. It has the best school system in the world, some of the most liberated women (the president is female), more cell phones per capita than anyone else, one of the world's best high-tech companies (Nokia), remarkable information technology of many kinds, great music from rock and jazz to classical." There was also an inspiring feeling of national self-confidence: "The Finns are proud of their generous welfare state, which provides, among much else, free health care and free education at every level." As is often said of all the Nordic countries, a main reason they are so widely admired is that they are seen as having been the most successful at achieving a modern society. As Kaiser thus reported, "We will try to figure out how the Finns have been so successful in so many different ways and why Finland appears to be one of the most modern and most adaptable societies anywhere." He also noted that any comparisons would have to take account of some large differences compared with the United States, especially the fact that "Finland is quite big, the size of Kansas and Iowa combined, but sparsely populated – 5.2 million souls, or about 10 percent smaller than metropolitan Washington, D.C."[2] So generalizing from a nation of around 5 million people to one of more than 300 million would not be easy.

In one of his first reports back to his American readers titled "Modest Finland," Kaiser wrote that for all their successes the Finns rarely bragged about it, reflecting an important side of their national culture. As he wrote,

> Finland has largely reinvented itself over the last generation. Its educational system, economy, technology and sense of itself have all been transformed. This is change on a scale rarely seen in the world; only China, perhaps, has under-

2. Kaiser, "Introduction to Finland Diary."

> gone a similar transformation in such a short period of time. But the Finns have not transformed their national personality, which remains pretty much intact. Sometimes it is helpful to the modernization going on here so intensely. For example, Finnish egalitarianism, a strong force, is ideally suited to a remarkable national education system that fosters what really seems to be equal opportunity for all, not just the lucky or privileged. On the other side of the coin, Finnish honesty and pragmatism combined with a quite profound shyness are ill-suited to the kind of salesmanship that America has made a hallmark of the modern global economy. Finns don't know how to hustle a customer. They don't seem very good at exaggerating their own successes or prospects, either.[3]

In other reports Kaiser delved in greater detail into the Finnish educational system, explaining that it is "very likely the best on Earth. Superb schools symbolize the modern transformation of Finland, a poor and agrarian nation half a century ago." He noted that "Finland finishes first in the Program for International Student Assessment (PISA) exams that test 15-year-olds in all of the world's industrial democracies." The high quality of education was an important contributor to Finnish successes in other areas: "Finland also finishes at or near the top in many global comparisons of economic competitiveness: Internet usage, environmental practices and more. Finland, where the modern cell phone was largely invented, has more cell phones per capita than any other nation – nearly 85 per 100 citizens."[4]

Although he covered many areas of Finnish life, one subject that Kaiser had little to say about was religion. This was partly because the many Finns he spoke with did not say much about religion. He asked a well-known Finnish philosopher and writer, Pekka Himanen, about the place of "prayer in schools, and the separation of church and state generally? Does religion play any role in public life?" Himanen re-

3. Kaiser, "Modest Finland."

4. Kaiser, "Focus on Education Helps Finns Build a Showcase Nation."

sponded that in Finland there is "no prayer in school. Finnish politicians don't refer to religion. You would never hear a Finnish politician say 'God bless Finland.' Finns want these things to be separated."[5] Reflecting a widespread way of thinking in Finland today, Himanen was saying in 2005 that religion in Finland is a private affair, everyone is freely entitled to their own private religious beliefs, but religion has essentially no role to play in deciding important matters of public policy and administration or other matters of significant concern to the Finnish state. Although religion had been largely excluded from public affairs, later in the series Kaiser did comment that Finland seemed to benefit from the inherited social capital of "a strong Lutheran work ethic, combined with a powerful sense of probity" that had deep roots in Finnish history.[6]

The recent Finnish and Nordic scholarship tracing the Lutheran roots of social democracy, as described earlier in this book, thus had yet to reach the wider Finnish public or even much of its educated elite (and still has not today). Himanen was seemingly blind to the fact that his own social democratic views might constitute an implicit religion, or even that such a thing as an implicit (or "secular") religion might be an actual form of religion that in many aspects might closely reflect an original Christian source. Kaiser was unlikely to ask about such matters because the American elite classes themselves have attitudes about religion similar to those so commonly found in Finland today – despite the writings as long ago as 1967 of the American sociologist Robert Bellah about the central importance of an American "civic religion," one that closely reflected Christian sources, to the national history.[7] Like much of the American elite, Kaiser is himself in many ways a true believer in the early twentieth-century American "progressive" religion, which anticipated the later arrival of social democracy in the Nordic countries in the 1930s and which also typically saw itself as leaving religion behind.

5. Kaiser, "Introduction to Finland Diary." See Castells and Himanen, *The Information Society and the Welfare State*.

6. Kaiser, "In Finland's Footsteps."

7. Bellah, "Civil Religion in America."

On returning to the United States, Kaiser wrote a final summary article for the *Washington Post* presenting his overall conclusions about Finland based on his three-week visit and extensive conversations and reading materials. He found a large "difference between what the Finns call a social democracy and our society. Finland is a leading example of the northern European view that a successful, competitive society should provide basic social services to all its citizens at affordable prices or at no cost at all. This isn't controversial in Finland; it is taken for granted." For Kaiser, who considered himself "a patriotic American, [...] the Finns present a difficult challenge: If we Americans are so rich and so smart, why can't we treat our citizens as well as the Finns do."[8]

Less favorably at least in typical American terms, as Kaiser wrote, "Finns live in smaller homes than Americans and consume a lot less. They spend relatively little on national defense, though they still have universal male conscription, and it is popular. Their per capita national income is about 30 percent lower than ours." The price of the Finnish social democratic state is that "Finns pay considerably higher taxes – nearly half their national income is taken in taxes, while Americans pay about 30 percent on average to federal, state and local governments." Overall, Kaiser asked himself, what "should we be learning from Finland" as Americans? As he wrote, this "question occurred to me repeatedly as I traveled around Finland this summer. Americans could easily get used to the sense of well-being that Finns get from their welfare state, which has effectively removed many of the tangible sources of anxiety that beset our society." But there would be no real chance that the United States could simply turn itself into another Finland, he concluded, because "too much of Finnish reality depends on uniquely Finnish circumstances. It is ethnically and religiously homogeneous." Another large national asset is that "Finns have extraordinary confidence in their political class and public offi-

8. Kaiser, "In Finland's Footsteps."

9. Ibid.

cials. Corruption is extremely rare."[9] Finns have a sense of social solidarity that does not exist in the United States. As would be the case for most American observers today too, it seemingly never occurred to him that he might be reporting the differences between a Finnish society shaped by a Lutheran ethic, and an American society shaped by a Calvinist ethic.

Instead, he saw things with little or no reference to religion; in the United States "ours is a society driven by money, blessed by huge private philanthropy, cursed by endemic corruption and saddled with deep mistrust of government and other public institutions. Finns have none of those attributes." Another large cultural difference is that Finns do not "tune in to American individualism. Groupthink seems to be fine with most Finns; conformity is the norm, risk-taking is avoided – a problem now, when entrepreneurs are so needed. I was bothered by a sense of entitlement among many Finns, especially younger people." But Kaiser nevertheless concluded that "if Finland can't be a blueprint for us, it can be an inspiration. Education struck me as the area where Americans could most profit by learning from Finland." Another area where "I think we could learn [is] from Finns' confidence that they can shape their own fate."[10]

Finns speak of "the Finnish National Project, an effort involving much of the country, and nearly all of its elites, to make the country more educated, more agile and adaptive, more green, more fair and more competitive in a fast-changing global economy." Kaiser noted that the "complicated Finnish language includes the word *talkoot*, which means, roughly, 'doing work together.' It's a powerful Finnish tradition, and reflects a national sense that 'we're all in the same boat,' as numerous Finns said to me. This idea has always appealed to Americans, but in this country it has nearly always been an abstraction. Finns seem to make it real," Kaiser concluded his final article.[11]

The attraction of the Nordic countries for many Americans was revealed once again in the 2016 presidential campaign in the United States. Hilary Clinton was put under a surprisingly strong challenge

9. Ibid.
10. Ibid.
11. Ibid.

by Bernard Sanders, a Senator from Vermont who had previously run for office as a "socialist," before seeking the nomination of the Democratic Party in 2016. Writing in the *Washington Post*, Christine Emba described how older Washingtonians were surprised at the extent to which American "millennials embrace 'socialism,'" as revealed, for example, by Sanders' popularity among this group. More broadly, as she wrote, "it seems that socialism is cool" in the United States of 2016. But the term "socialism" for these millennials did not mean the old-fashioned socialism in the sense of national ownership of the means of production. Rather, as Emba commented, for millennials "'socialism' is simply shorthand for 'vaguely Scandinavian in the best way' – free health care, free education, and subsidized child care, a state that supports its citizens rather than leaving them at the mercy of impersonal corporations bent on profit."[12]

Indeed, it was not only millennials who regarded the Scandinavian nations as a model for the world. In April 2016, *The Atlantic* magazine published a long retrospective on the Obama administration as its end was nearing, based in part on new lengthy interviews with President Obama. Obama discussed his large frustrations in attempting to bring greater order and progress to an unruly world, in places such as the Middle East – and frequently the United States as well. Despite his heroic efforts, seemingly irrational forces around the world were pervasive elements of the political and economic systems of most countries. There was one large exception that stood out for Obama, however. As Jeffrey Goldberg wrote, "Obama has always had a fondness for pragmatic, emotionally constrained technocrats, telling aids, 'if only everyone could be like the Scandinavians, this would all be easy.'" Despite new strains in Nordic societies, often related to the growing presence of Muslim and other immigrants, these countries for Obama and many other Americans remained models of good governance, strong national bonds, sound values and in general the ability to live the good life.

12. Emba, "Millenials Embrace 'Socialism'."

A Crisis of Finnish and Nordic Social Democracy?

For the citizens of the Nordic countries, admittedly, this international idealization of their nations can be something of a puzzle. This is partly a result of the national modesty that is one of their most attractive features for many outsiders. But the Nordic model of social democracy has also faced increasing strains since the 1980s. The murder of prime minister Olof Palme in Sweden in 1986 was a great shock to the nation and its core national assumptions about the peaceful solidarity of its society. More recently, both Norway and Denmark have experienced disturbing incidents of terrorism.

Finland originally lagged behind the other Nordic countries in its development of social democracy, partly owing to its less developed economy in the first half of the twentieth century and also to the unique problems for many years in the second half of the twentieth century relating to its relationship with the former Soviet Union, with which it shared a long border. The high point of social democracy in Sweden might have been in the 1970s; Kaiser might have picked Sweden if he had been looking for a paragon of successful national modernization then. Danish social democracy might have peaked later but it also began to experience difficulties in the 1980s and 1990s. Norway has been a special case since the discovery of oil and gas in the North Sea in the 1970s, giving it economic advantages that the other Nordic countries do not share. In 2005, as Kaiser described it, Finland by then was commonly seen as the leading example of the modern successes achieved by Nordic social democracies.

The year 2005, however, might have been the high point for Finland; things have not gone as well since then. Its educational system remains one of the highest ranked in the world but it no longer holds the number one position. Nokia made some significant strategic errors in the mid 2000s that left it floundering as sales of the old "clamshell" cell phones were displaced by Apple, Samsung and other smartphones with internet capacity and otherwise greater versatility. With the rise of email and other new electronic methods of communications, international demand for paper has declined, causing problems for the longstanding forestry mainstay of the Finnish economy. The Finnish economy in general has grown slowly in recent years, partly reflecting the general economic problems experienced by the nations of the European Union, a main consumer of Finnish exports. Adopting the Euro – Finland is the only one of the Nordic countries to do so – has not produced the benefits expected. Indeed, there is a growing view among economists that it is a main source of the problems in the Eurozone, depriving nations of the monetary and exchange rate flexibility to address their own economic problems in their own ways.

The Nordic welfare states achieved their greatest successes in times of rapid economic growth; it was their economic successes that made the generous provisions of their welfare states practically feasible. But the high growth rates of the 1950s through the 1970s have proven difficult to sustain, requiring government cutbacks. The high level of Finnish national confidence found by Kaiser has been succeeded by new doubts, and for some even a malaise in 2016 about the future.

Finland has faced difficult economic times before, however, such as in the early 1990s following the breakup of the former Soviet Union, until then a main market for its exports. It has always pragmatically improvised solutions, and may well do so again. Rather than the current economic downturn, the greater concern for Finnish social democracy may be a series of longer term and more fundamental developments that cannot be as easily resolved. These concerns extend beyond Finland to all the Nordic countries, even including Norway to the extent that they are cultural rather than economic. Perhaps the greatest issue is the West's declining faith in economic progress – in its power to save the world, going beyond its simple ability to produce higher and higher levels of material outputs and consumption. Some environmentalists now suggest that, short of radical changes in human thinking and behavior, a future hell on earth may be just as likely as a future heaven on earth.[13]

13. See Nelson, *The New Holy Wars*, Nelson, "Environmental Religion," Nelson, "Calvinism Without God."

Traditional religious fundamentalism in many forms has been seeing a resurgence in the United States and elsewhere as the optimistic premises of the various economic religions of the modern era have increasingly been called into question. As a form of economic religion, the faith of social democracy faces the same potential crises as other economic religions – and without a strong unifying national faith, many of the institutions of the Nordic world will no longer function as well as they did in the past. A main part of the vaunted "solidarity" of the Nordic countries has been derived from the powerful shared national belief in scientific and economic progress as a true solution to the problems of the world, the replacement for the lost unifying national faith in the teachings of the Lutheran church of old.

The membership of Finland, Sweden and Denmark in the European Union (and Norway is tightly bound to the EU by many common agreements, even if it is not a member) also poses fundamental issues of a long-term character. Many of the functions of the social democratic state, especially those relating to the regulation of private markets, have been transferred partially or even entirely from the Nordic states to the EU. The Nordic world is no longer the master of its own destiny, a matter not only of pragmatic but also potentially of existential concern. If a main part of the success of the Nordic countries has been their faith in their own capacity to shape the future for the better, and the strong sense of national solidarity that has resulted, it is difficult to see how any similar sense of European-wide solidarity will emerge to replace the Nordic national versions. Again, if Nordic countries suffer a loss of national confidence, this will be more than a matter of the future public mood of the nation; it could have many adverse practical political and economic consequences. Lacking the old solidarity, the dangers of heightened levels of political opportunism among the Nordic citizenry might increase. It is not only membership in the European Union, moreover, but also the economic forces of globalization that are working in general to undermine the ability of each Nordic nation to control its own fate, again with potentially damaging national psychic consequences.

Many Nordic intellectuals are well aware of these longer term and other more fundamental concerns. In their optimistic moments, some suggest that the substitute for eroding Nordic national solidarity will be European solidarity, and even in the very long run world solidarity. Indeed, this is a core part of their social democratic faith, as examined in Chapter 12. They may be naïve, however, in their confidence that the Nordic religion of social democracy will triumph across Europe (to say nothing of the whole world). This seems all the less likely when it is recognized that social democratic religion is to such a large extent a secularization of Lutheran religion. Martin Luther had great hopes for the universal triumph of his Lutheran version of the Reformation in his own time but few would today expect that a newly formed world order will be grounded in what in reality is now a newly implicit Lutheran religion.

Other countries have their own, non-Lutheran religious histories that also continue to exert a large influence on their current thinking and the organization of their societies. Indeed, in some of these countries such as those with Catholic religious histories, Lutheranism was long seen as a mortal religious enemy for significant parts of the past five centuries. Ecumenical ideals are widely held in the Nordic world today but they may effectively assume a continuing secularization of the world based on a common set of modern values. Lutherans and Catholics may finally be able to agree but only because they have lost much of their old powerful convictions that previously set them so distinctly apart. Deep traditional religious passions had to fade before much European agreement – now based heavily on economics – was possible.

But one way or another, the powerful sense of meaning of a religion may be a human necessity. In the Nordic world that source of meaning shifted in the twentieth century from traditional Lutheranism to a newly secularized form of social democratic "Lutheranism in disguise." But if social democratic faith is now fading in the twenty-first century, where next for religion? In part, the current malaise of social democracy in the Nordic world can been seen as reflecting an inability to see any clear answer. The Nordic world is a leading case of a much wider questioning of the modern project that is taking place in a number of nations and cultures around the world at the present time.

In conclusion, the crisis of social democracy in the Nordic world today – indeed, the beliefs and institutions of the whole EU – may thus be an intellectual and religious crisis more than an economic one. Addressing the intellectual and religious dimensions of social democracy may require a willingness to come to terms with some of the illusions of social democracy, including its outward rejection of religion (in any explicit form) as a central element of public discourse. Nordic elites are ill-prepared for a national public discussion actually centered around religion. Indeed, the vocabulary for such a discussion scarcely exists. Bringing such issues and concerns relating to the future of religion of the Nordic world explicitly into the wider arena of Nordic public debate would thus be a challenging task. It is my hope that this book may be of some limited help in sorting out these fundamentally interrelated questions of religion, national identity, and governance in the Nordic world.

Bibliography

Acemoglu, Daron, James A. Robinson and Thierry Verdier, *Can't We All Be More Like Scandinavians: Asymmetric Growth and Institutions in an Interdependent World*, Cambridge, MA, MIT Economics Department, Working Paper 12–22 (August 20, 2012).

Alapuro, Risto, "Comments on Sorensen's 'On King's, Pietism and Rent-Seeking in Scandinavian Welfare States'," *Acta Sociologica* 41:4 (1998), pp. 377-378.

Alapuro, Risto, "Nordic and Finnish Modernity: A Comparison," in Arnason and Wittrock, eds., *Nordic Paths to Modernity*, pp. 191-206.

Alapuro, Risto, *State and Revolution in Finland* (Berkeley, CA: University of California Press, 1988).

Alesina, Alberto, and Paola Giulano, "Culture and Institutions," *Journal of Economic Literature* 53: 4 (December 2015), pp. 898-944.

Alvey, James E., "The Secret Natural Theological Foundation of Adam Smith's Work," *Journal of Markets and Morality* 7:2 (Fall 2004)., pp. 335-363.

Anderson, Karen M., "The Church as Nation? The Role of Religion in the Development of the Swedish Welfare State," in Van Kersbergen and Manow, eds., *Religion, Class Coalitions, and Welfare States*, pp. 210-235.

Arnason, Johann Pall, and Bjorn Wittrock, "Introduction," in Arnason and Wittrock, eds., *Nordic Paths to Modernity*, pp. 1-23.

Arnason, Johann Pall, and Bjorn Wittrock, eds., *Nordic Paths to Modernity* (Oxford: Berghahn Books, 2012).

Association of Statisticians of American Religious Bodies, *U.S. Religion Census, 2010: Religious Congregations and Membership Study* (May 2012).

Backhaus, Juergen, ed., *The Reformation: As a Pre-Condition for the Development of Capitalism* (Berlin: LIT VERLAG, 2010).

Backstrom, Anders, and Grace Davie (with Ninna Edgardh and Per Pettersson), eds., *Welfare and Religion in 21st Century Europe: Volume 1, Configuring the Connections* (Burlington, VT: Ashgate, 2009).

Backstrom, Anders, and Grace Davie, "The WREP Project: Genesis, Structure and Scope," in Backstrom and Davie, eds., *Welfare and Religion in 21st Century Europe: Volume 1.*, pp. 1-23.

Backstrom, Anders, Grace Davie, Ninna Edgardh and Per Pettersson, eds., *Welfare and Religion in 21st Century Europe: Volume 2, Gendered, Religious and Social Change* (Burlington, VT: Ashgate, 2009).

Bailey, Edward, "'Implicit Religion?': What Might That Be?" *Implicit Religion* 15:2 (2012), pp. 195-207.

Bailey, Edward, "Implicit Religion," in Peter B. Clarke, ed., *The Oxford Handbook of the Sociology of Religion* (New York: Oxford University Press, 2009).

Bailey, Edward, "Implicit Religion," *Religion* 40:4 (2010), pp. 271-278.

Bailey, Edward, "Implicit Religion: A Bibliographical Introduction," *Social Compass* 37 (1990), pp. 483-498.

Bailey, Edward, *Implicit Religion in Contemporary Society* (Kampen, Netherlands: Kok Pharos, 1997).

Bailey, Edward, *Implicit Religion: An Introduction* (London: Middlesex University Press, 1998).

Bainton, Roland, *Here I Stand: A Life of Martin Luther* (Peabody, MA: Hendrickson Publishers, 2012 – first ed. 1950).

Ballor, Jordan J., "Dietrich Bonhoeffer, The Two Kingdoms, and Protestant Social Thought Today," *La Revue FAREL* 6/7 (2011–2012), pp. 62-75.

Barnett, Victoria, "Dietrich Bonhoeffer: Opposition," United States Holocaust Memorial Museum. http://www.ushmm.org/information/exhibitions/online-features/special-focus/dietrich-bonhoeffer/opposition.

Barnett, Victoria, *For the Soul of the People: Protestant Protest Against Hitler* (New York: Oxford University Press, 1992).

Basten, Christoph, and Frank Betz, "Beyond Work Ethic: Religion, Individual and Political Preferences," *American Economic Journal: Economic Policy* 5:3 (August 2013), pp. 67-91.

Becker, Carl, *The Heavenly City of the Eighteenth-century Philosophers* (New Haven, CN: Yale University Press, 1932).

Becker, Sascha O., and Ludger Woessmann, "Was Becker Wrong?: A Human Capital Theory of Protestant Economic History," *Quarterly Journal of Economics* 124:2 (May 2009)., pp. 531-596.

Bellah, Robert N., "Civil Religion in America," *Daedalus: Journal of the American Academy of Arts and Sciences* 96:1 (1967), pp. 1-21.

Blickle, Peter, *The Revolution of 1525: The German Peasant's War from a New Perspective*, trans. by Thomas A. Brady, Jr. and H. C. Erik Midelfort (Baltimore, MD: Johns Hopkins University Press, 1981).

Blosser, Joe, "Christian Freedom in Political Economy: The Legacy of John Calvin in the Thought of Adam Smith," in Oslington, ed., *Adam Smith as Theologian*, pp. 46-60.

Brady, Thomas, and Erik Midelfort, "Introduction: Interpretations, Problems, and New Perspectives," in Blickle, *The Revolution of 1525*, pp. 3-22.

Brandal, Nik, Oivind Bratberg, and Dag Einar Thorsen, *The Nordic Model of Social Democracy* (New York: Palgrave Macmillan, 2013).

Broberg, Gunnar, and Mattias Tyden, "Eugenics in Sweden: Efficient Care," in Broberg and Roll-Hansen, *Eugenics and the Welfare State*, pp. 77-149.

Broberg, Gunnar and Nils Roll-Hansen, eds., *Eugenics and the Welfare State: Norway, Sweden, Denmark and Finland* (Lansing, MI: Michigan State University Press, 2005).

Brooks, David, "Livin' Bernie Sanders' Danish Dream," *International New York Times*, February 13–14, 2016.

Brown, Mackenzie D., ed., *Ultimate Concern: Tillich in Dialogue* (New York: Harper and Row, 1965).

Buck v. Bell, 274 U.S. 200 (1927).

Castells, Manuel, and Pekka Himanen, *The Information Society and the Welfare State: The Finnish Model* (Oxford, UK: Oxford University Press, 2002).

Castles, Frances D., "On Religion and Public Policy, Does Catholicism Make a Difference?" *European Journal of Political Research* 25:1 (1994), pp. 19-40.

Chaker, Andre Noel, *The Finnish Miracle* (Helsinki: Talentum, 2011).

Christiansen, Niels Finn, and Klaus Petersen, "The Dynamics of Social Solidarity: The Danish Welfare State, 1900–2000," *Scandinavian Journal of History* 26:3 (2001), 177-196.

Clark, Christopher, *Iron Kingdom: The Rise and Downfall of Prussia, 1600–1947* (London: Penguin Books, 2007).

Clark, Norman H., *Deliver Us From Evil: An Interpretation of American Prohibition* (New York: Norton, 1976).

Cox, Harvey, *The Market as God* (Cambridge, MA: Harvard University Press, 2016).

Dahl, Robert A., and Charles E. Lindblom, *Politics, Economics and Welfare* (Chicago: University of Chicago Press, 1976 – first ed. 1953).

Dahl, Robert A., and Charles Edward Lindblom, *Politics, Economics, and Welfare: Planning and Politico-Economic Systems Resolved into Basic Social Processes* (New York: Harper, 1953).

Dalsgaard, Matias Mol, "Community and Individuality: Grundtvigian and Kierkegaardian Protestantism in Denmark," in Hall, Korsgaard and Pedersen, eds., *Building the Nation*, pp. 300-312.

De Long, J. Bradford, "Productivity Growth, Convergence, and Welfare: Comment," *American Economic Review* 78:5 (December 1988), pp. 1138-1154.

de Tocqueville, Alexis, *The Old Regime and the French Revolution* (Garden City, NY: Doubleday, 1955 – first ed. 1856).

Dillenberger, John, ed., *Martin Luther, Selections from his Writings* (New York: Anchor Books, 1962).

Doherty, Sean, *Theology and Economic Ethics: Martin Luther and Arthur Rich in Dialogue* (Oxford, UK: Oxford University Press, 2014).

Dworkin, Ronald, *Religion Without God* (Cambridge, MA: Harvard University Press, 2013).

Economist, "A Nordic Mystery: In the World's Most Female Friendly Workplaces, Executive Suites are Still Male-Dominated," November 15, 2014.

Ebner, Alexander, "Max Weber, the Protestant Ethics, and the Sociology of Capitalist Development," in Backhaus, ed., *The Reformation*, pp. 231-255.

Edwards, Mark U., *Printing, Propaganda, and Martin Luther* (Minneapolis, MN: Fortress Press, 2005).

Eire, Carlos M. N., *Reformations: The Early Modern World, 1450–1650* (New Haven, CN: Yale University Press, 2016).

Emba, Christine, "Millenials Embrace 'Socialism,'" *Washington Post*, March 25, 2016.

Erickson, Erik H., *Young Man Luther: A Study in Psychoanalysis and History* (New York: Norton, 1958).

Esping-Anderson, Gosta, "The Making of a Social Democratic Welfare State," in Mitgeld, et al, eds. *Creating Social Democracy*, pp. 35-66.

Esping-Anderson, Gosta, *The Three Worlds of Welfare Capitalism* (Princeton, NJ: Princeton University Press, 1990).

Fogel, Robert William, *The Fourth Great Awakening and the Future of Egalitarianism* (Chicago: University of Chicago Press, 2000).

Gentile, Emilio, *Politics as Religion*, translated by George Stanton (Princeton, NJ: Princeton University Press, 2006).

Glover, Willis B., *Biblical Origins of Modern Secular Culture: An Essay in the Interpretation of Western History* (Macon, GA: Mercer University Press, 1984).

Gorski, Philip S., *The Disciplinary Revolution: Calvinism and the Rise of the State in Early Modern Europe* (Chicago: University of Chicago Press, 2003)

Grant, Madison, *The Passing of the Great Race: Or the Racial Basis of European History* (Forgotten Books, 2012 – first ed. 1916).

Gregory, Brad S., *The Unintended Reformation: How a Religious Revolution Secularized Society* (Cambridge, MA: Harvard University Press 2012).

Gronlund, Henrietta, "Between Lutheran Legacy and Economy as Religion: The Contested Roles of Philanthropy in Finland Today," paper prepared for a "Symposium on 'Holy Money,'" Collegium for Advanced Studies, University of Helsinki, Helsinki, Finland, September 15–16, 2016.

Habermas, Jürgen, "Religion in the Public Sphere," *European Journal of Philosophy* 14:1 (2006), pp. 1-25.

Hall, John A., and Ove Korsgaard, "Introduction," in Hall, Korsgaard and Pedersen, eds., *Building the Nation*, pp. 3-26.

Hall, John A., Ove Korsgaard and Ove K. Pedersen, eds., *Building the Nation: N.F.S. Grundtvig and Danish National Identity* (Montreal: McGill-Queen's University Press, 2015).

Hallberg, Peter, "History and Ethics in Pre-revolutionary Sweden," in Arnason and Wittrock, *Nordic Paths to Modernity*, pp. 111-141.

Hammar, Inger, "From Fredrika Bremer to Ellen Key: Calling, Gender and the Emancipation Debate in Sweden, 1830-1900," in Markkola, ed., *Gender and Vocation*, pp. 29-67.

Hannson, Bjorn, "The Stockholm School and the Development of Dynamic Method," in Sandelin, ed., *The History of Swedish Economic Thought*, pp. 168-213.

Harrison, Peter, "Protestantism and the Making of Modern Science," in Howard and Noll, eds., *Protestantism after 500 Years*, pp. 98-120.

Harrison, Peter, *The Bible, Protestantism and the Rise of Natural Science* (New York: Cambridge University Press, 2001).

Harwood, John, *The Vikings* (Gloucestershire, UK: The History Press, 2010).

Hays, Samuel P., *Conservation and the Gospel of Efficiency: The Progressive Conservation Movement, 1890–1920* (Cambridge, MA: Harvard University Press, 1959).

Helliwell, John F., Richard Layard and Jeffrey Sachs, eds. *World Happiness Report 2015* (New York: Sustainable Development Solutions Network, 2015).

Hendrix, Scott H., *Martin Luther* (Oxford, UK: Oxford University Press, 2010).

Hendrix, Scott H., *Martin Luther: Visionary Reformer* (New Haven, CN: Yale University Press, 2015).

Henningsen, Bernd, "The Swedish Construction of Nordic Identity," in Sorensen and Strath, eds., *The Cultural Construction of Norden*, pp. 91-120.

Hietala, Marjatta, "From Race Hygiene to Sterilization: The Eugenics Movement in Finland," in Broberg and Roll-Hansen, eds., *Eugenics and the Welfare State*, pp. 195-258.

Hillerbrand, Hans J., "The Legacy of Martin Luther," in McKim, ed., *The Cambridge Companion to Martin Luther*, pp. 227-239.

Hilson, Mary, *The Nordic Model: Scandinavia Since 1945* (London: Reaktion Books, 2008).

Hitler, Adolf, *Mein Kampf*, translated by Michael Ford (Elite Minds: 2009 [1924]).

Hope, Nicholas, *German and Scandinavian Protestantism, 1700 to 1918* (Oxford, UK: Oxford University Press, 1995).

Howard, Thomas Albert, and Mark A. Noll, eds., *Protestantism After 500 Years* (New York: Oxford University Press, 2016).

Huntington, Samuel P., *The Clash of Civilizations and the Remaking of World Order* (New York: Simon and Schuster, 2011).

Huovinen, Eero, "Doctor Communis? The Ecumenical Significance of Martin Luther's Theology," in Holger Roggelin and Scott Gustafson, eds. *Lutheranism: Legacy and Future* (West Conshohocken, PA: Infinity, 2012), pp. 136-153.

Inglehart, Ronald, and Christian Welzel, *Modernization, Cultural Change, and Democracy: The Human Development Sequence* (New York: Cambridge University Press, 2005).

Jensen, Roger, "The Formation and Identity of the Church as a Present Challenge in Norway," in Anne-Louise Erikkson, Goran Gunner and Niclas Blader, eds., *Exploring a Heritage: Evangelical Lutheran Churches in the North,* Church of Sweden Research Series 5 (Eugene, OR: Pickwick Publications, 2012).

Johannson, Egil, "The History of Literacy in Sweden," in Harvey J. Graff, Alison Mackinnon, Bengt Sandin and Ian Winchester, eds., *Understanding Literacy in its Historical Contexts* (Lund, Sweden: Nordic Academic Press, 2009), pp. 28-59.

Johnson, Paul, *Modern Times: The World from the Twenties to the Nineties*, rev. ed. (New York: Harper, 2001).

Jones, Gareth Stedman, "Religion and the Origins of Socialism," in Ira Katznelson and Gareth Stedman Jones, eds., *Religion and the Political Imagination* (Cambridge, UK: Cambridge University Press, 2010), pp. 171-189.

Juntunen, Sammeli, "Sex," in Olli-Pekka Vainio, ed., *Engaging Luther: A (New) Theological Assessment* (Eugene, OR: Cascade Books, 2010), pp. 186-209.

Jussila, Osmo, Seppo Hentila and Jukka Nevakivi, *From Grand Duchy to a Modern State: A Political History of Finland Since 1809*, trans. by David and Eva-Kaisa Arter (London: Hurst and Company, 1999).

Kaariainen, Kimmo, "Religion and State in Finland," *Nordic Journal of Religion and Society* 24:2 (2011), pp. 155-171.

Kaariainen, Kimmo, Kimmo Ketola, Nati Niemela, Harri Palmu and Hanna Salomaki, *Facing Diversity: The Evangelical Lutheran Church of Finland from 2004 to 2007*, Publication 60, Church Research Institute, Tampere, Finland (2009).

Kahl, Sigrun, "Religious Doctrines and Poor Relief: A Different Causal Pathway," in Van Keesbergen and Manow, *Religion, Class Coalitions, and Welfare States*, pp. 267-295.

Kahl, Sigrun, "The Religious Roots of Modern Poverty Policy: Catholic, Lutheran and Reformed Protestant Traditions Compared," *European Journal of Sociology* 46:1 (April 2005), pp. 91–126.

Kaiser, Robert G., "Focus on Education Helps Finns Build a Showcase Nation," *Washington Post*, May 24, 2005.

Kaiser, Robert G., "In Finland's Footsteps," *Washington Post*, August 7, 2005.

Kaiser, Robert G., "Introduction to Finland Diary," *Washington Post*, May 23, 2005.

Kaiser, Robert G., "Modest Finland," *Washington Post*, May 23, 2005.

Kalberg, Stephen, *Searching for the Spirit of American Democracy: Max Weber's Analysis of a Unique Political Culture, Past, Present and Future* (Boulder, CO: Paradigm Publishers, 2014).

Katznelson, Ira, and Gareth Stedman Jones, "Introduction: Multiple Secularities," in Katznelson and Jones, eds., *Religion and the Political Imagination* (Cambridge, UK: Cambridge University Press, 2010), pp. 1-22.

Kaufmann, D., A. Kraay and M. Matruzzi, *The Worldwide Governance Indicators: Methodology and Analytical Issues, World Bank Group* (Washington, DC: World Bank, 2010).

Kaufmann, Daniel, Aart Kraay and Massimo Mastruzzi, *Governance Matters VIII: Aggregate and Individual Governance Indicators, 1996–2008*, Policy Research Working Paper 4978 (Washington, DC: The World Bank, Development Research Group, June 2009).

Kaufmann, Franz-Xaver, "Religion and Modernization in Europe," *Journal of Institutional and Theoretical Economics* 153:1 (March 1997), pp. 80-96.

Kautto, Mikko, Johan Fritzell, Bjorn Hvinden, Jon Krist and Hannu Uusitalo, eds., *Nordic Welfare States in the European Context* (London: Routledge, 2001).

Kautto, Mikko, et al., "Conclusion: Nordic Welfare States in the European Context," in Kautto et al., eds., *Nordic Welfare States in the European Context*, pp. 262-272.

Kent, Neil, *A Concise History of Sweden* (New York: Cambridge University Press, 2008).

Kersten, Lawrence L., *The Lutheran Ethic: The Influence of Religion on Laymen and Clergy* (Detroit, MI: Wayne State University Press, 1970).

Kettunen, Pauli, "The Nordic Welfare State in Finland," *Scandinavian Journal of History* 26:3 (2001), pp. 225-247.

Kettunen, Pauli, and Klaus Petersen, eds., *Beyond Welfare State Models: Transnational Historical Perspectives on Social Policy* (Cheltenham, UK: Edward Elgar, 2011).

Keynes, John Maynard, *Essays in Persuasion* (New York: Norton, 1963).

Kildal, Nanna, and Stein Kuhnle, "Introduction," in Kildal and Kuhnle, eds., *Normative Foundations of the Welfare State: The Nordic Experience* (Oxford, UK: Routledge, 2005), pp. 1-9.

Kirby, David, *A Concise History of Finland* (New York: Cambridge University Press, 2006).

Kleven, Henrik Jacobsen, "How Can Scandinavia Tax So Much?" *Journal of Economic Perspectives* 28:4 (Fall 2014), pp. 77-98.

Klinge, Matti, *A Brief History of Finland*, trans. by David Mitchell and Timothy Binham (Helsinki: Otava Publishing Co., 2000).

Klinge, Matti, *Let Us Be Finns: Essays on History*, trans. by Martha Gaber Abrahamson, Mary Lomas, Mirja Lavanne and David Morris (Helsinki: Otava Publishing Co, 1992).

Kolb, Robert, "Luther's Function in an Age of Confessionalization," in McKim, ed., *The Cambridge Companion to Martin Luther*, pp. 209-226.

Korsgaard, Ove, "The Danish Way to Establish the Nation in the Hearts of the People," in John L. Campbell, John A. Hall and Ove K. Pedersen, eds., *National Identity and the Varieties of Capitalism: The Danish Experience* (Montreal, CA: McGill-Queen's University Press, 2006), pp. 133-158.

Kuenzlen, Gottfried, "Religion and Modernization in Europe: Comment," *Journal of Institutional and Theoretical Economics* 153:1 (March 1997), pp. 97-99.

Kurrild-Klitgaard, Peter, "Classical Liberalism and Modern Political Economy in Denmark," *Econ Journal Watch* 12:3 (September 2015), pp. 400-431.

Kurtz, Ernest, *Not-God: A History of Alcoholics Anonymous* (Center City, MN: Hazelden, 1991).

Lagerquest, L. Deane, *The Lutherans* (Westport, CN: Greenwood Press, 1999).

Lears, Jackson, "The Usefulness of Cranks: Nature as a Standpoint for Social Criticism," *The New Republic*, October 7, 2009.

Leonard, Thomas C., *Illiberal Reformers: Race, Eugenics and American Economics in the Progressive Era* (Princeton, NJ: Princeton University Press, 2016).

Levine, Harry Gene, "The Alcohol Problem in America: From Temperance to Alcoholism," *British Journal of Addiction* 79:4 (1984), pp. 109-119.

Levinson, Sanford, *Constitutional Faith* (Princeton, NJ: Princeton University Press, 1988).

Lewis, Richard D., *Finland: Cultural Lone Wolf* (Boston, MA: Intercultural Press, 2005).

Lindberg, Carter, "Luther's Struggle with Social-Ethical Issues," in McKim, ed., *The Cambridge Companion to Martin Luther*, pp. 165-178.

Lindblom, Charles, "The Science of 'Muddling Through'," *Public Administration Review* 19:2 (Spring 1959), pp. 79-88.

Lo, Andrew W., and Mark T. Mueller, "WARNING: Physics Envy May Be Hazardous To Your Wealth," March 12, 2010. http:/ssrn.com. abstractl=1563882.

Lohse, Bernhard, *Martin Luther: An Introduction to His Life and Work*, trans. by Robert C. Schultze (Philadelphia, PA: Fortress Press, 1986).

Lowi, Theodore J., *The End of Liberalism: Ideology, Policy and the Crisis of Public Authority* (New York: Norton, 1969).

Lull, Timothy F., and Derek R. Nelson, *Resilient Reformer: The Life and Thought of Martin Luther* (Minneapolis, MN: Fortress Press, 2015).

MacCulloch, Diarmaid, *Reformation: Europe's House Divided, 1490-1700* (London: Penguin, 2004).

MacIntyre, Alasdair, *Marxism and Christianity* (Notre Dame, IN: University of Notre Dame University Press, 1984).

Manuel, Frank E., and Fritzie P. Manuel, *Utopian Thought in the Western World* (Cambridge, MA: Harvard University Press, 1979).

Markkola, Pirjo, "The Calling of Women: Gender, Religion and Social Reform in Finland, 1860–1920," in Markkola, ed., *Gender and Vocation*, pp. 113-145.

Markkola, Pirjo, "The Lutheran Nordic Welfare States," in Kettunen and Petersen, eds., *Beyond Welfare State Models*, pp. 102-118.

Markkola, Pirjo, ed., *Gender and Vocation: Women, Religion and Social Change in the Nordic Countries, 1830–1940* (Helsinki: SKS.FLS, 2000).

Markkola, Pirjo, and Ingela K. Naumann, "Lutheranism and Nordic Welfare States in Comparison," *Journal of Church and State* 56:1 (2014), pp. 1-12..

Marklund, Staffan, and Anders Nordlund, "Economic Problems, Welfare Convergence and Political Instability," in Kautto et al., eds., *Nordic Social Policy*, pp. 19-53.

Martin, David, *Religion and Power: No Logos without Mythos* (Burlington, VT: Ashgate, 2014).

Martin, David, *Tongues of Fire: The Explosion of Protestantism in Latin America* (Hoboken, NJ: Wiley-Blackwell, 1993).

McCloskey, Deirdre N., *The Bourgeois Virtues: Ethics for an Age of Commerce* (Chicago: University of Chicago Press, 2006).

McCloskey, Deirdre N., *Bourgeois Dignity: Why Economics Can't Explain the Modern World* (Chicago: University of Chicago Press, 2010).

McCloskey, Deirdre Nansen, Bourgeois Equality: *How Ideas, Not Capital or Institutions, Enriched the Modern World* (Chicago: University of Chicago Press, 2016).

McCloskey, D. N., "The Rhetoric of Economics," *Journal of Economic Literature* (June 1983).

McCloskey, Deirdre Nansen, "The Great Enrichment: A Humanistic and Social Scientific Account," *Scandinavian Economic History Review* 64:1 (2016), pp. 6-18.

McGovern, William Montgomery, *From Luther to Hitler* (Cambridge: Riverside Press, 1941).

McKim, Donald K., ed., *The Cambridge Companion to Martin Luther* (New York: Cambridge University Press, 2003).

Meinander, Henrik, *A History of Finland*, trans. by Tom Geddes (London: Hurst and Company, 2011).

Methuen, Charlotte, *Luther and Calvin: Religious Revolutionaries* (Oxford, UK: A Lion Book, 2011).

Misgeld, Klaus, Karl Molin, and Klas Amark, eds., trans. by Jim Teeland *Creating Social Democracy: A Century of the Social Democratic Labor Party in Sweden* (University Park, PA: Pennsylvania State University Press, 1992).

Mueller, William A., *Church and State in Luther and Calvin: A Comparative Study* (Garden City, NY: Anchor Books, 1965).

Nasaw, David, *Andrew Carnegie* (New York: Penguin Press, 2006).

Naumann, Ingela K., "Consensus, Conflict, or Compromise?: Church-State Relations in the Swedish 'People's Home' During the 1920s and 1930s," *Journal of Church and State* 56:1 (Winter 2014), pp. 36-59.

Nelson, Robert H., "Calvinism Without God: American Environmentalism as Implicit Calvinism," *Implicit Religion* 17:3 (2014), pp. 249-273.

Nelson, Robert H., "The Economics Profession and the Making of Public Policy," *Journal of Economic Literature* 25:1 (March 1987), pp. 49-91.

Nelson, Robert H., "Environmental Religion: A Theological Critique," *Case Western Reserve Law Review* 55:1 (2004), pp. 51-80.

Nelson, Robert H., "Is Max Weber Newly Relevant?: The Protestant-Catholic Divide in Europe Today," *Finnish Journal of Theology* 5 (2012), pp. 420-445.

Nelson, Robert H., "Max Weber Revisited," in Ilkka Pyysiainen, ed., *Religion, Economy, and Cooperation* (Berlin: Mouton de Gruyter, 2010), pp. 157-217.

Nelson, Robert H., "Mythology Instead of Analysis: The Story of Public Forest Management," in Robert T. Deacon and M. Bruce Johnson, eds., *Forestlands: Public and Private* (San Francisco: Pacific Institute for Public Policy Research, 1985), pp. 23-76.

Nelson, Robert H., "The Office of Policy Analysis in the Department of the Interior," *Journal of Policy Analysis and Management* 8:3 (Summer 1989), pp. 395-410.

Nelson, Robert H., "The Public Lands," in Paul R. Portney, ed., *Current Issues in Natural Resource Policy* (Washington, D.C.: Resources for the Future – distributed by the Johns Hopkins University Press, 1982), 14-73.

Nelson, Robert H., "The Secular Religions of Economic Progress," *The New Atlantis* 39 (Summer 2013), pp. 38-50.

Nelson, Robert H., "The Secularization Myth Revisited: Secularism as Christianity in Disguise," *Journal of Markets and Morality* 18:2 (Fall 2015), 279-308.

Nelson, Robert H., "What is 'Economic Theology,'" *The Princeton Seminary Bulletin* 45:1 (February 2004), 58-79.

Nelson, Robert H., *Economics as Religion: From Chicago to Samuelson and Beyond* (University Park, PA: Pennsylvania State University Press, 2001).

Nelson, Robert H., *God? Very Probably: Five Rational Ways to Think about the Question of a God* (Eugene, OR: Cascade Books, 2015).

Nelson, Robert H., *The New Holy Wars: Economic Religion versus Environmental Religion in Contemporary America* (University Park, PA: Pennsylvania State University Press, 2010).

Nelson, Robert H., *Private Rights and Public Lands: The Failure of Scientific Management* (Lanham, MD: Rowman & Littlefield, 1995).

Nelson, Robert H., *Reaching for Heaven on Earth: The Theological Meaning of Economics* (Lanham, MD: Roman & Littlefield, 1991).

Nestingen, James Arne, "Approaching Luther," in McKim, ed., *The Cambridge Companion to Martin Luther*, pp. 284-298.

Noll, Mark A., *Protestantism* (Oxford, UK: Oxford University Press, 2011).

Norager, Troels, "Crisis of Religion and Nineteenth-Century Spiritual Reform: Varieties of Nation Building in Grundtvig and Emerson," in Hall, Korsgaard and Pedersen, eds., *Building the Nation*, p. 284-299.

Oberman, Heiko A., "The Nationalist Conscription of Martin Luther," in Carter Lindberg, ed., *Piety, Politics and Ethics* (Kirksville. MO: Sixteenth Century Journal Publishers, 1984), pp. 65-73.

Oberman, Heiko A., *Luther: Man Between God and the Devil*, trans. by Eileen Walliser-Schwarzbart (New York: Doubleday, 1992 [1982]).

Offer, Avner, and Gabriel Soderberg, *The Nobel Factor: The Prize in Economics, Social Democracy, and the Market Turn* (Princeton, NJ: Princeton University Press, 2016).

Opielka, Michael, "Christian Foundations of the Welfare State: Strong Cultural Values in Comparative Perspective," in Wim van Oorschot, Michael Opielka and Birgit Pfau-Effinger, eds., *Culture and Welfare State: Values and Social Policy in Comparative Perspective* (Cheltenham, UK: Edward Elgar, 2008), pp. 89-114.

Oslington, Paul, "Divine Action, Providence and Adam Smith's Invisible Hand," in Oslington, ed., *Adam Smith as Theologian*, pp. 61-74.

Oslington, Paul, "Introduction: Theological Readings of Smith," in Oslington, ed., *Adam Smith as Theologian*, pp. 1-16.

Oslington, Paul, ed., *Adam Smith as Theologian* (New York: Routledge, 2012).

Østergåard, Uffe, "Lutheranism, Nationalism and the Universal Welfare State, " in Katharina Kunter and Jens Holger Schiørring, eds., *Europäisches und Globales Christentum / European and Global Christianity: Herausforderungen und Transformationen im 20. Jahrhundert / Challenges and Transformations in the 20th Century*,
Arbeiten zur Kirchlichen Zeitgeschichte, series B vol. 54 (Göttingen, 2011), pp. 78-101

Ostergard, Uffe, "The Danish Path to Modernity," in Arnason and Wittrock, eds., *Nordic Paths to Modernity*, pp. 49-68.

Ostergard, Uffe, "The Geopolitics of Nordic Identity – From Composite States to Nation States," in Sorensen and Strath, eds., *The Cultural Construction of Norden*, pp. 25-71.

Ostergard, Uffe, "The Nation as Event: The Dissolution of the Oldenburg Monarchy and Grundtvig's Nationalism," in Hall, Korsgaard and Pedersen, eds., *Building the Nation*, pp. 110-133.

Partanen, Anu, *The Nordic Theory of Everything: In Search of a Better Life* (New York: Harper Collins, 2016).

Pettegree, Andrew, *Brand Luther: 1517, Printing, and the Making of the Reformation* (New York: Penguin Press, 2015).

Pettersson, Per, "Majority Churches as Agents of European Welfare: A Sociological Approach," in Backstrom et al., *Welfare and Religion in 21st Century Europe, Volume 2*, pp. 15-59.

Peukert, Helge, "Martin Luther: The First Modern Economist," in Backhaus, ed., *The Reformation.*, pp. 13-63.

Pinchot, Gifford, *Breaking New Ground* (New York: Harcourt, Brace and Co., 1947).

Portman, Anneli, *From Might to Mandate: Values in Rulers' Public Speeches in Finland in 1809-2000*, Ph. D. dissertation, Faculty of the Social Sciences, University of Helsinki, Finland, April 2014.

Press release, *Reader's Digest Online*, September 14, 2013. http://www.rda.com/news/reader%E2%80%99s-digest-reveals-the-most-and-least-honest-cities-in-the-world-with-the-wallet-drop-project

Proctor, Robert N., *Racial Hygiene: Medicine Under the Nazis* (Cambridge, MA: Harvard University Press, 1988).

Redles, David, *Hitler's Millennial Reich: Apocalyptic Belief and the Search for Salvation* (New York: New York University Press, 2005).

"Requiem for Civil Religion," *Christian Century*, unsigned editorial, March 1, 2017, p. 7.

Rhein, Stefan, *Philipp Melanchthon* (Lutherstadt Wittenberg: Drei Kastanien Verlag, 2008).

Richardson, Cyril C., "Prophesy and Politics: A Study in Martin Luther," *The Review of Religion* (1937).

Rokkan, Stein, "Nation-Building and Language," in Peter Flora, ed., *State Formation, Nation-Building, and Mass Politics in Europe: The Theory of Stein Rokkan* (Oxford, UK: Oxford University Press, 1999).

Roll-Hansen, Nils, "Conclusion: Scandinavian Eugenics in the International Context," in Gunnar Broberg and Nils Roll-Hansen, eds., *Eugenics and the Welfare State*, pp. 259-271.

Roper, Lyndal, *Martin Luther: Renegade and Prophet* (London: Bodley Head, 2016).

Sandelin, Bo, "Beyond the Stockholm School," in Sandelin, ed., *The History of Swedish Economic Thought*, pp. 214-224.

Sandelin, Bo, ed., *The History of Swedish Economic Thought* (London: Routledge, 1991).

Schjeldahl, Peter, "Knock on Wood: The Five-Hundredth Anniversary of Luther's Ninety-Five Theses," *New Yorker*, November 14, 2016, pp. 92-93.

Sejersted, Francis, *The Age of Social Democracy: Norway and Sweden in the Twentieth Century*, trans. by Richard Daly (Princeton, NJ: Princeton University Press, 2011).

Siemon-Netto, Uwe, *The Fabricated Luther: Refuting Nazi Connections and Other Modern Myths, second edition* (Saint Louis, MO: Concordia Publishing House, 2007).

Sinha, Manisha, *The Slave's Cause: A History of Abolition* (New Haven, CT: Yale University Press, 2016).

Skinner, Quentin, *The Foundations of Modern Political Thought: Volume 2, The Age of Reformation* (Cambridge, UK: Cambridge University Press, 1978).

Slagstad, Rune, "The Metamorphoses of Norwegian Reformism," in Arnason and Wittrock, eds., *Nordic Paths to Modernity*.

Smith, Christian, *The Sacred Project of American Sociology* (New York: Oxford University Press, 2014).

Sorensen, Aage B., "On Kings, Pietism, and Rent-Seeking in Scandinavian Welfare States," *Acta Sociologica* 41:4 (1998), pp. 363-375.

Sorensen, Oystein, and Bo Strath, "Introduction: The Cultural Construction of Norden," in Sorensen and Strath, eds., *The Cultural Construction of Norden*, pp. 1-24.

Sorensen, Oystein, and Bo Strath, eds., *The Cultural Construction of Norden* (Oslo: Scandinavian University Press, 1997).

Spencer, Nick, *The Evolution of the West: How Christianity Has Shaped Our Values* (London: SPCK, 2016).

Spiro, Jonathan Peter, *Defending the Master Race: Conservation, Eugenics, and the Legacy of Madison Grant* (Lebanon, NH: University of Vermont Press, 2009).

Spolaore, Enrico, and Roman Wacziard, "How Deep are the Roots of Economic Development?" *Journal of Economic Literature* 51:2 (June 2013), pp. 325-369.

Stackhouse, Max, "Weber, Theology, and Economics," in Paul Oslington, ed., *Oxford Handbook of Christianity and Economics* (New York: Oxford University Press, 2014), pp. 307-336.

Steigmann-Gall, Richard, *The Holy Reich: Nazi Conceptions of Christianity, 1919–1945* (New York: Cambridge University Press, 2003).

Steinglass, Matt, "Martin Luther, Church Splitter," *The Economist: The World in 2017* (December 2016).

Stenius, Henrik, "Paradoxes of the Finnish Political Culture," in Arnason and Wittrock, *Nordic Paths to Modernity*, pp. 207-228.

Stenius, Henrik, "The Good Life is a Life of Conformity: The Impact of Lutheran Tradition on Nordic Political Culture," in Oystein and Strath, eds., *The Cultural Construction of Norden*, pp. 161-171.

Stjerna, Kirsi, *Women and the Reformation* (Oxford, UK: Blackwell, 2009)

Strath, Bo, "The Normative Foundations of the Scandinavian Welfare States in Historical Perspective," in Nanna Kildal and Stein Kuhnle, eds., *Normative Foundations of the Welfare State: The Nordic Experience* (Oxford, UK: Routledge, 2005)

Sulkunen, Irma, "Suffrage, Gender and Citizenship in Finland," *NORDEUROPAforum* 1/2007

Sulkunen, Irma, "Suffrage, Nation and Political Mobilization – The Finnish Case in an International Context," in Sulkunen, Nevala-Nurmi and Markkola, eds., *Suffrage, Gender and Citizenship*.

Sulkunen, Irma, Seija-Leena Nevala-Nurmi and Pirjo Markkola, *Suffrage, Gender and Citizenship: International Perspectives on Parliamentary Reforms* (Newcastle upon Tyne, UK: Cambridge Scholars Publishing, 2009).

Sulkunen, Pekka, and Katariina Warpenius, "Reforming the Self and the Other: The Temperance Movement and the Duality of Modern Subjectivity," *Critical Public Health* 10:4 (2000), pp. 423-438..

Sulkunen, Pekka, Caroline Sutton, Christoffer Tigerstedt and Katariina Warpenius, *Broken Spirits: Power and Ideas in Nordic Alcohol Control* (Helsinki: Nordic Council for Alcohol and Drug Research, 2000).

Sulkunen, Pekka, *The Saturated Society: Governing Risk and Lifestyles in Consumer Culture* (Los Angeles: Sage, 2009).

Talmon, J. L., *Political Messianism: The Romantic Phase* (Boulder, CO: Westview Press, 1985 [1960]).

Thorkildsen, Dag, "Religious Identity and Nordic Identity," in Sorensen and Strath, eds., *The Cultural Construction of Norden*, pp. 138-160.

Thorkildsen, Dag, "Unconditional Christian Loyalty Towards the Rulers?" in Katharina Hunter and Jens Holger Schjorring, *European and Global Christianity: Challenges and Transformations in the 20th Century* (Gottingen: Vandenhoeck & Ruprecht, 2011).

Treu, Martin, *Katherine von Bora: Luther's Wife*, trans. by Stephen P. Glinsky, Jr. (Lutherstadt Wittenberg: Drei Kastanien Verlag, 2013).

Treu, Martin, *Martin Luther in Wittenberg: A Biographical Tour* (Wittenberg: Luther Memorial Foundation of Saxony-Anhalt, 2013).

Troeltsch, Ernst, *Protestantism and Progress: A Historical Study of the Relation of Protestantism to the Modern World* (Boston: Beacon Press, 1958 – first English ed. 1912).

Troeltsch, Ernst, *The Social Teaching of the Christian Churches*, Vol. 2 (Chicago: University of Chicago Press, 1981 – first ed. 1911).

Truman, David B., *The Governmental Process: Political Interests and Public Opinion* (New York: Knopf, 1951).

Van Kersbergen, Kees, "From Charity to Social Justice: Religion and the European Welfare State Traditions," in Kettunen and Petersen, *Beyond Welfare State Models*, pp. 102-119.

Van Kersbergen, Kees, and Philip Manow, eds., *Religion, Class Coalitions, and Welfare States* (New York: Cambridge University Press, 2009).

Vitz, Paul C., *Psychology as Religion: The Cult of Self-Worship, second ed.* (Grand Rapids, MI: William B. Eerdmans, 1994).

Von Drehle, David, "The Demon Drink," *Time*, May 24, 2010.

Waldo, Dwight, *The Administrative State: A Study of the Political Theory of American Public Administration* (New York: Holmes and Meier, 1984 – first ed. 1948).

Wannenwetsch, Bernd, "Luther's Moral Theology," in McKim, ed., *The Cambridge Companion to Martin Luther*, pp. 120-135.

Warburton, Clark, "Prohibition and Economic Welfare," *Annals of the American Academy of Political and Social Science* 163:1 (September 1932), pp. 89-97.

Waterman, A. M. C., "Economics as Theology: Adam Smith's *Wealth of Nations*," *Southern Economic Journal* 68:4 (2002).

Weber, Max, *The Protestant Ethic and the Spirit of Capitalism* (New York: Charles Scribner's, 1958).

Weikart, Richard, *Hitler's Ethic: The Nazi Pursuit of Evolutionary Progress* (New York: Palgrave, MacMillan, 2011).

Witte, Jr., John, "From Gospel to Law: The Lutheran Reformation and its Impact on Legal Culture," in Howard and Noll, eds., *Protestantism After 500 Years*, pp. 52-74.

Wittrock, Bjorn, "Modernity: One, None, or Many? European Origins and Modernity as a Global Condition," *Daedalus* 129:1 (Winter 2000), pp. 31-60.

Wittrock, Bjorn, "The Making of Sweden," in Arnason and Wittrock, eds., *Nordic Paths to Modernity*, pp. 89-110.

Woodberry, Robert D., "The Missionary Roots of Liberal Democracy," *American Political Science Review* 106:2 (May 2012), pp. 244-274.

World Economic Forum, *The Global Gender Gap, 2014* (Geneva, Switzerland: 2014).

Wuorinen, John H., "Finland's Prohibition Experiment," *Annals of the American Academy of Political and Social Science* 163:1 (1932), pp. 216-226.

Yeung, Anne Birgitta, "The Finnish Lutheran Church as an Agent of Welfare – the Case of Lahti," in Anne Birgitta Yeung, Ninna Edgardh Beckman and Per Petterson, eds., *Churches as Agents of Welfare – Sweden, Norway and Finland*, WREP working paper 2, Volume 1 (Uppsala, Sweden, 2006).

Zetterberg, Seppo, *Finland After 1917*, translated by Malcolm Hicks (Helsinki: Otava Publishing Company, 1991).

Index

n denotes notes
t denotes table

O

Y

Z